A Revolution Gone Backward

Recent Titles in
Contributions in Afro-American and African Studies
Series Advisers: John W. Blassingame and Henry Louis Gates, Jr.

Wilson Harris and the Modern Tradition: A New Architecture of the World
Sandra E. Drake

Portrait of an Expatriate: William Gardner Smith, Writer
LeRoy S. Hodges, Jr.

Race, Politics, and Culture: Critical Essays on the Radicalism of the 1960s
Adolph Reed, Jr.

The White Press and Black America
Carolyn Martindale

Africa and the West: The Legacies of Empire
Isaac James Mowoe and Richard Bjornson, editors

A Black Elite: A Profile of Graduates of UNCF Colleges
Daniel C. Thompson

"De Lawd": Richard B. Harrison and *The Green Pastures*
Walter C. Daniel

Health Care Issues in Black America: Policies, Problems, and Prospects
Woodrow Jones, Jr., and Mitchell F. Rice, editors

The Character of the Word: The Texts of Zora Neale Hurston
Karla F. C. Holloway

Surprizing Narrative: Olaudah Equiano and the Beginnings of Black Autobiography
Angelo Costanzo

Conscientious Sorcerers: The Black Postmodernist Fiction of LeRoi Jones/Amiri Baraka, Ishmael Reed, and Samuel R. Delany
Robert Elliot Fox

Alexander Crummell: Pioneer in Nineteenth-Century Pan-African Thought
Gregory U. Rigsby

A REVOLUTION GONE BACKWARD

The Black Response
to National Politics, 1876–1896

BESS BEATTY

Contributions in Afro-American and African Studies,
Number 105

Greenwood Press
New York • Westport, Connecticut • London

Library of Congress Cataloging-in-Publication Data

Beatty, Bess, 1947-
    A revolution gone backward.

    (Contributions in Afro-American and African
studies, ISSN 0069-9624 ; no. 105)
        Bibliography: p.
        Includes index.
        1. Afro-Americans—Politics and government.
2. United States—Politics and government—1865-1900.
3. Afro-Americans—History—1877-1964. I. Title.
II. Series.
E185.6.B38   1987   973'.0496073   86-25747
ISBN 0-313-25533-4 (lib. bdg. : alk. paper)

Library of Congress Catalog Card Number: 86-25747
ISBN: 0-313-25533-4
ISSN: 0069-9624

First published in 1987

Greenwood Press, Inc.
88 Post Road West, Westport, Connecticut 06881

Printed in the United States of America

∞

The paper used in this book complies with the
Permanent Paper Standard issued by the National Information Standards
Organization (Z39.48-1984).

10 9 8 7 6 5 4 3 2 1

For Eleanor Rankin Spratt,
my first and best history teacher

Contents

Preface

This book is a study of the black response to a revolution gone backward; it is about the erosion of black political rights from 1876 to 1896. The Reconstruction amendments, mandating black freedom and black rights, were the most important result of Union victory in the Civil War. Within a few years of their emancipation, southern freedmen could vote and elect members of their race to office. Northern blacks likewise enjoyed an upsurge in political freedom. But the revolution was short-lived. In April 1877, the last federal troops stationed in the South to protect freedpeople and the Republican governments they elected were withdrawn, bringing Reconstruction to a symbolic end. Almost twenty years later, Booker T. Washington made a speech before the Atlanta Exposition which catapulted him into the forefront of black leadership. He muted the political demands of Radical Reconstruction with a philosophy of economics-before-politics. Morgan Kousser has described the twenty years between the Compromise of 1877 and the Washington era as years of "transition, uncertainty, fluctuation" for blacks politically. Understanding how blacks responded to the change and uncertainty is essential for a complete understanding of the varying patterns of black political response and the development of black political ideology.[1]

The purpose of this study is to view the aftermath of Reconstruction through the eyes of blacks. This perspective is necessary, but the difficulties in pursuing it are considerable. It is difficult but important to focus on black participants in a confrontation where whites had more power and thus greater impact. As Willie Lee Rose explains, when dealing with the Reconstruction era we must consider black people not only as "powerless participants" but as individuals, each "struggling unsuccessfully to control his own problems."[2]

A second major problem inherent in analyzing the ideas of a large group of people tied together by circumstances rather than by intellectual commitment is the tendency to generalize about the thought of a "talented tenth"—in this case those few black men and women who were both literate and in a position to disseminate their ideas—as though it were representative of the entire group, and to assume that those whose ideas are readily available in newspapers, letters, speeches, and memoirs are typical of those who thought about the same issues but left no written record, and of those who hardly thought about them at all. One of the best, although extreme, analyses of the problem of treating the black elite and the black masses as interchangable is found in Nell Painter's *Exodusters*. Painter correctly warns that "danger lies in confusing the views or rhetoric of 'representative colored men' with the authentic voices of rural blacks." She claims that "so-called" leaders such as Frederick Douglass, Blanche K. Bruce, and Pinckney Pinchback were not really leaders of the rural masses, and that "rural Southern black voters faced dangers virtually unheard of in Northern or Southern cities, for bulldozing was a characteristically rural phenomenon." Some black leaders, some of the time, were conservative accommodaters, out of touch with the majority. At times they were even the anti-black puppets that white America wanted them to be. There is abundant evidence that black leaders did sometimes put their own security ahead of the interest of the masses. Their negative response to the exodusters, the subject of Painter's book, is one example. Painter, however, has exaggerated the degree and impact of class division among blacks and the conservatism of black leaders. Black leaders could be quite conservative in coping with white America's retreat from Reconstruction, but many articulate blacks, who were sometimes conservative and even self-serving, were at other times quite militant, risking their own precarious positions when confronting the plight of the poor black majority. Most "representative colored men," from both the North and South, were intensely aware of bulldozing and worked mightily to stem its course. A common attribute of most black leaders during this period was inconsistency. In their desperate search for the most efficacious course to pursue in an increasingly proscribed society, black leaders might counsel accommodation at one time—resistance the next. And although poor rural blacks could indeed be quite independent, they often looked to men such as Bruce and Douglass for guidance. Many black political leaders had direct contact with the masses through churches or schools. It is impossible to determine how many blacks read, influenced, and were influenced by the black press, but evidence suggests that their numbers extended beyond the small literate middle class. Lewis Suggs, editor of the most comprehensive study of the southern black press, writes that newspapers "were passed from family to family and read aloud in barber shops, pool halls, and informal civic and religious gatherings." And while black leaders often pursued their own political interests, as Leon Litwack observes, they were always united with the masses of blacks and divided from most whites in one profoundly important way: their "determination to preserve the gains of Reconstruction." If the small cadre of black leadership "was never independent of white carpetbag influence," as Willie Lee Rose has written, it "nevertheless gave voice to needs and attitudes of newly enfranchised people.[3]

In this work I have tried to emphasize that blacks were active participants in the debate about their political future but that ultimately they were largely powerless. Although the analysis emphasizes that small, articulate elite which left behind a written record of its own fears and aspirations, it nevertheless reflects the responses of the masses who shared them.

During the rather long time it has taken to complete this book, I have become indebted to many people. The staffs of all libraries consulted were almost unfailingly helpful; I particularly thank those at the Robert Manning Strozier Library at Florida State University who so often assisted me. My family, particularly my mother Eleanor Spratt Hacker, has long provided support and encouragement. Historians Glen Jeansonne and David Bennetts both gave the manuscript a careful reading and made constructive suggestions. Robert Gardner, Wilson Hall, Margaret Whitworth, and Sara Wingard, colleagues at Shorter College, all proofread the entire manuscript to its considerable benefit. Two colleagues at the University of Iowa, David Schoenbaum and Jonathan Walton, have helped with the final third-floor revisions the best they could. I wish to thank the History Department of Oregon State University for its financial support. My greatest debt, one of long standing, is to three of my teachers at Florida State University. William I. Hair and William W. Rogers both read various versions of the manuscript. Joe M. Richardson gave me hours of assistance in the early years of this work. His expertise in this field, his cooperation, and his consistently sound advice have made my work much easier and are deeply appreciated.

A Revolution Gone Backward

1

A Revolution Goes Backward: The Election of 1876 and the Hayes Administration

In the spring and summer of 1865, as it became increasingly clear that northern victory in the Civil War would result in emancipation, there were days, sometimes stretching into weeks, when southern blacks could savor the profound fact of freedom. But as southern whites strengthened their resolve to concede nothing to their former slaves except the name of freedom, many freed-people turned their attention from jubilation to practical matters of survival. All across the South blacks met to organize their new lives. A first prerequisite, many quickly recognized, was assuring the right to vote. Political participation was a genuine possibility in 1865, but one few people could have imagined only four years earlier. The Civil War, however, had radically transformed per-ceptions—northern and southern, black and white—of the place of blacks in American life. As focus shifted from emancipation to social, economic, and political realities, black suffrage became central to postwar debate. Although some blacks joined the ma-jority of whites in denouncing their right to vote, many more recognized it as a fundamental base of freedom. "Our work will not be done," wrote preeminent black leader Frederick Douglass in 1863, "until the colored man is admitted as a full member in good and regular standing in the American body politic." His sentiments were echoed by blacks in all walks of life. "We's got to hab a voice in de 'pintin' of de law-makers," a recently freed

North Carolina black man insisted. "Den we knows our frens, and whose hans we's safe in."[1]

Black politicization began with federal occupation of the South. White Republicans formed Union clubs to indoctrinate southern blacks politically; increasingly, however, blacks took charge of their own political affairs. All-black Republican clubs replaced the Union clubs in many areas and began, a black Louisianian recalled, "teaching the people what they were to vote for." In time, local activity expanded to statewide freedmen's conventions, "the political debut of southern blacks." Initially some blacks were reluctant to press for the ballot, emphasizing instead the need for trial and jury rights, but most agreed with a Virginia Freedmen's Convention that "the only salvation for us besides the power of the Government is the 'possession of the ballot.' "[2]

Many blacks regarded Abraham Lincoln as a virtual Messiah, but some recognized that his policy of leniency toward the defeated South would deliver the race back into the hands of former masters and render political gains unlikely. Although deeply grieved over Lincoln's assassination, many blacks were initially optimistic that President Andrew Johnson, who was well known for his hatred of southern slave owners, would be, as he promised, "your Moses." Hope quickly turned to despair, however, when Johnson inaugurated a program of reconstruction in the South that was almost as lenient as Lincoln's while far less tolerant of black equality. State governments, formed under Johnson's leadership while Congress was out of session, reelected the planter class to office and passed a series of black codes starkly circumscribing black freedom.[3]

But Johnson's control of Reconstruction proved short-lived. By early 1866, congressional Republicans, led by the radical faction which was determined to prevent a restoration of southern Democratic power, had begun to stymie the Johnson program. They nullified the new state governments, organized the South into military districts, and mandated black suffrage. In April 1866, shortly after Congress had passed a civil rights act over Johnson's veto, Richard H. Cain, a black minister who had recently moved to South Carolina, proclaimed, "Never was there a bright prospect before any people than that presented to the colored people of the Southern states." With passage of the Reconstruction Act in March 1867, it appeared that this bright prospect had indeed become reality. By reversing the restoration of white political power fostered by the Johnson plan and guaranteeing southern blacks the vote, the radical Republicans created a political revolution that was immediate and viable. The revolution seemed secure with the ratification of the Fourteenth Amendment, which assured black civil rights, and two years later the Fifteenth Amendment, which prohibited disfranchisement on the basis of race.[4]

The radical Republicans wrought this political revolution for a variety of reasons. Political expediency was clearly evident in their calculations. As John and Lawanda Cox have explained, although they realized "Republican sponsorship of Negro suffrage meant flirtation with political disaster in the North," they also knew that the southern black vote was necessary to curb resurgent southern Democratic power. Generally the Republicans were adept at turning the suffrage question into a partisan one by linking opposition with Democratic treason. Some Republicans also assumed that ratification of the Fifteenth Amendment was sound political strategy for winning in the North because it would appease "pietistic Yankee Protestants" who believed in black political equality as well as put northern black votes in Republican columns. Undoubtedly some radical Republicans supported the Fifteenth Amendment because they believed in the rightness of political equality. But if Republican support of black suffrage stemmed at least in part from principle, their aspirations for the impact of that vote were far more limited than those of blacks themselves. Whites rarely supported the social and economic revolution that blacks hoped to achieve.[5]

A minority of blacks, due to inexperience or fear of reprisal, avoided politics. The most prescient among the race recognized the flimsy base of their political rights; they knew that they were protected by largely selfish interests. The majority, however, viewed the Fifteenth Amendment as political salvation. In all the southern states, the majority of blacks, once introduced to their rights, participated in elections and were remarkably successful in acquiring nascent political skills. Thomas Holt's study of South Carolina offers impressive evidence refuting the long-standing contention that blacks were merely the tools of white politicians.

Holt writes that "Negroes themselves made the initial moves toward politial participation. They organized and paid for their own exclusive conventions, wrote their petitions, identified their leadership, and generally fashioned the basis for the Republican party of later years." Leon Litwack's study of the immediate black response to emancipation and political rights and J. Morgan Kousser's statistical study of southern political behavior following Reconstruction concur that the black political participation rate was high.[6]

Most of the newly enfranchised blacks, recognizing the role of the Republican party in their emancipation, enfranchisement, and continued protection, embraced that party. The emotional response of many blacks to the assassination of Lincoln and the resulting "Great Emancipator" legend further assured their support. In 1872 Frederick Douglass expressed a popular sentiment when he claimed that for blacks, "the Republican party is the ship, all else the sea." Widespread black support for the Republicans was also the result of negative response of blacks to the Democrats. Many found truth in the Republican charge that "the only test of Democratic soundness is hatred of the Negro." In 1870, a group of New York blacks denounced black Democrats as "an enemy to our race forever." Although some northern and southern whites predicted that the freedmen would follow their former masters into the Democratic party, in reality, as Joel Williamson has explained, "the Negro had no real choice; for him, freedom and Radicalism were one and inseparable."[7]

But if black support for the Republican party was inevitable, it was rarely uncritical. Occasionally, black leaders and newspapers urged the masses to vote Republican out of a sense of obligation to the North and the Republican party. In 1867, for example, the Augusta *Loyal Georgian* proclaimed that "he [the black man] owes it to the great Union Republican Party of the land, that would enshrine the principles of truth and liberty, repurchased and reconstructed in the late war, to vote, and vote to a man for that party." But more commonly blacks demanded that the relationship between the party and its black partisans be one of mutuality and were sharply critical when they perceived that it was not. Even among the masses of uneducated blacks, those most likely to deify the Republican party, there were demands that they be allowed to participate and hold office as equal members and that their political loyalty lead to changes in their economic status.[8]

Black criticism of the Republican party accelerated as Republican support for Radical Reconstruction waned. In 1868, most blacks rejoiced that Ulysses S. Grant, perceived as a friend of blacks, had been elected president. Grant, however, had limited moral commitment to black rights. In Congress the radicals were increasingly replaced with a new breed of Stalwart Republicans who emphasized partisan needs and conservative economic policies while deemphasizing black rights. The general amnesty granted by Grant and Congress meant that in a number of southern states the Democrats were voted back into office. Furthermore, following passage of the Fifteenth Amendment in 1870, many Republicans determined that nothing more needed to be done for the black population. When in 1872 a number of disgruntled Republicans, many of them former radicals who now despaired of black men as voters, split from the regular Republicans over the issues of corruption and formed the Liberal Republican party, it was clear, as Kenneth Stampp explains, that "the crusade for Negro rights had lost its vitality." Although the Liberals nominated Horace Greely, once an outspoken abolitionist and champion of black rights, a party that condemned radical policy held limited appeal for black voters. There were several groups of black Greelyites organized, but few prominent black leaders supported the Liberals; the vast majority of black voters voted for Grant.[9]

But if they anticipated support from Grant, theirs proved to be an empty vision. The president continued to maintain troops in the South but they were rarely effective in protecting black rights. A series of force acts, passed in 1870 and 1871 to curb the violence of the Klan and other southern vigilante groups, were only erratically enforced. As a result, Democratic violence rapidly accelerated, and an increasing number of blacks were disfranchised de facto. Growing northern opposition to even the limited force Grant exerted in the South combined with economic recession and revelations of corruption in government to bring about, in 1874, the first Republican congressional defeat since pre–Civil War elections. Some Republicans naïvely assumed that protecting black rights could reverse their loss, and in 1875, during a lame duck session, they pushed through a civil rights bill, the last major piece of Reconstruction legislation. But the bill was of limited significance because it made no reference to education and included only limited means of enforcement. A growing number of Republican politicians concluded that it was politically more expedient to forget the South in order to win in the North. In the fall of 1875, President Grant, under advice that the use of federal force in the South would jeopardize Republican electoral success in the North, refused to send troops to deal with particularly violent elections in Mississippi.[10]

Black criticism of Republican retrenchment in the early seventies did have limited impact. White concern with black political defection was a major motivation behind passage of the ineffective 1875 Civil Rights Act. Blacks, however, were justifiably skeptical of the renewed goodwill of the Republican party. In the 1875 state elections, violence toward southern blacks accelerated, allowing further "redemption" by the Democratic party. In the spring of 1876 a white newspaper correspondent reported from the Nashville National Colored Convention that the delegates were "sick of the Republican party...it has deceived them, betrayed them insulted them."[11]

While some black politicians, dependent on Republican patronage, remained Republican sycophants, others increasingly expressed their disillusionment. John R. Lynch, a Republican congressman from Mississippi, counseled blacks to remain loyal Republicans on the national level but to divide according to their interests on the state and local levels. Pinckney B.S. Pinchback, lieutenant governor of Louisiana in the early 1870s, became even more vitriolic in attacking the Republicans. After being denied a seat in a Republican-dominated Senate, he charged that blacks "as a race are between the hawk of Republican demogogism and the buzzards of Democratic prejudices."[12]

Despite their growing disillusionment, the majority of blacks remained Republican; a minority, however, endorsed the Democratic party. Northern support for the Democrats was rendered somewhat easier after 1868 when moderates gained control of the party and launched a "new departure" which included at least theoretical acceptance of the Reconstruction amendments.

Democratic leaders recognized that despite extensive northern prejudice, too much blatant emphasis on race was often interpreted as intent to overthrow the results of the war. As a result, northern Democrats began deemphasizing racism at the same time that Republicans were deemphasizing black rights. Northern blacks continued to stress the southern situation in their political rhetoric, but their more liberal environment largely divorced their state and local political response from that of southern blacks. The black Democratic vote in northern local and state elections rose steadily in the seventies although it remained a minority of the total black vote. Northern blacks who voted Democratic commonly labeled themselves independents. Peter Clark, principal of a Cincinnati school and a leading northern advocate of independence, condemned the Republicans for their diminishing zeal in supporting black needs and particularly urged independence on the local level. George T. Downing, a wealthy Rhode Island businessman, was another northern leader who recommended independence on the grounds that a divided black vote would not be taken for granted.[13]

Southern blacks, who faced increased violence rather than a moderate "new departure," had no such incentive to support the Democratic party voluntarily. Still, for a variety of reasons, a small minority of southern blacks did vote Democratic. August Meier identifies southern black Democrats during this period as generally "of the old servant class, or successful, conservative farmers and businessmen who identified their interests with those of upper-class whites." A few former slaves, accustomed to heeding the dictates of their masters, followed them into the Democratic party; others were bribed or forced to become Democrats. There were also black Democrats who sincerely believed that southern Democracy rather than alien Republicanism could best solve the unique problems of the South or that self-imposed segregation would be the result of excessive adherence to one party.[14]

The minority of southern blacks who voted Democratic often met with sharp criticism and even violent reprisal from black Republicans. A staunch Republican from Mississippi explained, "We don't believe they have a right to acquiesce with a party who refuse to recognize their right to participate in public af-

fairs." But the number of blacks who voluntarily voted Democratic remained small. Because of general black distrust of the
Democratic party and considerable southern white Democratic
opposition to any black voting, most blacks in the North and
South considered themselves Republican and voted for that
party if at all possible.[15]

By 1876, blacks were well aware that freedom did not mean
political equality because they knew that the Fifteenth Amendment did not in reality protect their vote. Proscription and violence had already eroded black suffrage, particularly in rural
areas. But extralegal means of disfranchisement were not yet as
effective as white Democrats wished; most qualified black voters
in the North and South could still vote. For them, the 1876
presidential election loomed as pivotal in determining whether
or not the precarious political rights they still enjoyed could be
maintained in the face of resurgent Democratic power. Although
the presidency had less power and prestige in this period than
before or since, many blacks, facing diminishing political power
on the state level, looked to the president for redress of their
grievances. Blacks were generally disappointed that Grant was
not seeking a third term despite his inept handling of the enforcement acts. In the preconvention months, there was considerable debate among them as to which Republican candidate
they should support. Despite the rise of southern terrorism and
the resulting de facto disfranchisement, many retained enough
confidence in the efficacy of black political participation to discuss potential black candidates for the vice-presidential nomination. No one seriously suggested a black presidential nominee,
but blacks did agree that their endorsement of a candidate
should be on the basis of his stand on black rights. Their opinions
were not without weight. Blacks dominated or played powerful
roles in most southern Republican party organizations and
would be delegates to the Republican convention. Also, some
white Republican politicians still believed that the black vote in
both the North and South could make a difference in the outcome of the election.[16]

In the months prior to the Cincinnati convention, Senator
Oliver P. Morton, a leader in the fight for black suffrage, was
the candidate most frequently endorsed by blacks as the best

alternative to Grant. Frederick Douglass used his considerable influence to convince a majority of southern black delegates to support Morton. The Nashville Colored Convention, meeting in early 1876, endorsed Morton on the grounds that he was the candidate most sympathetic to the particular problems of blacks. And in April the Washington *People's Advocate* reported that Morton was held in the highest regard by local blacks because of his efforts to assure their rights, although the paper later switched its own support to Zachariah Chandler, another radical who was chairman of the Republican Congressional Committee.[17]

A majority of the southern black delegates attending the Republican National Convention, held in Cincinnati in June, voted for Morton on the first ballot. P.B.S. Pinchback seconded Morton's nomination and described him as a man who "will strike terror to the hearts of those monsters in the South." Blacks were not, however, unanimous for Morton. Senator James G. Blaine, who had supported black suffrage but opposed continued military protection, was prominent among other candidates they endorsed. Henry M. Turner, Georgia minister and editor, was one of several speakers who seconded Blaine's nomination.[18]

In reality, none of the potential Republican nominees was likely to "strike terror to the hearts" of southern redeemers. Even Morton, previously a staunch radical, now called the radical program at best a necessary evil. Most white delegates were now more interested in the issue of corruption in government than they were in Reconstruction policy. With the exception of a speech by Douglass in which he called on Republicans to be true to their principles, convention speeches emphasized reconciliation.[19]

Governor Rutherford B. Hayes of Ohio had rarely been mentioned by black leaders as an acceptable candidate, but when he and William A. Wheeler were nominated, most blacks gave the ticket their enthusiastic approval. The *People's Advocate* insisted that, contrary to reports that there seemed to be an erosion of black support for the Republican party, "the colored men of the South, the North and the West, will with very rare exception be found supporting Hayes and Wheeler against anything the Democrats may set up." Senator Blanche K. Bruce, who claimed to

have headed a solid delegation for Hayes, congratulated the
nominee on behalf of four million blacks and predicted "an
administration of the government of the nation as fruitful in
glorious results to all the people as was that of the martyred
president."[20]

Blacks could point to evidence from Hayes's past to justify
their support. As a young lawyer he had defended fugitive slaves.
After the war, he had generally endorsed radical Republican
policy. In 1867 Hayes ran for governor of Ohio on a platform
favoring black suffrage, a position still unpopular in much of
the North. But he also had a record, typical of many northern
Republicans in the seventies, of vacillating between support for
the radical policy of the sixties and reconciliation with the South.
To many blacks reconciliation was synonymous with abandonment. That Hayes was now the Republican candidate, however,
was for the majority enough to elicit their support. They were
initially reassured by Republican canvassers, notably Robert G.
Ingersoll, who repeated the "bloody shirt" rhetoric of earlier
campaigns. Although Hayes himself usually maintained a
guarded silence, he instructed his campaign workers to emphasize the horrors of "rebel rule" as a counterbalance to the focus
on national depression.[21]

Despite general awareness that the election would be close, in
the preconvention months few blacks expressed concern that the
first Democratic president since before the Civil War might be
elected and accordingly they showed little interest in whom the
Democratic nominee would be. Despite efforts by northern Democrats to mute their racist image, most blacks, North and South,
fully intended to vote Republican and were confident that their
party would retain the presidency. When Samuel Tilden was
nominated with Thomas Hendricks, who had opposed emancipation on the grounds of black inferiority, as his running mate,
they were given much less attention in the black press and by
black political spokesmen than the Republicans received. The
People's Advocate's negative assessment, which condemned Tilden
as "a monster in the art of cunning" and Hendricks as "a hopeless
democrat," was typical of the limited coverage.[22]

Early in 1876 Pinchback warned that "the prospects of a bloody
campaign are daily increasing and consequently colored voters

are becoming more and more demoralized." But despite a growing awareness that their status in the South had so degenerated
that their participation in some areas could result in violent retaliation, the majority of politically active southern blacks openly
supported and often campaigned for the Republican ticket.
Hayes received a number of requests for financial assistance
from blacks who wished to campaign for him. Isaac H. Smith of
New Bern, North Carolina, wrote that "in a campaign like this
if the colored men had proper information they would vote a
Republican ticket," but he doubted they could continue fighting
the wealthier Democrats without some assistance.[23]

Frederick Douglass promised to take an active part in a contest
he viewed as "the same old conflict, liberty, union and civilization
on the one hand, disunion and barbarism on the other." Some
blacks, however, were less certain that the line between good
and evil was so clearly drawn in this campaign and often qualified
their support for the Republicans. Pinchback's *Weekly Louisianian*, which proclaimed itself "Republican in All Times and
Under All Circumstances," was prominent among black papers
in supporting the Hayes ticket, but Pinchback was also typical
of many black Republicans when he hedged his support by condemning the party for selfishly using black votes. George Washington Williams, an Ohio minister with political aspirations,
warned that the slights and frustrations blacks were encounter-
ing in the campaign promoted a sense of self-reliance that could
lead to independence. He demanded that if black loyalty was to
be retained, "primitive Republicanism in its letter and spirit must
be resuscitated."[24]

Some blacks went beyond criticism of the Republicans and
demands for the resuscitation of earlier idealism to active support of the Democrats. A conscious effort by northern Democrats
to downplay racism and win over disgruntled black Republicans
won black supporters in northern cities, although they were still
a small minority. Some agreed with the three black men from
Baltimore who claimed that the Republican mission to end slavery was over and that "the Democratic party is the party of
reform." At the Nashville Colored Convention, John Shaw, a
black Democrat from New York, insisted that the Democrats
should gain adherents as Republican abandonment progressed,

but in 1876 such ideas were still roundly condemned by most black leaders and voters in the North.[25]

Southern blacks, directly confronted with Democratic "redemption," had less incentive to leave the Republican party although some southern Democrats recruited their support. Northern Democrats, recognizing the possibility of a backlash if there was excessive campaign violence, urged the southern wing of their party to cease the use of violence. In Louisiana, one of the most violent states, some state Democratic leaders heeded these warnings and replaced earlier terrorist tactics with parades, barbecues, and speeches emphasizing Democratic concern with black rights. All across the South, Democrats tried to persuade blacks to abandon the Republicans by linking Hayes to the corruption of the Grant administration and by claiming that the collapse of the Freedmen Saving's Bank, created by a Republican Congress to help blacks financially, was proof that northern Republicans cared nothing for them. Some blacks did willingly join Tilden clubs. But for the most part Democratic appeals to blacks were not successful, as the South Carolina Black Oak Democracy inadvertently admitted when resolving to protect "the few colored democrats who have & will join the party."[26]

As a result, despite warnings from the North, southern Democrats continued using fraud, intimidation, and violence to prevent black Republican voting. Buying black votes was another method successfully used in both the North and South. According to the *People's Advocate*, this was sometimes accomplished with the aid of "unprincipled, but shrewd and experienced colored men," but it was also made possible by a general awareness that the Republicans had fallen short of patronage promises. It was also often a result of economic necessity. In Barnwell County, South Carolina, some blacks claimed that they were forced to sell votes "to keep starvation off." Economic coercion—threatening blacks with the loss of jobs and land—persuaded large numbers that they could not vote.[27]

Violence persuaded many others. All across the South whites resorted to the Mississippi Plan—the successful use of intimidation and violence to destroy the black vote. Congressman Robert Smalls charged South Carolina Democrats with fraud, murder, and more "inhuman brutality" than he had ever thought possible. Attorney D. Augustus Straker labeled the situation "organized chaos." In Louisiana the term "bulldozing" was coined to describe the racial outrages that occurred. A U.S. marshall in the state reported that blacks "are politically in a state of siege." The violence came to a head in Hamburg, South Carolina, where on the fourth of July a parade of black militiamen resulted in the massacre of six black men and the looting of black homes. The incident had the impact northern Democrats feared: briefly southern violence was again a viable issue with northern Republican voters.[28]

In light of such violent opposition, it is remarkable how many blacks remained politically active. Most northern blacks focused on race relations in the South and thus overwhelmingly concluded that the Republicans must be reelected. Despite the possible repercussions, blacks in both the North and South formed clubs to work for Hayes. The few southern black Democrats who openly acknowledged their political allegiance had to contend with ostracism and even physical abuse from loyal black Republicans for their unorthodox views. In North Carolina, Garland H. White, a Baptist minister and leading black Democrat, became so unpopular that he was forced to go north to campaign for Tilden. When black Democrats in Nashville tried to organize, black Republicans broke up their meeting with "eggs, potatoes, and heavier missiles." Southern black Republicans were also tenacious in their determination to vote. In South Carolina, the most violence-ridden state, over 90 percent of the eligible black population voted, and the vast majority of them, as in other southern states, cast their votes for the Republicans. Despite all obstacles, James A. Garfield observed, the black voter "almost universally inclines" to vote against former masters.[29]

A major reason many blacks were unwilling to make good on threats to desert the Republicans was an awareness of how close the 1876 election would be and the real possibility that a Democrat might win the White House. Robert Marcus has observed that the closeness of elections in the late nineteenth century "supported party regularity by raising the cost of expressing one's dissatisfaction with the party above what most voters were willing to pay." This was particularly true of black Republicans. Although they increasingly hedged their support for the GOP with qualifications and warnings, they were generally unwilling to express their dissatisfaction by voting Democratic.[30]

The outcome of the election was uncertain from November to March. Early returns indicated that Tilden, by carrying all of the southern states, had won the electoral college by one vote. Continued Republican control in Florida, South Carolina, and Louisiana, however, enabled their Republican electoral supervisors to claim victory for Hayes. The resulting dual electoral returns, plus a disputed vote from Oregon, gave both parties a claim to the presidential victory. For nearly four months the country was uncertain whether Hayes or Tilden had been elected. Democrats and Republicans both demanded that their particular candidate be inaugurated, and some even threatened war if he was not.

Some blacks, initially confident that Hayes had been electeq, wired him their congratulations. John Langston, former vice-president of Howard University and in 1876 a member of the Board of Health of Washington, D.C., claimed to speak for all black Americans when he congratulated the Republican nominee on his victory. The Thanksgiving program of the St. Paul A.M.E. Church in Urbana, Ohio, proclaimed, "The political status of the Negro is something to make us thankful." Lew Wallace, sent by the Republican party to investigate conditions in Florida, reported that blacks there retained hope and confidence in "freedom and God."[31]

A number of blacks soon realized, however, that the election might be settled in favor of the Democrats. A southern black man wrote Hayes that his people, having first heard that Tilden won and then that Hayes had won, were bewildered. Fears that slavery would be restored if Tilden was elected and demands for violence if necessary to assure a Hayes victory were reported in some parts of the country. A black Mississippian wrote, "What a hell of a fix the country is in," and questioned whether the southern "bulldozers" would be so bold if blacks fought back. W. W. Dedrick insisted that "Hays has a right to be declared president having received 185 electoral votes. To doubt or hesitate on this proposition is to be damned. The triumph of Tilden is the triumph of murder as an element in politics." Ex-judge Grandison Harris assured Hayes that if the Investigating Committee came to Georgia it would discover that the state had been counted Democratic only because Republicans had been driven from the polls. John Lynch, congressman from Mississippi during the electoral crisis, recalled years later that he voted against the establishment of a commission because he believed that Hayes had been duly elected and that Grant should use force if necessary to assure his inauguration.[32]

The election result, publicly settled by an Electoral Commission drawn from Congress and the Supreme Court, was covertly influenced by the maneuverings of special interest groups which brought together northern Republicans and their potential southern Democratic allies. These majority factions of both parties had come to recognize their common interests, particularly their mutual desire for conservative economic policy, federal internal improvements, and the suppression of labor strife. Once the southern Democrats had effected a compromise which included southern home rule, aid to southern internal improvements, southern representation in the administration, and most important, removal of the last troops from the South, they tacitly supported a pro-Hayes count. Although southern Democrats had agreed to respect southern black rights, many blacks immediately recognized the pejorative implications of the compromise. Even before the new president was inaugurated, they warned against Republican abandonment. Pinchback charged the Republican party to "be brave enough" to insure the citizenship that it had conferred upon blacks. To leave the South alone, he admonished, "would be to turn the lamb over to the wolf." Perception that this was exactly what the Compromise of 1877 had done would grow over the next decade until "the betrayal of 1877" became synonomous to blacks with Republican abandonment and racism.[33]

Most whites in both the North and South welcomed this symbolic end to a decade of Radical Reconstruction. The *Nation*, which generally expressed opinions more sympathetic to black rights than most Northerners held, predicted "the negro will disappear from the field of national politics." But despite widespread awareness of the possible ramifications that the compromise and Hayes's developing southern policy had for them, many blacks initially rejoiced at the Republican victory and expressed confidence that they would not be betrayed. On the South Carolina coastal island of St. Helena "smiles, laughter, hand-shakings, huggings ... tears of joy" and "fervent thanks to heaven" greeted the final electoral count. On Hayes's inauguration day the Vidalia (La.) *Concordia Eagle* praised the Republicans for handling the controversy with "admirable skill" and criticized the Democrats for showing "as little political generalship as honesty." Some of this optimism stemmed from a tendency to rationalization and wishful thinking following political setbacks. The New Orleans *Republican* insisted that the president would not "abandon his political friends and supporters in the South for the personal advantage he would be likely to derive from the conciliation of his utterly routed enemies." Several blacks writing congratulations to Hayes noted the president's concern with their status when his election was in doubt and expressed confidence that with his victory the race's best interest would be considered. But there was also uncertainty. Not infrequently optimism was joined with reminders of the sacrifices that blacks had made to bring Republican victory about.[34]

In April, the last troops were withdrawn from Louisiana, and quickly thereafter the Hayes administration began implementing its southern policy. This policy was predicated on the idea that the Republican party, in order to win in the South, must switch its emphasis from wooing black voters to converting the "Whiggish" element—antebellum southern Whigs and other Southerners who were primarily concerned with industrial development. The new southern Republican party would be secured by dispensing patronage to potential native white converts rather than to carpetbaggers and blacks. This policy had roots dating back to Lincoln's administration and had been periodically proposed ever since by Republican politicians. They were prodded by conservative northern businessmen who had come to the conclusion that under Radical Reconstruction they were "estranged from their natural allies." These businessmen hoped for economic reasons to restore stability to the South and to establish ties with "New South" businessmen who were in accord with them on most economic issues. President Hayes's own belief that the "best people" should dominate public affairs fit well with this conservative strategy. His southern policy was a profound change from radical Republican thought, but, as C. Vann Woodward explains, many Republicans had concluded that "old Radical Southern policy" was "quite out of line with its [the party's] true nature."[35]

Initially some black leaders counseled accepting the president's policy. John Langston of Virginia, Richard T. Greener of South Carolina, and J. Willis Menard of Florida, were typical of southern black Republicans who were dependent on the northern party for protection of their political and journalistic endeavors—a dependency that undoubtedly influenced their defense of Hayes's policy. Langston, who held a Republican appointment, described "peaceful reconstruction" as a blessing to blacks. Greener, a professor at the University of South Carolina which was dependent on Republican support for its precarious integrated status, wrote Hayes that "the policy that you have so simply outlined, if honestly, impartially and rigidly carried out, will give the only harmony, peace and true moral development which at the present time is so badly needed among both races in the South." Menard, a Florida editor and politician, admitted that a cursory examination of Hayes's policy could cause blacks some concern but denied that there was any alternative. Like most other black politicians, however, his ability to rationalize support for conservative Republican policy had limits. Blacks, he said, should work to shape their own political destiny by considering both parties and should also give more attention to non-political endeavors.[36]

Organized blacks also tried to remain optimistic and sent the president assurance of their continued support in the early months of his administration. A Memphis group passed a resolution endorsing Hayes's policy with only two dissenting votes. A group from Virginia resolved, "That we hail with joy the dawn of a new era fraught with signs and promises of peace and prosperity to the entire people of our distressed country." Louisiana black Baptists offered a prayer of thanks that "the wise policy of our ruler is cementing the white and colored races." But groups also expressed reservations about Hayes's policy. A complimentary resolution from Alabama was tempered by the conclusion that "it is the earnest wish of the colored citizens of the South to fully enjoy the blessings of civil and political liberty—without any curtailment or proscription—allotted to any other class."[37]

Some northern blacks were also initially optimistic about the prospect of Hayes's southern policy, and because they were less directly aware of its potentially regressive ramifications, were less qualified in their praise. Shortly after the inauguration, Douglass was invited to confer with President Hayes on southern affairs; the president later recorded in his dairy that Douglass approved his policy. Douglass's silence at the removal of federal troops and his acceptance of a position in Hayes's administration do indicate his tacit support. John Bagwell claimed to speak for New Jersey blacks in celebrating this "triumph of Truth, Justice and Liberty." Blacks from Hayes's native Ohio were particularly outspoken in their defense and urged southern blacks to remain loyal when many in that section grew pessimistic. George W. Williams headed a group of Ohioans who issued a circular letter calling on southern blacks to support the administration. If Southerners violated their promise to protect black rights, the circular assured, Hayes would turn from pacification to force. James Poindexter, Benjamin Arnett, John P. Green, and Alfred Anderson were also black Ohio leaders who defended the president. Poindexter urged an economic alliance between black labor and southern capital with less emphasis on politics.[38]

Some black leaders continued supporting Hayes and defending his southern policy throughout his presidency. Almost two years after Hayes took office, Williams claimed that a large number of southern blacks accepted the southern policy. John Lynch claimed to verify this from the more proximate perspective of Mississippi. Hiram Revels, a Mississippi senator from 1869 to 1871, agreed that Hayes's policy was successful and predicted that it would lead to a day when there would be mutual confidence between southern blacks and whites. James L. Herbert, another Mississippian, claimed two years after it was initiated, that the president's policy was the best promotion of racial and sectional harmony since the war. About the same time George Hull of Virginia wrote Hayes that the "poor ignorant colored race" was "almost to a man . . . Stalwart Republican but had no one to instruct them politically." They would never vote contrary to the wishes of the northern Republican party, he assured the president, if they knew those wishes. C. C. Antoine, former state senator and lieutenant-governor of Louisiana, offered a more typically mixed reaction: He praised Hayes for efforts to punish violators of black suffrage but despaired that there had been a general failure to convict.[39]

Most black defenders of Hayes's southern policy were conservatives who hoped for political appointments. The majority of blacks were less reluctant to criticize a Republican president. As it became increasingly clear that promises to protect black rights were not being kept, their frustration and criticism increased. Anxiety about what Hayes's policy meant for southern black rights proliferated in the North. This was even true in Ohio. Robert Harlan reported in August 1877 that "nineteen out of every twenty colored men I know believe that the Republican party wishes to unload them." Fred Roney tried to give substance to the criticism when he organized a boycott of elections in Columbus. Philadelphian Abraham Barber wrote Hayes of his concern that not enough had been done for southern blacks. A group in New York refused to endorse Hayes unless he guaranteed protection of all people in the South. Although a New Jersey Colored Convention failed to pass a resolution against Hayes's policy, several speakers condemned it.[40]

Criticism continued to be most common in the South where blacks experienced firsthand the impact of Hayes's southern policy. In letters to the president as well as to black leaders, southern blacks described the lawlessness and violence they confronted and made both pleas and threats that something be done. South Carolina Congressman Joseph R. Rainey told Hayes that in some counties of his state intimidation and violence were effectively disfranchising his people and that they were "depressed beyond measure" when popular state leader Robert Smalls was unjustly convicted of fraud. D. Augustus Straker predicted that the Republican party would soon be wiped out in the state and determined to leave the South for good. "The promise of peace by the Democrats," he insisted,

is a promise to the race to be broken to the heart. I do not question the good will of President Hayes towards us as a race. I admire, agree with, and am willing to uphold his hands in reconciling the conflict

between the races in the South and making our motto E pluribus unum
not merely words but a veritable fact, but let him be certain that there
is mutuality in the contract.

Congressman Lynch also began to exonerate the president.
Hayes's policy, he rationalized, did not correspond to the president's personal convictions but was necessitated by preinaugural
pledges.[41]

Although it was generally black leaders and editors who publicly criticized Hayes's southern policy, the masses were most
dramatically aware of its impact and they also protested. Benjamin Johnson of Arkansas wrote, "We are suffering very bad
in the South. We have no rights hear among the white people
they dont consider we colored people no more than dogs. We
need protection. We want our Republican friends to do all they
can for us black people the Democrats kill us and there aint
anything dont about it." A citizen of Booneville, Mississippi,
urged Blanche K. Bruce, the only black man in the Senate, to
work for a bill guaranteeing the freedom to vote because every
black in the state from former officeholders to the "small Republican in the cotton field" was denied that right. Another
Mississippian asked Bruce if he expected any protection for the
black vote in 1878, warning that "the party is dead as Hector
without it." There were also charges more serious than disfranchisement. In East Felisiana, Louisiana, activitist James Laws was
reported as one of possibly hundreds murdered "because he was
a Republican nigger."[42]

H.C.C. Astwood led the New Orleans Young Men's Protective
Association in complaining about the outrages committed against
blacks in the 1878 Louisiana elections. By 1878 many of the
state's black political leaders, particularly in rural areas, had been
forced either to cease political activity or to flee the state, and
some had been killed. Black voters in some sections of the state
were given badges to protect them from violence after being
forced to vote Democratic. Pointing to the growth of such outrages against black Republicans since the last presidential election, the Protective Association determined that their earlier
faith in the president had been ill-founded. Although Hayes was
described as personally "honest, honorable and humanitarian,"

his southern policy was condemned as a threat to the very lives of black Americans. The group claimed loyalty to the Republican party but declared itself ready to cooperate with white Louisianians "whenever such cooperation does not interfere with our cardinal principles."[43]

Proposals that blacks leave the Republican party and make the best possible terms with the Democrats, although still rare, became more common in the later years of Hayes's administration as blacks desperately searched for a viable way to stem the growing disfranchisement and violence they confronted. Gilbert Myers of Mississippi is an example of a small number of wealthy southern blacks who became Democrats in order to protect their property. He reported to a Senate committee in 1879 that he voted Democratic, "because I sympathize with my own self, knowing that I expected to stay with them [white Democrats] to make property if I could, and the South has always been kind to me." Pragmatic P.B.S. Pinchback, whose advice to southern blacks ranged from the most radical to the most conservative, at this time lobbied in his New Orleans paper for accommodation with the Democrats. The *Weekly Louisianian*'s Washington correspondent condemned northern Republicans for their betrayal and virtually advocated support for the Democrats when he wrote, "All things considered, it is better to trust those with which you live, even if they are stained with your blood, than to link your political fortunes to a set of cold, heartless and hypocritical leaders in the north, as represented by the present executive and the class of men he has called around him." Another correspondent for the paper claimed that if blacks would "vote for the conservative and independent thinkers of the South" they could "break down the wall of prejudice which surrounds the Democratic party." The relatively benevolent regime of Democratic governor Wade Hampton in South Carolina fostered the movement of some blacks into the Democratic party, a response repeated in some other parts of the South. The Montgomery (Ala.) *Advance*, in what was probably an effort to reform the Democrats by flattery, claimed that under Bourbon control the South was a haven for the race, but this was a view roundly condemned by most southern blacks.[44]

Most blacks still stopped far short of actual endorsement of the Democrats; their qualified praise was usually veiled criticism directed at the Republicans. More common than Republican apostasy was continuation of a tenuous relationship that often included harsh criticism and warnings that the party must accept its moral obligations. Pinchback, possibly motivated by a desire for lucrative patronage, typified this sentiment when he threatened, "The Republicans must either do the proper thing by me, or I will make them rue the day they forced me to take arms against them.... I am as true a Republican as treads the earth, and you know it well, but by the eternal, I will have recognition or revenge."[45]

As blacks became increasingly frustrated by Republican policy and at the same time remained opposed to the Democrats, affiliation with a third party was proposed as an alternative. The Greenback party, which had been formed in response to postwar economic dislocations and which had by the late seventies broadened its platform to include a variety of social issues, was the first major third party to be endorsed by blacks. In the later years of the Hayes administration it attracted some southern blacks on the state level. In the 1878 Texas state elections, almost half of the blacks voting supported the Greenbackers. But their allegiance was ephemeral, and the majority, perhaps heeding warnings that the Greenbackers were merely "forlorn Democrats," were back in the Republican fold by 1880. On the national level the Greenbackers had little appeal for black voters, but they did play a role in conditioning poor black and white southern farmers to the possibility of seeking solutions to economic problems through alternative political routes. Occasionally there were radical proposals that blacks launch a new party as well as conservative suggestions that they abandon politics altogether. George T. Downing, for example, although generally adamant about black rights, proposed shortly after Hayes's election that the race should become better educated and more skilled in the art of government before becoming active politically. But in the seventies, when many blacks still believed that political participation could be effective, such advice was given little consideration. Although blacks were becoming increasingly critical of Republican treatment, most still believed that this party was the most efficacious vehicle for assuring their rights.[46]

Prominent among the rights demanded was the right to hold political and appointive offices. Blacks had become accustomed to having representation in the federal government during the Reconstruction era and continued to demand a recognition many considered symbolic of the race's citizenship and equality. Although the fight for patronage was most tenaciously pursued by leaders who stood to profit personally, blacks with little chance for recognition also demanded black appointments. When Frederick Douglass was appointed marshall of the District of Columbia in 1877, some accepted this as proof that Hayes would consider black interests. Henry Highland Garnet, New York pastor and former minister to Liberia, wrote that in New York the appointment was viewed as the most complete acknowledgment of black rights yet given by a president. The appointment was also labeled "another shot heard around the world," and "another degree on the dial." Douglass responded to his own appointment by praising Hayes as "a just man whose policy embraces the welfare of both races." Soon after, John Langston was named minister to Haiti. The two appointments, affirmed a Virginia group, were "honest fulfillment" of Hayes's "declared purpose as to our race." The appointment two years later of James Hill to be internal revenue collector of Mississippi was heralded by the New Orleans *Weekly Louisianian* as a timely and important appointment that would be most helpful in retaining black support for the Hayes administration.[47]

Not all blacks, however, considered symbolic appointments as the fulfillment of Republican obligations. Alexander Crummell, Episcopal divine and noted intellectual, more pessimistically noted, following the Douglass appointment, "I have the most serious misgivings, for President Hayes putting one black man forward does not compensate for his pulling back 4 1/2 million black men in the south and giving supremacy . . . to the old power-holding body." Such criticism became more common as blacks became aware of the administration's "lily-white" policy. Despite considerable evidence by 1879 (including defeat in the 1878 congressional elections and a Senate investigation into southern election illegalities) that his southern policy was not building a viable white southern party, Hayes continued to pursue a "genteel strategy." Robert Elliott, former congressman from South Carolina, reported that black Southerners were everywhere concerned that Hayes was filling most federal offices in the South with Democrats or white Republicans whom blacks could no longer trust. Norris Wright Cuney, the leading black Republican in Texas, complained that, although blacks made up four-fifths of the state's Republican party, they held no federal appointments. Six months after praising the Republican appointment of Hill, the *Weekly Louisianian* condemned white Republicans for intimidating blacks in the state so that they feared seeking appointive positions and warned that attempts to obligate blacks by harkening back to the Emancipation Proclamation and at the same time denying them recognition would bring the most intelligent of the race into revolt. Black men who themselves aspired to office were particularly bitter in their denunciation of Republican policy. Edwin Belcher, a leader of black Republicanism in Georgia and an inveterate office seeker, had concluded by 1879 that no black Georgian could ever expect an appointment from a president who had solicited their votes and then ignored them for three years. William Pledger, shortly before he was elected chairman of the Georgia Republican party, scorned Hayes's promises to appoint a black man as collector of revenue by suggesting that "the man to whom it is tendered ought to hurl it back into the face of the administration that it may grow to a larger size." J. M. Bynum of Mississippi included Senator Bruce when he condemned the Republicans for ignoring black Republicans while trying to appease southern Democrats. He wrote Bruce, "It is humiliating to us who have stood to our principles to have the cold shoulder turned to us. I want to see Republicans in office that have stood by their guns through the thickest of the fight.[48]

As black leaders became increasingly disenchanted with the Republican administration they had helped to elect, they organized to protest. Organizations formed in the seventies epitomize the ambivalence many blacks felt as to the best means to the desired end of "effective liberty." While they generally stressed integration rather than separation, they also stressed black self-help and unification. They were conservative in that they commonly urged adapting to middle-class social and economic standards. Despite emphasis on conformity and self-help, however, many of these groups continued appealing to and even demanding that the Republican party fight for their rights. The American Protective Society to Prevent Injustice to the Colored People was typical. Pinchback, Lynch, Bruce, Cuney, Isaac Myers, J. W. Cromwell, J. C. Napier, and J. S. Hinton were leaders at a conference in Nashville which founded the organization. They resolved:

We the colored people of the United States of America do declare the first principle of a republican government to be equality of its citizens before the law and the obligation of the government to protect all classes of citizens by its laws; that we recognize with profound regret the existence of a race distinction, having caste and prejudice as its principle directed toward the colored people of this country with such force of discrimination as to nullify the constitution and render law enacted thereunder unoperative; that the civil, political and intellectual advancement of our race is thereby seriously impaired, and the life and property of our people are unjustly abused.[49]

Organizations to work for an end to racial proscription became common, but they were not supported by all black people. Some were fearful of any harsh rhetoric directed toward whites. Henry Scroggins, for example, condemned the Nashville convention on the grounds that protest could only make matters worse, possibly even leading to reenslavement, and demanded that the race seek redress of its grievances only through the established governmental process.[50]

On the other hand, more radical blacks were convinced that proper channels would never serve to ameliorate conditions in the South. While the black elite registered its protest in print and at conventions, thousands of poor black Southerners determined that the only viable course left was to leave. Steady erosion of political rights, combined with social and economic woes, fed the exodus. In 1877, several months after the last federal troops were withdrawn from Louisiana, a colonization council met in the state and decided that "the whole South— every State in the South—had got into the hands of the very men that held us slaves," and that "there was no hope for us and we had better go."[51]

Some aspiring emigrants concluded that black rights would

never be respected in any part of the United States and proposed settlement in Africa, particularly in Liberia. In South Carolina the Liberian Exodus Joint-Stock Steamship Company was formed to facilitate large-scale immigration to Africa. In 1878, the Louisiana-based National Colored Colonization Council sent a petition with three thousand signatures to President Hayes, asking for aid in relocation in Liberia or a separate black territory unless protection could be assured to southern blacks. D. D. Bell of Mississippi wrote Bruce of the despair in his state. "There are hundreds of colored people here," he lamented, " 'refugees' from the southern part of the state driven here by the bulldozers. I hope you will do all you can to help us to Africa as we never can get justice in the U.S. Senate."[52]

Some blacks opposed a return to Africa but supported the creation of a separate territory in the United States. In the summer of 1877 a group in Charlotte, North Carolina, asked the president for information concerning colonization, "for we find that you are about to shake hands with the South. If you do that you are putting us in a worse condition than we were when we were slaves. The only way that we see to obtain our freedom is colonizing into a country of our own." John Williamson, North Carolina leader for colonization, introduced a resolution in the North Carolina House demanding a separate territory for blacks as the only way they could receive their fair share of rights and honors.[53]

The majority of would-be emigrants, however, wanted to remain American citizens but relocate outside the South, particularly in Kansas, considered "the quintessential free state." This alternative generated a national debate when, in January 1879, Senator William Windom of Minnesota proposed that blacks who were not allowed to vote and exercise their constitutional rights be federally assisted in emigrating from the southern states. Possibly in part motivated by Windom's resolution, thousands of blacks left or attempted to leave the South in the Exodus of 1879.[54]

Although some southern whites supported the exodus of blacks as good riddance, many others, fearful of losing their cheap labor supply, worked to stem the migration. Thomas W. Conway, a former Freedmen's Bureau official and superintendent of education in Louisiana who now lived in New Jersey, wrote the president about southern obstruction. "This is bondage," he told Hayes. "We may have to cry aloud to you Mr. President, as we cried to your illustrious predecessor, Mr. Lincoln, to issue our emancipation proclamation, for surely our colored brethren in the South have not been emancipated except on paper." Although some planters used force to curb the exodus, others counseled a more benign course. In May 1879, a group met in Vicksburg, Mississippi, and pledged to seek protection of black suffrage as a means of keeping black labor in the South. Their fear of a labor shortage did prompt some improvement for southern blacks, but the change was limited and generally short-lived.[55]

The idea of migration also generated debate among blacks. Nell Painter points out that "respectable Blacks' opinion on the Exodus ran the gamut from conditional criticism, through conditional approval, to enthusiastic acclaim." The most strident critic was Frederick Douglass, who argued that the race's enemies would claim that ignorant blacks were imported into the North to outvote intelligent whites, a charge that was in fact frequently made. Douglass was also concerned that emigration would become an alternative to demanding rights in the South. Some southern black political leaders, who were dependent on the masses for a political base and whose higher economic status gave them a quite different perspective, agreed with Douglass and opposed the exodus. Benjamin "Pap" Singleton, an exodus leader, claimed that it included only working men—that "not a political Negro was in it." A number of these black politicians were at the Vicksburg meeting and cooperated with whites in seeking ways to keep black labor in the South. But other black political leaders, including Joseph Rainey of South Carolina, James T. Rapier of Alabama, and J. C. Napier of Tennessee, gave no credence to the Vicksburg pledge and supported the exodus out of the South.[56]

Many northern Republicans, black and white, championed the movement. Senator Windom headed the National Emigration Aid Society to aid the refugees, and Richard Greener, removed from the faculty of the University of South Carolina by the Hampton administration, served as the society's secretary. In

Missouri, J. Milton Turner's Colored Immigration Aid Society competed with the Colored Relief Board in giving direct relief to the exodusters. John Cromwell, editor of the *People's Advocate*, and John Smyth, former minister to Liberia, were among the leaders in forming the Southern Emigration Company "for the purpose of aiding the colored people of the Southern States in moving from their present abodes of misery and poverty."[57]

Private aid, however, was far too limited to support massive emigration, so many would-be Kansas emigrants also appealed to the federal government for help. President Hayes, who expressed sympathy for the movement, received numerous requests for assistance. W. H. Mann of Battleboro, North Carolina, asked for pamphlets and aid for black North Carolinians to immigrate to Africa, Kansas, or, inexplicably, Arkansas. Twenty blacks from Hinds County, Mississippi, petitioned the president for help in moving to Kansas because they were so oppressed that they could no longer endure. Thomas Farmer, speaking for blacks in Arkansas who had been so badly swindled and outraged "that starvation and neckedness had almost overtaken us," also requested assistance. Edward Bailey demanded that Hayes provide the needed aid because the race's condition had greatly worsened since he took office. A. H. Johnson of Laurens County, South Carolina, wrote Senator John Sherman that he was "forced to the conclusion that the treatment we receive at the hands of our Southern White friends will never be better—that our rights of citizenship can never be employed under Democratic rule in the South" and appealed to Sherman either to buy land in Kansas for black emigrants or in some way to advance the funds needed to start a colony. But little aid was forthcoming, and in 1880 most blacks remained in the South, where they continued to confront political and economic discrimination.[58]

T. Thomas Fortune, a prominent black editor of the period and author of several books, described the chain of events set in motion by the election of 1876 and the Compromise of 1877 in a terse and dramatic phrase: "a revolution gone backward." In *The Negro in Politics* (1886) he asked "What did the party gain by its open barter and sale in 1876," and responded "It gained Rutherford B. Hayes. . . . It gained scorn and contempt for abandoning the vital principle which had made it invincible; it gained discredit with the honest voters of the country which entailed upon it as succession of defeats up to the present." The Republican party, Fortune asserted, "had sacrificed principle to perpetuate its control of the Federal power and patronage."[59]

Although blacks would be critical of future Republican administrations for failing to stem the tide of disfranchisement, segregation, and violence in the South, Hayes's Compromise of 1877 would remain the event most symbolically representative of Republican abandonment. Fortune's assessment of the Hayes administration was predictive of those offered by black leaders in the eighties and nineties. Even some blacks who had defended Hayes's policy during his administration were critical in later years. When asked in 1885 about the effect of the election of Grover Cleveland on black rights, Frederick Douglass claimed that the Hayes years, rather than the election of a Democratic president, had brought an end to black political rights in the South. In 1896, the twentieth anniversary of Hayes's election, the Omaha *Gazette* insisted, "This country does not want any Hayes in the White House. It would have been better for Tilden to have been seated than for the rights of the negro to have been surrendered by Hayes."[60]

When this editorial appeared in 1896, the southern black vote had been virtually eliminated. In 1880, however, many southern blacks could still vote and they continued to look to the national government for protection from proscription and violence and to the Republican party as the most promising source for that government. As the election of 1880 approached, blacks rationalized that a new Republican president would reverse the setbacks of the Hayes years. This hope was given voice by W. D. Sherman, Jr. [?] of Springwood, Georgia, who in a barely literate but very insightful letter, described the sentiments of many southern blacks in 1880: "Under Grant's administration the Republicans were more in power than under mr Hays though this present govnt administration yet so has proved energy to my judgment to all with the exception of the Southern policy." But because of this southern policy, Sherman was hopeful that a new president would be elected. "The gentlemen at the North doesn't understand the swindling killing ant cheating at these rates the white people here can and does take 10 whites and pools more votes than 100 colored can." Still Sherman was optimistic. "The day will soon be here," he wrote, "when we shall hear from Chicargo Illinois we hope to that Hon. Sherman are president."[61]

2

Still Necessarily a Republican: The Election of 1880 and the Garfield Administration

In 1880, blacks confronted the first presidential election since Hayes's removal of federal troops. In February Pinchback wrote Senator Bruce that in Louisiana, "the masses are in arms and eager for the fray to begin." But a letter in Pinchback's paper more pessimistically reported that "as to the political affairs of our parish there is but little to say. If we are to have a free ballot and fair count, Grant would be our choice for President, but the people are despondent. They don't take much interest in politics. They seem to care more for the future, and are trying to move to a land where bulldozing is unknown." In South Carolina a white reporter less sympathetically claimed that "black political aspirations are nearly if not entirely at an end." The truth lay between these two extreme conjectures. Events of the previous four years had spawned both political apathy and fear. Blacks had been badly disillusioned by the erosion of Radical Reconstruction, and some had been forced to abandon politics. But despite bitter confrontations with the limits of national political power, an approaching presidential election inspired many blacks to rationalize that a new Republican president would protect their rights.[1]

In reality the Republican party in 1880 was vastly different from the mythical party of Lincoln and was more akin to the Democrats than ever. As northern interest in the reconstructed South and the rights of the freedmen faded, so too did ideological differences between the two major parties. Both were becoming increasingly factionalized and decentralized and more concerned with organization and power than with promoting specific policies. In 1880 the name "Stalwart" was applied to the Republican party's largest faction which had first coalesced as the congressional power center during the Grant years. Although the Stalwarts were primarily concerned with fostering their own power in the North, they did condemn reconciliation with the Democratic South and continued to give lip service to the protection of black rights. Because of their opposition to both Hayes's southern policy and his interest in reform, their power had waned considerably since his election. Led by shrewd and egotistical Senator Roscoe Conkling of New York, who was well liked by many blacks for his courtesy to Senator Bruce, the Stalwarts hoped to restore their power by making Grant president again in 1880.[2]

Although Grant's southern policy had been almost as responsible as Hayes's for reversing the radical political revolution, he was still associated with federal enforcement of Reconstruction and was therefore the favorite candidate of many blacks in the North and South. George Ruffin, a Boston lawyer and leader for Grant, promised support from New England blacks "even if they have to wade through seas of blood." In the South, where blacks would be more likely to wade through seas of blood, many viewed Grant as second only to Lincoln as a champion of black rights. Although Pinchback had insisted in 1878 that Grant cared "not a continental for the negro, further than to use him," the *Louisianian* was, by 1879, a leader among southern black supporters of the ex-president's nomination. Grant was viewed by the masses as a savior, the paper contended, and the one man who would break the solid South and give the race real political freedom—a correct assessment of Grant's popularity, at least for many poor southern blacks. Even some black officeholders who were indebted to Hayes concurred that Grant's name stirred up more enthusiasm among southern blacks than any except Lincoln's.[3]

Black loyalty, however, was not limited to any faction of the Republican party; many blacks readily supported Stalwarts. John

Sherman was second to Grant in popularity among southern blacks. A senator from Ohio during Reconstruction, Sherman had consistently supported radical measures and was generally considered sympathetic to black interests. As Hayes's secretary of the treasury, he had emphasized sound fiscal policy rather than sectional and racial matters as the government's primary concern, but his appointment of several prominent southern blacks to key Treasury Department positions enabled him to retain some black allegiance. In the preconvention months, Sherman received letters from numerous southern black leaders assuring him of widespread enthusiasm for his candidacy. Some of these Sherman enthusiasts were Treasury Department appointees who were virtually bribed to be faithful and who tended to exaggerate Sherman's strength. Would-be appointees also campaigned for the secretary. Fellow Ohioan George W. Williams was chastized by an Alabama paper when he came South to speak for Sherman for looking after his own "gold mine." But the southern paper agreed that Sherman "is the most available candidate the Republicans can nominate." C. C. Antoine, former lieutenant-governor of Louisiana, wrote that in his state blacks considered Sherman "the special champion of their rights and privileges." Robert Elliott, one of Sherman's appointees, acknowledged, after talking to black leaders in North and South Carolina, that Grant was still the leading contender there but found that Sherman and James G. Blaine were second. Former Congressman Joseph H. Rainey concluded a few months later that South Carolina blacks were shifting their support to Sherman. Another former congressman, James T. Rapier of Alabama, who now held a Treasury Department position, urged blacks in his state to support Sherman because he had played a role in writing the Reconstruction acts, had long championed black political rights, and had condemned racial violence. In Mississippi, the issue of the party's candidate threatened to split the triumvirate of Republican leaders—Blanche K. Bruce, John Lynch, and James Hill. Bruce and Hill were for Sherman, but Lynch supported Grant. Enemies of the three hoped that their differences could be used to destroy their party leadership, but a compromise was worked out. Bruce and Hill were chosen delegates to the convention while Lynch was chosen to run for Congress. This meant that the Mississippi delegation was solid for Sherman.[4]

James G. Blaine, leader of the largest anti-Stalwart faction, "the Half-Breeds," and early front-runner, followed Grant and Sherman in popularity among blacks. Although the Half-Breeds were generally more interested in economic questions than in the southern question, Blaine's own record in support of black suffrage and in opposition to reconciliation assured him of some black support. Elihu B. Washburne, former minister to France, and Ohio Congressman James A. Garfield were also mentioned as men worth supporting for their records on black rights.[5]

To some blacks, the person nominated by the party was less important than the party's general support of black rights. It was even advocated that blacks endorse Grant only if Senator Bruce was named his vice-presidential running mate. Although often preoccupied with such unrealistic demands, the preconvention rhetoric did convince many, at least temporarily, that there could be political solutions to the problems of black people. Several weeks before the Republican convention, Blanche K. Bruce reported that "the colored people are thoroughly aroused and will not be found wanting on election day."[6]

A number of prominent southern blacks were again delegates to the convention and they were particularly courted by the Sherman forces. When the Sherman star began to fade, however, some, notably George W. Williams, shifted to Grant or other candidates. Several black men played significant roles. Bruce was nominated by John Lynch for the vice-presidency and received eight votes. The Mississippi senator was also honored by being elected temporary chairman. At a time when rival delegates wanted the floor, Chairman Bruce recognized Garfield; Garfield's subsequent speech was considered a key factor in his nomination. An equally important result of Bruce's chairmanship was the pride and assurance it afforded black people. Robert Elliott, who served as Sherman's floor manager for black delegates and seconded his nomination, was also prominent at the convention.[7]

Despite the recognition accorded Bruce and Elliott, however, most of the major decisions made at Chicago were far removed from the needs and wishes of black Republicans. Although the party's platform did brag of having elevated "4,000,000 human beings from the likeness of things to the rank of citizen," it also defended Hayes's policy of reconciliation. Because of a deadlock between the Stalwarts, who favored Grant, and the Half-Breeds, who supported Blaine, the nominee was a compromise candidate—James A. Garfield. Chester A. Arthur, a Stalwart, was nominated for the vice-presidency to appease that faction of the party. Blacks familiar with the Ohio congressman knew that his record on black rights was similar to those of the more favored candidates. He had been an abolitionist before the war and, as a member of Congress since 1863, a supporter of most Radical Reconstruction policy. In 1878 he had criticized Hayes's policy in the South as "a give-away" and had called for a return to protection of black votes. But as a staunch believer in a laissez-faire policy, he generally gravitated to support of less government in southern affairs. Although Garfield continued to believe that the Republican party needed black votes, he was ambivalent about black rights generally. Like Sherman, he increasingly prodded the Republican party to focus on industrial development and other economic questions.[8]

For the most part, disappointment that the black-supported candidates had not won quickly gave way to traditional black Republican allegiance. Black leaders from all over the United States sent congratulations to the Republican ticket and promised support. Even the staunchly pro-Grant *Weekly Louisianian*, while reporting considerable black disappointment at the convention outcome, called on all blacks to close ranks behind the Republicans. George W. Williams spoke for many when he wrote, "I am a republican and therefore always support the successful candidate." Despite the setbacks of the Hayes years, Democracy had as yet made few permanent inroads into this Republican bastion of support. Most blacks were still, as one West Virginia man described himself, "necessarily a republican."[9]

Again, blacks had little interest in the Democratic convention since no blacks were delegates and few anticipated supporting whomever was chosen. The Democrats chose Winfield Scott Hancock, a compromise dark-horse candidate who had been a

Union general, in part to convince northern voters that their party would abide by the results of the war. Blacks were generally complimentary, despite Hancock's weak enforcement of martial law in Louisiana and Texas when he headed the military government there during Reconstruction and despite his considerable support among southern Democrats. One paper suggested that the nomination of a prominent northern general meant two candidates so similar that it was not worth dying over the difference. The *People's Advocate* called the nomination of "that valient union soldier" one of the best that the Democrats had ever made but felt that its merit had unfortunately been expunged by the nomination for the vice-presidency of William H. English, best known for his advocacy of a pro-slavery constitution for Kansas before the Civil War. It was a judgment often repeated in other black newspapers.[10]

When the campaign began, many blacks fervently supported a party with which they were badly out of step. Although white Republicans occasionally waved the bloody shirt and spoke for black rights, they more commonly addressed other issues—particularly the tariff question which they related to national prosperity and made the key issue of the day. Black Republicans, however, naturally continued to be preoccupied with old issues of southern politics and black rights, and they often unrealistically acted as if white Republicans were equally concerned. The New York *Times* found that blacks were enthusiastically joining the southern campaign because of their as yet unshaken loyalty to the Republican party.[11]

The black press was nearly unanimous in endorsing the Republican ticket. Some new papers, John Bruce's *Weekly Argus* for example, were founded specifically to work for the Republicans and received financial aid. The older and more independent papers, whose support was more commonly ambiguous, were at once filled with praise and despair. The Topeka *Tribune* typically observed that because of history and circumstances "our politics will be uncompromisingly Republican," but also indicted the Republicans for being either too weak or too cowardly to insure black safety and a fair ballot. The paper's attitude shifted again just before the election when it insisted that the party should be supported, not out of gratitude, but because it was at the time the only progressive party in America.[12]

Groups and individuals worked for the Republican ticket. The Fisk Jubilee Singers performed for Garfield at his Mentor, Ohio, home. Black Garfield clubs, indicative of the segregation of black Republicans, sprang up in even the smallest towns. John Bruce, who formed a Republican glee club in Washington, asked Garfield for money to buy uniforms for his group, claiming that he "preached the gospel of Republicanism to the children of darkness." In Trenton, New Jersey, a Garfield and Arthur club with over one hundred members adopted uniforms of "a black cap with a red border, white shirt and blue front, and the letters T.G. and A.C., black pants, white leggings and ballot box torches." These exclusively black groups and meetings were criticized by some blacks who condemned them as Jim Crowism or denounced them as merely forums for those seeking prominence in the party. In Lawrence, Kansas, formation of a black Garfield club was voted down because of opposition to a segregated club and fear that it would stifle political independence. In the South, organization of black Republican clubs was also limited by the possibility of violent white retaliation. Because of effective white opposition to black grass-roots organization, southern black leaders had begun to emphasize a state or national approach to politics in hopes of pressuring Republicans to meet their obligations to the race.[13]

In several states Committees of Colored Republicans endorsed the Republican ticket with reservations. The Colored Republican State Committee of New Jersey, for example, praised the party and resolved to support Garfield and Arthur, but also it contended that the black vote was essential if the Republicans were to carry New Jersey and threatened that to guarantee this vote, the party must give equal representation to blacks. The black New Jersey Republicans also urged that, rather than writing off the South, white Republicans be sent down to campaign while blacks stumped in the North.[14]

Other black groups and the black press also demanded that white Republicans campaign in the South. In August, Pinchback, while acknowledging to leaders at a National Republican Committee meeting that the black Republican majority was not a safe basis for political power in the South, also asserted that if leading Republicans such as Blaine, Conkling, and Sherman went South to campaign "and let these ignorant Black people see that Republicanism is not a sham that its protection to them is not a mere name you will not stand in such need of electoral vote." Whites must go into the South, he stressed, because black spokesmen would be branded as incendiary and possibly lynched. In late September, a group of prominent northern blacks wrote the National Republican Committee, urging a southern canvas. To do otherwise, they claimed, would be to show the cowardice of the Republican party.[15]

Undoubtedly many southern blacks were afraid to take an active role on behalf of the Republicans. Former South Carolina Congressman Robert Smalls assured the Republican Campaign Committee of black support in his state but expressed doubt that it could help the ticket. He requested from Garfield adequate corroboration that South Carolina would receive a fair count because many blacks required assurances that they could vote safely before they would make the effort. The Colored Men's Protective Union of Louisiana also reported that while blacks there still expressed devotion to the Republican party, the threat of violence prevented many from voting.[16]

Although southern Democrats increasingly used white supremacy rhetoric and tactics to solidify white support, they also both overtly and covertly solicited black votes. In an effort to lure blacks away from the Republican party, they again emphasized the collapse of the Freedmen's Bank and other alleged Republican failures and promised southern blacks that voting Democratic would protect their lives. Several southern black Hancock clubs were formed during the campaign. Despite Republican harassment, black Democrats in Nashville persevered and midway through the campaign were able to draw more than two hundred blacks to a meeting. One member explained that he joined because he thought it was time for blacks to think for themselves. This lure of independence, rather than of Democratic policy or effectiveness, was again characteristic of black Democratic allegiance.[17]

But Nashville was not typical. It was generally assumed that the few blacks who joined southern Democratic organizations in 1880 did so because of fear or ambition for office rather than from personal conviction. The Albany (Ga.) *Watchman* offered a free newspaper subscription to anyone who could prove that a black man could be a Democrat. Another black newspaper merely disregarded the matter, stating, "There are so few Democratic Negroes that they are hardly worth mentioning." Those who did affiliate with the Bourbon party were again roundly condemned by other blacks. John Langston admonished anyone who advised the race to vote Democratic that "Judas Iscariot went mad and hanged himself and I would to God the pretended friend who asks a negro to vote the Democratic ticket had so much sense."[18]

Although in the North also the majority of blacks remained loyal to the Republicans, changing racial attitudes of northern Democrats, which had enhanced their black support on the local and state levels, now brought some additional support for the national ticket. This was particularly true in close states such as New York, New Jersey, Ohio, and Indiana where the Democrats increasingly regarded the small black vote as potentially significant. Black Hancock clubs were formed in each of these states although they were generally small and ineffective. In Garfield's native Ohio, even traditionally independent Peter Clark was temporarily back in the Republican fold.[19]

The number of black Democrats remained too small to be of much concern to Republican leaders. Most blacks rationalized that Garfield represented their interests at least moderately well. For many less-involved southern blacks the matter was simpler than the complexities of campaign rhetoric. J. H. Smith of Meridian, Mississippi, explained, "the fact is the greatest interest I feel in this thing is to defeat our W. S. Hancock and my reason for wishing his defeat is that he is not a Republican.[20]

In most of the South, despite the removal of federal troops and the serious encroachments on black rights that had occurred during the previous four years, a majority of southern blacks could still vote in 1880, and a majority of them voted Republican. Only in particularly violent Mississippi and in Georgia, which had instituted a cumulative poll tax, did less than a majority of eligible blacks vote. In some areas of Mississippi the black vote had been virtually eliminated. In Yazoo County, for example, only 155 Republican votes were cast, compared to 2,433 cast in 1872. In Louisiana, the end of federal protection meant that in 1880 a slightly higher percentage of black votes was counted for the Democrats than for the Republicans. In every other southern state, however, the Republicans still received the majority. In the South at large 66 percent of eligible blacks voted, and more than two-thirds of their votes went to the Republicans.[21]

This political clout gave blacks some leverage with Bourbon Democrats. Through fusion arrangements they were sometimes given minor state and local positions in areas the Democrats controlled. Unfortunately, however, despite the intrepid black loyalty to the Republican party, continued protection of their right to vote was undermined by the fact that the Republicans won the 1880 election without any southern electoral votes. As a result, some Republican strategists were further convinced to write the section off and concentrate on economic issues, particularly industrial protection. This was not true of all Republican leaders, however; some, noting the thin margin of their victory, continued to seek southern votes.[22]

Following Garfield's decisive victory, black Republicans from all over the country sent their congratulations. The world-famous and effusive Fisk Jubilee Singers wired the president-elect, "March on you have gained the victory rise and shine and give god the glory . . . we have redeemed when the righteous are in authority the people rejoice." Richard Greener congratulated the victory on behalf of younger black Republicans who, he claimed, looked to Garfield as their fathers had to Abraham Lincoln. Former Congressman Joseph Rainey only regretted that Garfield had failed to carry the South, which, he claimed, was because "you have been defrauded out of it by every conceivable device that Satan himself could have devised or planned."[23]

Blacks were determined that their efforts on behalf of the Republican ticket would receive recognition. In 1881, many blacks still rationalized that the setbacks of the Hayes years were a temporary hiatus, attributable to the presence of the wrong man in the White House. A change, therefore, could be expected to restore their rightful share of patronage, particularly if the Republicans were reminded often enough of their moral obligation to blacks. The depth of this rationalization is indicated by the considerable attention given demands for a black cabinet appointment. The *People's Advocate* insisted that blacks would settle for nothing less. The Trenton *Sentinel* proclaimed that putting a black man—preferably Douglass, Bruce, Langston, Elliott, or William Wells Brown—in the cabinet could best demonstrate to the world the achievements of blacks. Daniel Murray, a Library of Congress worker, contended that even some Democratic papers believed that blacks were justified in asking for a place in the cabinet. "It is submitted to the judgement of the Republican party," he wrote, "to take into consideration, in a spirit of fairness, the claim of colored voters and not to ignore them in giving out representative places (i.e.) such as having patronage and power attached." Southern lobbyists generally backed Langston or Bruce, who had declined to make the futile fight for a second senate term. Bruce's candidacy was particularly pushed by J. B. Bagwell, editor of the Washington *Exodus*; W. A. Pledger, chairman of the Georgia Republican State Committee and editor of the Athens *Blade*; and Bruce's fellow Mississippians, James Hill and John Lynch. A committee of Mississippi blacks sent Garfield a petition requesting Bruce's appointment. Support for Langston was particularly strong in Tennessee, largely because of the influence of his son-in-law J. C. Napier.[24]

Although there was discussion by Garfield's advisors of a black cabinet appointment, it was not seriously considered. Just prior to the inauguration, the *Sentinel* concluded that "Garfield hasn't the backbone enough to put Bruce in the cabinet, but it won't do Garfield any harm to let him know that we would like him to do it." Despite this disappointment, the months following the election and inauguration were generally optimistic ones for blacks. Garfield's inaugural speech gave considerable attention to black suffrage, condemning infringements of voting rights as "a crime which, if persisted in, will destroy the government itself."[25]

Both before and after the inauguration, black groups, optimistically determined to make this Republican administration work for them, visited the newly elected president. Most publicized was a group from North and South Carolina headed by Robert Elliott. Blacks, Elliott stressed, were the majority in parts of the South and had been loyal to the country and to the Republican party. Garfield, who had not yet decided on a southern strategy, claimed that the race question would be solved when blacks were as well educated as whites. The meeting ended amicably with Elliott agreeing that education should be the major concern of blacks. Two months later, Garfield gave similar advice to a fifty-member delegation from Louisiana. Both meetings were widely praised in the black press. Such advice left a question in the minds of some blacks, however, as to whether Garfield was indeed a champion of equal rights. Samuel Lee argued that changes in the federal jury and election laws must come first; then increased educational facilities might work.[26]

President Garfield continued to receive numerous trivial personal requests. John Bruce asked that his Black Republican Glee Club, which he claimed had "touched the souls of the disciples of money and strengthened the hearts of the stalwarts" during the campaign, be allowed to sing for the president and his family. But most blacks writing Garfield in the months following his election inquired about federal positions for themselves or for other blacks. Receiving federal jobs not only assisted individuals but also enhanced general racial pride. Friends of Pinchback in Louisiana and James Hill in Mississippi urged their appointments as a way of restoring waning black support for the Republican party. The *People's Advocate* called on the president to remember faithful campaigners including Douglass, Elliott, Bruce, Greener, and Williams for the same reason.[27]

Black political activists often inquired into their own chances for federal positions. James Poindexter of Ohio tried to convince the president that his appointment would help northern blacks remain loyal Republicans by refuting changes that the party only appointed southern blacks to office in order to humiliate southern whites. George W. Williams, who had recently become the first black elected to the Ohio legislature, recalled his seventy-seven speeches for the Republican party when he appealed for a position. He also claimed that earning a government salary was the only way he could afford to complete his *History of the Colored People in the United States from 1620 to 1880*. Even well-established Republican leader Frederick Douglass, after hearing rumors that he was to be removed from his position as marshall of the District of Columbia on racial grounds, appealed to the president with flattery, describing the incoming administration as one of "justice, liberty, humanity and good."[28] Garfield did not retain Douglass as marshall but appointed him recorder of deeds, one of the most lucrative positions in the capital city.

Douglass's new appointment was hailed as a great compliment to the race, but many blacks also insisted that it was not enough. The *Weekly Louisianian* told blacks, "Now we must look for the appointment of such men as Pinchback, Bruce, and Elliott." The *Sentinel*, which found little of positive significance even in Douglass's appointment, charged that Republicans were using the black vote and then "Mr. Douglass is handed a fifth-rate appointment, bows his venerable head, smiles and retires, perfectly delighted with the Presidential condescension." Additional appointments, including that of Bruce as registrar of the treasury and Elliott as special agent of the treasury, suggested to some that Garfield might make black preelection efforts worthwhile. Blacks were also encouraged by Garfield's reluctance to extend patronage to southern Democrats as Hayes had done. Still, despite a few good appointments, many blacks were complaining by the spring of 1881 that the race had received "just crumbs."[29]

Although Garfield devoted less attention to the South than had Hayes in his first months, he did begin fashioning a southern policy. He rejected reconciliation, looking instead for more efficacious means to revitalize the southern Republican party and defeat the southern Bourbons. The rise of independent groups in the South, disgruntled with Bourbon rule, offered a possible alternative. By 1880, the Readjusters, an independent party in Virginia led by General William Mahone, had become a major challenge to Bourbon hegemony. A number of Virginia blacks, impressed by pro-black stands taken by the Readjusters, voted for the new party. A delegation of black Mahonites visited Garfield and urged his support of the independents. Not all black Virginians, however, agreed that abandoning the Republicans was justified. Black officeholders, politicians, editors, and others who benefited from Republican largess feared the consequences if large numbers of blacks abandoned the regular Republicans. A second group visited the White House to protest any support of the independents. Garfield considered recognizing Mahone as a political expedient but, largely because of his abhorence of the debt readjustment demanded by the Mahonites, never firmly resolved to do so.[30]

Garfield never finished designing his new southern policy or clarifying how he would respond to the demands for black rights. On July 2, 1881, he was shot by Charles Guiteau, a deranged office seeker. Black criticism of his patronage policy, which had proliferated in the late spring, was suspended throughout the summer as Garfield fought for his life. The *Sentinel* spoke for thousands of blacks when it proclaimed there is "no party, no faction, no class but Americans, all equally imbued with the patriotic feeling, all equally concerned for the safety of the President." Letters from blacks horrified at Guiteau's act were among the hundreds received by the striken president. Richard D. Cross of Covington, Kentucky, wrote Bruce that "the colored people of this city is down with sorrow and are anxious to get a letter from the capital from one who has seen President Garfield. So I thought that you was the man to write and tell me what you think of his condition I am anxious to now we spelt our blood here for him and the party."[31]

On September 19 President Garfield died, and blacks joined the rest of the country in mourning. After Garfield's funeral, blacks in Washington met and offered resolutions of sorrow and respect. Many also expressed confidence in Chester A. Arthur, although Frederick Douglass later recalled that he had greeted the announcement of Arthur's nomination for the vice-presidency with a shudder of despair.[32]

James A. Garfield was not president long enough to leave blacks with a strong impression of his commitment to their rights. The circumstances of his death precluded most criticism. As a result, Garfield was generally absolved from the blame directed toward Harrison, Arthur, and particularly Hayes in the coming decades for betraying the black political revolution. Still, many remembered his paucity of patronage and his conservative advice to blacks to seek solutions to their problems through education rather than demanding enforcement of laws, and doubted that this Republican president would have effectively championed their cause.

3

Between Scylla and Charybdis: The Arthur Administration

Although blacks, like most Americans, were astounded that "Chet" Arthur was now president, the circumstances under which he assumed the office, combined with the optimism that usually greeted a new administration, initially forestalled most criticism. Pinchback, after several interviews with the new chief executive, claimed that "the party can now boast of a president who will protect the rights of those who elected him, who will not prostitute his office for Democratic plaudits." Even when Arthur largely ignored the plight of blacks in his first message to Congress, few were critical; the speech was even praised by some as one of the most able ever presented to Congress. The Huntsville *Gazette* maintained that "the Negro has a fixed, abiding faith in President Arthur" and rationalized that the president probably assumed all classes were protected.[1]

Although Arthur's credentials as a proponent of black rights were less impressive than those of his two Republican predecessors, he had supported abolitionism before the war and, in an important prewar segregation case in New York, had successfully defended a black woman. Otherwise, as organizer of the New York Republican political machine and as collector of customs for the port of New York, Arthur had been largely removed from black affairs. In the early months of his administration, Attorney General Benjamin H. Brewster had vigorously, but unsuccessfully, pursued an elections violation case in

Charleston, South Carolina. While his effort reinforced initial black optimism, it was an optimism that was to prove largely unwarranted. Arthur had less interest in black rights than either Garfield or Hayes. He viewed the South primarily as a source of Republican strength and pro-Arthur delegates in 1884.[2]

The new president quickly determined that support of the independent movement in the South, the strategy that Garfield had rejected, was the most viable way to defeat the southern Bourbons, enhance Republican strength, and secure his own power within the party. His secretary of the navy, William E. Chandler, an expert on southern affairs and the leading Republican critic of Hayes's "genteel strategy," was put in charge of this new southern policy. Chandler had once extolled the protection of black rights as the high purpose of the Republican party; he now defended a fusion policy as the most practical way to defend those rights while restoring Republican power in the South. It was a strategy that often created strange bedfellows for the Republicans. The sound-money party was forced to support readjusters, greenbackers, agrarians, and other groups across the South whose only commonality with the Republicans was a desire to overthrow Bourbon hegemony. But it was political expediency, not orthodoxy, that Arthur and Chandler sought. Their southern strategy varied considerably from state to state; independents were supported in some states but rejected in others in favor of the regular Republicans.[3]

Some blacks, impressed that the Virginia Mahonites supported black civil and political rights and disillusioned by white Republicans, believed that independent movements in other states could be advantageous to the race. The Cleveland *Gazette* claimed that "if some of our prominent Republicans were more like Mahone of Virginia, the colored press throughout the country would not be advising the colored voter to be independent and, as is the case with some, be Democrats." Some staunch black Republicans, including Frederick Douglass and John Langston, were even complimentary of Mahone. Langston, who had been appointed minister to Haiti by Arthur, asserted that "the success of the Mahone movement in Virginia means education, liberty, a free ballot, and a fair count for the colored man and the abolition of the whipping-post and I am for it heart and soul and not against it."[4]

Independent movements in other states, however, while commonly supporting black suffrage and other inducements to black voters such as aid to education, generally relegated blacks accustomed to considerable power within the southern Republican party to minor roles. Some independent leaders, particularly James R. Chalmers of Mississippi, notorious for the Fort Pillow massacre of black Union soldiers, were feared and detested. Arthur and Chandler, while giving lip service to continued protection of black rights, often supported these lily-white independents and even fostered lily-whitism among southern Republicans. "Negro officials," Arthur asserted, "do not help the party as much as white officials." In Georgia, another state in which a split between lily-whites and blacks marked the rise of independence, Arthur offered William Pledger, head of the Georgia State Republican Committee, a federal position in order to remove him from Republican politics. Arthur then recognized the white, independent wing of the Georgia party.[5]

This lily-white aspect of Arthur's southern policy confronted blacks with a dilemma which created a kind of class division among them. Successful defeat of the Bourbons by independents could lead to improved conditions for the masses of southern blacks. The Arkansas *Weekly Mansion* pointed out that the race stood to benefit from white political dissatisfaction because "the greatest danger that threatens democratic [Democratic] supremacy in the South is that the 'out faction' always gravitates toward the Negro and secures his aid to route the 'ins.' " But independence also threatened to destroy southern Republican parties, the source of the limited patronage and political power blacks possessed. In 1880, for example, the Republicans had carried a majority of the Virginia counties with a black majority; in 1882, when the Readjusters took former Republican votes, the Republicans carried none. The result was that, while the masses frequently voted for independent candidates when they could, black political leaders were generally less supportive. They were particularly outraged when the president discussed his policy with independents, including former Confederate officers, while ignoring black leaders. "What does Mr. Arthur care for Douglass, Bruce, Pinchback, Lynch, Quarles, Straker, Downing, or Ruffin?" questioned journalist Thomas Fortune, Arthur's most acrimonious critic. The Athens (Ga.) *Banner-Watchman* said of Arthur's support of white independents, "It is the initial step made by the Republican party to shake off the Negro, now that they can no longer use him."[6]

Despite the racial exclusiveness of many independents, southern Democrats often fought and defeated them with cries of "Negro domination." Racial violence in Danville, Virginia, and Copiah County, Mississippi, was successfully exploited by the Democrats as indicative of the racial turmoil that would follow independent success. It was a tactic that worked and all across the South the independents were defeated in 1883.[7]

Despite its rapid demise, the independent movement continued to be significant to blacks as an indication of President Arthur's racist attitudes. His approach to independence combined with other slights to erode his black support. To many blacks, patronage was the symbol of a president's racial views. As soon as Arthur was inaugurated, some blacks optimistically revived discussion of a cabinet position. It again centered on Bruce, but Richart T. Greener, former dean of the Howard Law School, was also frequently mentioned. In the first year of his administration, Arthur did make a few black appointments. The February 1882 selection of Pinchback as surveyor of customs of the port of New Orleans prompted the flamboyant Louisiana politician to proclaim that racial harmony now prevailed in his state. But, despite a few such appointments, the trend was to reduce blacks to relatively minor roles in the Republican party and in the federal bureaucracy, and black criticism grew accordingly. In early 1883, the Huntsville *Gazette* warned "It may not be worth the attention of Republican leaders now to accord to colored Republicans a just recognition. The hour of retribution, however, will come."[8]

As their disillusionment with the Arthur administration grew, blacks increasingly talked about their own brand of "independence." In April 1883, J. Willis Menard, editor of the Key West *News*, claimed that all blacks now favored party independence. Although Menard exaggerated, blacks were closer to political independence in 1883 than ever before. Despite its common usage, however, the term "independence" never developed a definitive meaning. It might at one time or for one individual mean continued but critical Republican allegiance. Another independent view might suggest disavowal of the Republican party in non-election months, but support of the party at the polls. Some independents genuinely advocated supporting all parties to avoid subservience to any one. Finally, independence might mean complete independence from the Republican party and, therefore, de facto support of the Democrats. The first two interpretations were the ones held by the majority who claimed to support independence. The Boston *Advocate*'s conclusion that "it is safe to presume that the Negro Independents will do in the future as in the past; talk Democracy—vote Republican" was as generally correct in 1883 as it was throughout this period.[9]

Black intellectual leaders in the North and Midwest were particularly receptive to independence. In New England, prominent independent leaders included, in addition to pioneers Clark and Downing, William Wells Brown, James M. Trotter, and George Ruffin. New England independence was especially boosted when Ruffin was appointed judge of the city court in Charleston, Massachusetts, by Democratic Governor Benjamin Butler in November 1883. The same year nearly fifty blacks met in Rhode Island to condemn Republican indifference and to espouse independence. The New York *Globe*, one of the most influential papers nationally, expressed the varied, but almost always independent, sentiments of its editor, T. Thomas Fortune. In Pennsylvania two of the three black papers endorsed independence as did William Still and Robert Purvis, two of the state's most prominent black leaders. By 1882 independence was so strong in the state that the Colored Independent Party was formed, but the violent opposition that confronted the group indicated that it was yet an unpopular course with many. Independence was occasionally supported in New Jersey by the Trenton *Sentinel* which, although ostensibly Republican, also asserted: "If by supporting Independence, we aid a free ballot and justice before the courts, we say it is the proper thing to do."[10]

In the Midwest some of the most important black papers— including the Chicago *Conservator*, St. Louis *Advance*, Kansas City

Enterprise, and Louisville *Bulletin*—endorsed varying degrees of independence. Separation from Republicans, sometimes to the point of supporting Democrats, was particularly strong in Ohio where blacks were angered by the racism of Republican Governor Joseph Foraker. In 1883 a majority of Ohio blacks, led by Peter Clark (who was at one time a member of the Socialist Workingman's party) and encouraged by the Cincinnati *Afro-American,* voted for the Democratic party. Black Republicans in Missouri, led by J. Milton Turner, a leading convert to independence and eventually to Democracy, met in Jefferson City and resolved "that we hereby announce as the new Monroe Doctrine of the era of emancipation that the negro voter in the United States shall not henceforth consider himself a subject for colonization and appropriation for any party, but shall be untrammeled by party claims." Independence became extensive enough in the state to prompt one Missourian to claim that all blacks there supported it.[11]

Independence also grew in the South throughout the Arthur years. The Savannah *Echo,* edited by T. T. Harden, was often credited with being the only southern independent paper, but many others included strong condemnations of the Republicans and occasionally suggested wholesale apostasy from the party. Their dissatisfaction was often directed toward the disintegrating and increasingly lily-white state and local parties. In Alabama, forty-five disillusioned blacks issued a complaint about Republican racism in the state but pledged continued support of the Arthur administration. It was a typical postscript to any announcement of southern black independence.[12]

In these first years following the end of Reconstruction, thousands of poor rural southern blacks also exhibited a kind of independence that, while not as well articulated as that proclaimed in the black press, demonstrated considerable political savvy. Although most continued to consider themselves Republican because they associated the party with Lincoln, and although they continued to look to black and white Republican leaders for counsel, many rural blacks knew their own political minds and interests. In 1882, shortly after he arrived in Alabama to begin building the Tuskegee Institute, Booker T. Washington learned about this kind of black political independence when an elderly black man explained politics in the black belt to him:

You can read de newspaper and most of us can't, but dar is one thing dat we knows dat you don't, and dat is how to vote down here; And we wants you to vote as we does. I'll tell you how we does, we watches de white man; we keeps watching de white man; de nearer it gets to 'lection time de more we watches de white man. We watches him till we find out which way he gwine to vote. After we find out which way he gwine'r vote, den we votes 'zactly de other way; den we knows we's right.[13]

Although such independence was undoubtedly widespread, there were still many blacks, both educated and not, who continued to cling tenaciously to the party of Lincoln. Frederick Douglass was the most prominent Republican partisan. In 1883, in a speech entitled "The United States Cannot Remain Half-Slave and Half-Free," he asserted that "the grand old party of liberty, union and progress, which has been his [the black man's] reliance and refuge for so long, though less cohesive and strong than it once was, is still a power and has a future."[14]

The two sides, supporters of independence in its various guises and staunch Republicans, continuously and sometimes acrimoniously debated the efficacy and validity of their positions. Press support for independence was led by Fortune and the New York *Globe*; Calvin Chase's Washington *Bee* was the most adamant defender of the Republicans. Chase was inconsistent and later in his career far more independent, but in his first year as editor of the *Bee* he was unabashedly a Republican. Those who cried independence were denigrated as disappointed office seekers. Fortune replied in kind, calling Chase "not only a violent Republican partisan, but a tenacious Republican office seeker." The debate between Chase and the independents became so embittered that Chase was sued for libel by Robert Purvis after the *Bee* editor condemned Purvis's membership in the Pennsylvania Colored Independent party. The split was particularly obvious at the twentieth anniversary celebration of the Emancipation Proclamation held in January 1883. Fortune, who praised the new spirit of independence, was followed by Richard Greener, who toasted "the negro's adherence to the Republican party."[15]

By mid–1883, few still believed that independence was an insignificant force. By this time Arthur's policy of lily-white Republicanism and support of racist independents was obvious. John E. Bruce, still a Republican and now Washington correspondent for the *Globe*, observed widespread discontent among Washington blacks in 1883 and predicted that Republican leaders would soon answer for their indifference. In the summer of 1883, the *Globe* pointed to five recent events as proof of the new spirit of independence: (1) a black convention in Rhode Island at which the Republican party was denounced; (2) extensive non-Republican voting in Pennsylvania, Connecticut, Massachusetts, and New York; (3) opposition to the National Colored Convention based on the fear that it would promote the interests of Republican politicians; (4) the Declaration of the Colored Press Association meeting in St. Louis that it was non-partisan; and (5) condemnation of the management of the Republican party by a black convention held in Charleston, South Carolina.[16]

Even the *Bee* acknowledged in 1883 that independence was rapidly growing. The paper seemed almost ready to sanction the movement when Chase wrote, "We still believe the President means to do what is right, and will wait a little longer before we join in the chorus. But we beg leave to respectfully remind President Arthur that the time is at hand for him to do something proper for the ever faithful allies." Two letters received by Douglass in the spring of 1883 also reflect the dichotomy of black attitudes. "I have no patience with the independent nonsense," George Pierce wrote, "when you and I know so well that independence means isolation and that means ruin to the race." George Downing, on the other hand, wrote that as long as Republicans could be sure of black allegiance, the party would remain indifferent to their plight. He left the Republican party because "I desire a division of the colored vote, because I believe it will be better to have more than one party anxious, concerned and cherishing the hope that at least a part of that vote may be obtained, because a division would result in increased respect from all quarters and create general competitive concern."[17]

Political desperation continued to mean occasional overtures to the Democrats. John Quarles, a black New York lawyer, suggested that 1883 was a good year for Democrats to win support among blacks because, whether the GOP realized it or not, blacks were drifting away. Getting uncoerced Democratic support from blacks in the South was far more difficult than in New York but not impossible. Some southern blacks voted Democratic but only a minority of them did so out of conviction. Thomas Hamilton, an educated and moderately wealthy black South Carolinian, was virtually alone when he claimed that the Democrats had done the most to educate and elevate blacks. Even the independent *Globe* disputed Hamilton's radical claim, countering that if South Carolina Republicans had done little for blacks, the Democrats had done even less. More commonly, southern blacks who voted Democratic did so because of economic necessity or because they were coerced by threats and demonstrations of violence. Alabama educator William Councill, for example, called on blacks in his state to either vote Democratic or abstain from politics altogether as a way of appeasing the Democrats.[18]

Still, while many southern blacks resented Republican betrayal and often condemned the party, a majority probably agreed with the *Bee* that "the democratic [Democratic] party should be branded as the most brutish of all parties in this civilized world. ... Its record is as black as the hinges of hades, the crimes perpetrated will never be blotted from the pages of history." The *Globe* more succinctly proclaimed, "The Democratic party is a huge humbug."[19]

Diverse and contradictory political pronouncements reflected the impossible political situation in which blacks found themselves. The *Globe* bemoaned that "the blacks now flounder about, ignorant of where they stand, fearful of moving to the right or the left ... the poor and oppressed of the land have no refuge in either camp. They stand between Scylla and Charybdis."[20]

Several black conventions met in 1883 to search for some way out of this political morass. The South Carolina State Convention of Colored Men, which met in Columbia in July, was particularly significant for its articulation of southern black opinion. Convention delegates focused on the Republican policy of ignoring southern blacks in order to win white support. The first speaker, D. Augustus Straker, claimed that the extension of American ideals rather than the Republican party had given blacks their freedom. Unification, he insisted, should now become the great concern of the race, and unification could be most readily achieved if blacks were independent in every realm, including politics. The Committee on Resolutions, less radical than Straker, acknowledged a debt to the Republican party for securing black citizenship and for at least partial protection of the rights implied. Nevertheless, they indicted the party "for its omission in the past six years, as far as it related to its administration in connection with our race."[21]

A national convention was called to meet in Washington in September to consider similar issues, but the proposed meeting soon became almost as controversial as the issue of independence itself. John Bruce accused convention leaders of only seeking jobs for themselves. Conservative Richard Greener, a man often accused of being a Republican sycophant, opposed the meeting because, as he said, "we are free, have citizenship, have educational advantages, some degree of civil rights. What more do these men want?" George W. Williams was anti-convention because he saw it as self-segregation. "I am opposed to Negroes asking or demanding anything as Negroes," he asserted. "We want race lines abolished!" J. Willis Menard asked what a convention with "brilliant resolves and windy speeches" could do that Congress, president, federal courts, army and navy could not do. Finally, a Georgia convention rejected the proposal with a rationale increasingly common in times of despondency—that blacks would be better off ignoring politics and conventions while they concentrated on making their fortunes. Plans for the convention finally became so entangled that it was relocated in Louisville, Kentucky. Part of the opposition, claimed Frederick Douglass, who supported the meeting, was fear that it would be anti-Republican. The independents, on the other hand, were concerned that it would be controlled by the Arthur administration.[22]

Apparently a majority of blacks favored a convention, and throughout September delegates were chosen in every part of the country. Alabama blacks, one observer claimed, were more politically enthusiastic than ever. The *Bee*'s Louisville correspondent predicted that a majority of delegates would be independents, but he also expected to see considerable support for Arthur. Chase was one of the delegates and announced he intended to support "the Stalwart, straight Republicans against all isms and notions, with independent, greenback, or democratic tendencies." A New York *Times* correspondent, viewing preparations, concluded that while the independents might not control the convention, they would be heard, and the result could be bitter antagonisms. The rising new black man, the *Times* concluded, does not mind attacking the GOP.[23]

Preconvention critics correctly predicted a pronounced ideological division at the convention. When it opened on September 24, a fight immediately broke out over who would be chairman. Many delegates supported Douglass, but William H. Young of Nashville led the opposition because, ironically, he perceived Douglass as too independent. Douglass was elected and did speak in a more independent vein than usual. He concluded with his most direct assault on his party: "If the Republican Party cannot stand a demand for justice and fair play it ought to go down. We were men before the party was born, and our manhood is more sacred than any party can be." The speech was too independent for the majority of delegates at a convention ostensibly called for non-political purposes. Douglass had difficulty explaining his remarks and finally insisted that "I am an independent inside of the Republican Party."[24]

That Frederick Douglass, traditionally the leading defender of black Republicanism, was challenged as too independent reflected the hopelessness many of the convention delegates felt. One speaker concluded that blacks "have been abandoned by the government and left to the laws of nature. So far as they are concerned, there is no Government or Constitution of the United States." The convention passed a memorial calling on Americans to protect black rights and proposed another convention to be held prior to those of the major parties in 1884 to plan black strategy and involvement.[25]

Few concrete decisions were made in Louisville, but the convention was important for publicizing continued violation of black rights and for promoting a sense of racial pride and self-sufficiency. Although not officially independent, the convention helped consolidate that position. The *Globe* concluded that "no convention held since the emancipation of the colored race gave rise to such general feelings of interest and was considered of greater national significance as regards the colored citizen."[26]

The Louisville convention revealed how far the political revolution of the 1860s had receded. Shortly after it adjourned, revolutionary gains were further eroded by a Republican Supreme Court which declared the Civil Rights Act of 1875, the last major legislation passed by the Republicans to guarantee black rights, unconstitutional. A minority of black spokesmen justified the decision. The *Bee*, still staunchly Republican, claimed that the party was not responsible and that the decision would not materially affect blacks. The Arkansas *Weekly Mansion* even claimed that the decision was a correct one, that the Civil Rights Act was "a law conceived in humbuggery and enacted in fraud." Rev. William B. Derrick agreed that the race was now too strong to require such special legislation.[27]

But protest was far more common as blacks struggled to comprehend this latest Republican perfidy. Political pessimism was as extensive as at any time since the end of Reconstruction. A Georgia paper predicted that the day was not far removed when the Emancipation Proclamation would be declared unconstitutional. The *Globe*, reporting a great flood of protest mail, lamented that the decision left the race with the ballot but no laws for its protection. The *People's Advocate* predicted a political revolution among blacks, and the Wheeling (W.V.) *Pilot* counseled that the decision should lead all blacks to independence.[28]

Several protest meetings were held. In New York City fifteen hundred blacks met to condemn the decision. In late October, over two thousand people gathered in Lincoln Hall in Washington to consider the implications of the Supreme Court's action. Douglass, who had earlier mourned, "This blow was dealt us in the house of our friends," now absolved the Republicans from blame until it could be determined if the party generally endorsed the decision. He was still convinced, however, of the profound significance of the court's ruling which "has swept over the land like a moral cyclone." The Washington meeting resolved to hold the Republicans to the task of enforcing liberty and equality and also called on blacks to support whichever party best served their interests. Another group of over one thousand gathered at the First Congregational Church in Washington to hear John M. Langston condemn the decision. Langston bemoaned the demise of humanitarianism in the modern party but also rationalized that this failure had forced blacks to be more self-reliant. In response to party counsel that blacks be patient, Langston could only say, "My God! how long a time are we to wait?" Still, it was ultimately to the Republicans, "the noble party of freedom," that Langston looked to remedy black ills.[29]

The most scathing attack was delivered by A.M.E. Bishop Henry M. Turner. Consistently one of the most outspoken and radical blacks, Turner had long supported black nationalism, including migration to Africa. He now proclaimed, "the eight million of my race and their posterity will stand horror-frozen at the very mention of their [the Supreme Court justices'] names." Over a year later, he still fulminated that the Supreme Court decision was "a crime more infamous in its character than was ever charged upon the devil or any of his subalternates." As for the United States, he declared, "I care nothing for it, wish it nothing but ill and endless misfortune, wish I could only live to see it go down to ruin and its memory blotted from the pages of history."[30]

The Civil Rights decision was a further impetus to the independent movement. To many blacks it was new evidence that they must themselves assume responsibility for dealing with the profound problems confronting them. In 1884, T. Thomas Fortune published *Black and White: Land, Labor and Politics in the South*, the most able defense of independence written in the wake of the Civil Rights decision. Fortune denounced the Republican party for degenerating "into an ignoble scramble for place and power" and suggested that independence was vital to black progress because "the independent colored man, like the independent white man, is an American citizen who does his own thinking. When some one else thinks for him he ceases to be an intelligent citizen and becomes a dangerous dupe." Fortune did not expect blacks to support that "curse to our land" the Bourbon Democrats, but he did believe that they could and should support "independent, progressive Democrats as frequently as Republicans."[31]

Fortune was also a leading lobbyist for the creation of a na-

tional black independent organization that would support candidates for either party and ideally become the balance of power.
He did not yet have the resources to start his organization, but
several regional groups promoting black unification and self-
help were launched. In December, George T. Downing formed
the Sumner Independents of Boston, which he hoped to build
into a national organization. Harry C. Smith, editor of the Cleveland *Gazette*, although condemning Downing's group as too close
to Democracy, also proclaimed that "an independent party must
arise and take command ere it be too late or this country, from
a political standpoint, will speedily go to the dogs." All-black
political groups were indicative of the trend among blacks to
move away from an integrationist ethos toward support for all-
black institutions.[32]

In the wake of the Supreme Court decision, there was also a
resurgence of advice that blacks abandon politics altogether.
John Bruce, usually actively involved in politics, despaired, "We
have already paid too much attention to politics." Education, he
counseled, should be the primary concern of the race. But such
counsel was still usually condemned.[33]

In the fall of 1883, D. Augustus Straker summarized the causes
of black resentment toward the Republican party: (1) the betrayal
of 1877, (2) continued failure to protect the ballot, (3) fostering
a caste system, (4) exclusion of blacks from office, (5) permitting
separate schools, (6) Republican industrialists' exclusion of
blacks, (7) failure to enforce the Constitution, and (8) prevalence
of bossism in the Republican party. The fostering of lily-white
Republican organization in the South and the 1883 Supreme
Court decision were additional causes of resentment by 1884.
During the Arthur years, blacks had sought new strategies to
deal with these and other encroachments on their political rights.
Support of southern white independents was sometimes advocated, but the independents were regarded by many blacks as
racists, and ultimately they failed. More commonly blacks called
for their own brand of independence which ideally would free
the race from blind Republicanism and make it a powerful bar-
gaining force. Black independence, however, also failed to have
much political impact, in part because blacks were not united,
but more importantly because the Republicans under President

Arthur had little interest in blacks as a source of political power. "The Republican party," Fortune wrote in the summer of 1883, has "eliminated the black man from its politics." Furthermore, blacks were seeking federal support at a time when most of the rest of the country firmly rejected the Reconstruction legacy of federal involvement in state and local affairs. The Supreme Court decision was indicative of both the demise of Republican moral and political interest in the plight of blacks and of the growing entrenchment of a laissez-faire philosophy in the country at large. To blacks, the decision was an unmistakable sign of the continued reversal of the black political revolution. Still, many blacks retained faith in political solutions. By early 1884, their attention began to focus again on an upcoming presidential election.[34]

4

The Age of the Negrowump: The Election of 1884 and the First Cleveland Administration

The continuing deterioration of black political and civil rights was exemplified in early January 1884 when black North Carolina Congressman James E. O'Hara proposed an amendment to the Constitution empowering Congress to guarantee all citizens the right to vote and to assure them equal protection of the laws. Over a decade had passed since the passage of the Reconstruction amendments and blacks were acutely aware that the political revolution of the 1860s had been seriously eroded. But despite this burgeoning de facto disfranchisement, blacks clung tenaciously to their political rights. In 1882, John Lynch, serving his last term as a congressman from Mississippi, assured his colleagues that blacks "have bravely refused to surrender their honest convictions, even upon the altar of their personal necessities." There was widespread optimism that participation in the 1884 presidential election could still halt political reversal. The Savannah *Echo* proclaimed in early 1884, "The American Negro is going to hold a mighty big hand in the coming Presidential contest, and don't you forget it." Frederick Douglass optimistically predicted that black votes would serve their cause as never before.[1]

As the presidential election approached, blacks renewed their loyalty to the Republican party. The *Globe* explained that although blacks were now convinced that the Republicans were not their champions, the Democrats, rather than capitalizing on this disillusionment, had continued to oppress, rob, and murder blacks. In a January 1884 meeting of the Colored Republican Central Committee of New York, President William Derrick spoke for many blacks when he declared that regardless of some defections from the Republican party, "Yet it is our mother."[2]

Many blacks renewed their insistence, however, that loyalty must be rewarded. Marylander J. R. L. Diggs wrote Douglass for advice on the upcoming election. "It is the greatest joy of the colored man to support the republican party," Diggs claimed, but he also insisted that the race must not stand for white refusal to have a black on the ticket. Was it proper, he queried Douglass, for blacks to make such a demand? While Douglass's reply is unknown, many black leaders would have responded affirmatively. In April, Professor William Scarborough of Wilberforce University analyzed the political status quo. There still existed, he claimed, servitude in the South and ostracism and caste in the North. The time had come for blacks to rise up and strike back. Scarborough was particularly insistent on unity in the fight for equality, a fight he feared might in time mean meeting force with force. He agreed that blacks might cooperate with the Democrats on local matters but insisted that nationally they should "stick to the old ship." Scarborough did not, however, advocate unquestioning allegiance to the Republicans; he warned party leaders to consider black interests equally with all others or risk losing the black vote. J. Willis Menard suggested that the upcoming Republican convention might be the last chance to restore rights lost in the last few years, and that, as the balance of power, the race might force the selection of a candidate favorable to its interests. As early as February 1883, the *Bee* agitated for the election of delegates from Washington to the national convention who would stand for principle and pledge themselves to demand universal suffrage. In a more militant vein than usual, the paper concluded that if issues were not resolved at Chicago, "it were better that we die under a shot-gun policy fighting for liberty than it would be to live in a country styled a republic where its citizens are denied their rights and butchren like hogs." The *Globe* was also a leader in making demands on the Republicans, even asserting that it might be necessary to subject the party to defeat to assure that black needs were met in the future. The *Mail and Express* warned that if justice was not assured at the ballot box in the upcoming election, violence might be expected.[3]

There was some early black support for nominating President Arthur. Black state conventions in Alabama and Florida endorsed the administration of a president labeled by the Floridians as "the life-long friend of our people." Mifflin Gibbs, judge and Republican leader in Arkansas, praised the administration as one "signalized by its justice, eminent statesmanship and wise direction," and the Huntsville *Gazette*, reversing earlier criticism, asserted that all blacks agreed Arthur was a good leader. But many could not forget the slights and setbacks of the Arthur years. Both the *People's Advocate* and the *Bee*, although praising Arthur, endorsed other candidates. The *Globe* continued to editorialize on the president's lack of concern for the race and once concluded: "Away with President Arthur, who combines the weaknesses of his predecessors without possessing their slim stock of virtues." The *Globe* refuted the Huntsville *Gazette*'s contention that southern blacks were as attached to Arthur as they had been to Republican presidents of the past but predicted that if Arthur were nominated, blacks would support him.[4]

By the summer of 1883 blacks were everywhere debating the 1884 Republican ticket. Initially there was considerable support for a ticket headed by Robert T. Lincoln, son of the former president and Arthur's secretary of war, with Blanche K. Bruce as his running mate. The *People's Advocate* maintained that a black vice-presidential nomination was necessary to bring disgruntled black Republicans back into the party and thus ensure victory. Although the *Bee* claimed that all black papers joined in this demand, there was some opposition. The *State Journal* feared that demands for a black Republican candidate would bring Republican ingratitude "too appalling ever to be forgotten." By the fall of 1883, many editors were questioning a Lincoln nomination. The realities of the campaign increasingly forced them to consider who among the leading contenders was most likely to support their interests rather than to promote an ideal racial ticket.[5]

By 1884, considerable black support was shifting to Illinois

Senator John A. Logan, primarily because of Logan's sponsorship of a bill to investigate the condition of southern blacks.
Frederick Douglass praised Logan's "pure Republicanism." The
Peoria (Ill.) *Daily Transcript* contended that Logan could call forth
a larger black vote than any candidate since Abraham Lincoln.
The *Bee* continued to advocate a Robert Lincoln ticket in early
1884 but acknowledged Logan as a viable alternative. The paper
insisted, "It is an undeniable fact that no Republican President
can be elected without the colored vote" and predicted defeat if
neither Lincoln nor Logan was nominated. When the Stalwarts
advocated Grant, the *Globe* responded that, while it had a tender
spot for the general, blacks would not support him as he probably
could not be elected. There was considerable support for Grant
among the masses of blacks, but most leaders agreed with the
Globe. The Logan boom grew until a majority of black papers
endorsed him.[6]

Some blacks were most concerned that James G. Blaine not
receive the nomination. Blaine's presidential ambitions had
prompted him to shift from support of black aspirations in the
South to support of lily-white Republicans and reconciliation
with southern Democrats. The *Bee* warned that Blaine could not
carry the black vote, and the Harrisburg (Pa.) *State Journal* appealed to the party "to save us the humiliation of having to vote
for James G. Blaine for President."[7]

There was less interest in Democratic activity in the preconvention months in part because many still believed, as the *Globe*
declared in mid-May, that the Democratic party had no more
chance of winning the presidency than did the Greenbackers or,
as the *Bee* expressed it, "the devil has a greater chance for
heaven." Talk that Benjamin Butler might be the Democratic
candidate stimulated some interest since the former Union general and radical Republican had long been regarded as a friend
of the race. It was even suggested that if the Democratic party
nominated Butler and the Republicans nominated Blaine and
endorsed the recent Supreme Court decision, blacks should support the Democrats.[8]

A small minority of blacks gave at least qualified support to
the Democratic party in the preconvention months. George
Downing called on the race to "take pains to let the Democratic

party understand that though it has outraged us in a shameful manner, it may have support at our hands on the condition that it change its policy and treat us with the consideration that is our due." John W. A. Shaw led in the formation of the New York Colored Democratic Association, which proclaimed that it was better to have both parties protecting the race. In Ohio the Democrats made such a strong effort to win over blacks that a Republican complained about the "black sheep among us." The motives of black Democrats were frequently criticized. The Cleveland *Gazette* claimed that many of the blacks who voted Democratic in its city had sold their votes.[9]

In April, black leaders held a conference in Pittsburg to organize for the upcoming election. Although Robert Jackson, the temporary chairman, attempted to repulse any partisan schemes and urged the convention to take no action favorable to any political party, there were several who spoke favorably of Democracy. George Elliott of Indiana pushed for the formation of an independent party and the support of a Democrat for president on the grounds that in the last six months Indiana Democrats had done more for blacks than had the Republicans in the last ten years. Rev. C. S. Smith of Bloomfield, Illinois, declared that the day the Republicans could command the entire black vote was over and called for support of Benjamin Butler. George Downing condemned the managers of both parties for ignoring black problems and called for a committee to meet after the conventions to coordinate black political activity in the campaign. Most speakers offered at least qualified support for the Republicans, but the convention adjourned without an official endorsement of either party. Because of the considerable division among the delegates, they also had little success in planning effective campaign strategy. But the Pittsburgh convention did successfully dramatize the growing conviction that blacks must begin operating as a distinct political interest group.[10]

Despite considerable criticism of the Republicans, the majority of blacks still supported them. The *State Journal* concluded, in a typical analysis of the political situation in the spring of 1884, "After mature deliberation, that no greater calamity could befall the people of this country, and their every endearing interest, than the defeat of the Republican party in this Presidential cam-

paign of '84." This did not mean that the *State Journal* was un-
aware of Republican shortcomings. The paper noted that the
Republican party often afforded the race insulting treatment
and asserted: "While we have no faith in Democracy, we are fast
losing confidence in Republicanism."[11]

When the Republican convention opened in Chicago in June,
a number of southern blacks were delegates. The convention
highlight for them was the nomination of John Lynch as temporary chairman, a selection engineered by anti-Blaine "Mugwump" reformers as part of their effort to defeat the Maine
senator. The Topeka *Tribune*, representing near unanimity in
the black press, observed that "to the masses it will come as a
ray of hope faintly glimmering through a cloud of despair as
they endeavor to construe it as indicating a northern sentiment
against Bourbon intolerance and open murder of black men."[12]

President Arthur, estranged from both his own Stalwart faction and from the Half-Breeds, was unable to garner his party's
nomination. Largely because of the Stalwart division, Blaine won
the nomination. Four black men—Lynch, Perry Carson, Samuel
Lee, and N. Wright Cuney—were placed on the committee to
notify him. Other than these appointments and the Lynch election, the convention proceedings gave blacks little reason for
optimism. Blaine's nomination prompted a revolt of Mugwumps,
but, despite Mugwump support of Lynch and their own antipathy toward Blaine, few blacks followed suit. Although the Mugwumps were led by former abolitionists and supporters of black
suffrage, most of them had become disillusioned with black voters and now favored reconciliation with the white South. Most
blacks, seeing no alternative, swallowed their disappointment
and encouraged acceptance of Blaine and the Republicans.[13]

Some consolation was found in the nomination of Logan for
the vice-presidency. The *Bee* called for support of the ticket
because "honorable John A. Logan on the ticket means victory
without a doubt," and concluded: "The *Bee* is happy. Amen!"
But the *Bee* was not completely appeased. Although the paper
supported the ticket, it often insinuated that it did so only because Logan was the vice-presidential nominee and that without
him the party could not win. The Cleveland *Gazette* was also
more enthusiastic about Logan than Blaine. The *Globe* found

Blaine objectionable for a number of reasons but sought to rationalize support on the grounds that he had stood by blacks in the slavery era.[14]

Other black Republican papers enthusiastically supported the ticket. In late June, the *Globe* announced that the colored press was unanimous for the Blaine-Logan ticket. In the deep South, the *Montgomery Citizen* enthusiastically proclaimed, "Blaine is our choice, and we join in three cheers for the grand old statesman. He is the choice of a large majority of the people and will be elected." The Republicans again supported newspapers founded for the duration of the campaign, including John Bruce's Washington *Grit* and C. A. Simpson's St. Louis *Plumed Knight*.[15]

As blacks rationalized their acceptance of Blaine, they turned their attention to the Democratic convention. When Grover Cleveland became the party's nominee, he was acknowledged by many blacks as a man superior to the party's average membership. The *Globe* doubted he was the choice of the Democratic leadership because "he represents all that is opposed to traditional Democratic cussedness." Vice-presidential nominee Thomas A. Hendricks, still remembered as a foe of emancipation, was again nominated for the vice-presidency and was more commonly the target of black vituperation than was Cleveland. Fortune condemned him as "a bigoted Democrat of the ancient school." The Democratic platform, which called for equality before the law regardless of race, color, or religion and for "a free ballot and a fair count," was generally acceptable to blacks. But few were convinced that many Democrats had any intention of abiding by such platitudes. The San Francisco *Elevator* warned blacks not to be deceived by the apparent liberality of the Democratic platform because "platforms are like molasses to catch flies."[16]

The *Bee* set the tone for blacks early in the campaign by declaring that "our standard bearers, Misters Blaine and Logan, are men of brilliant dash and valiant courage and will arouse the greatest kind of enthusiasm throughout the country." Fortune, because of his past independence, had to fight accusations that he now supported the Democrats. Although admitting he was a reluctant Republican, Fortune insisted that black voters "will prefer to feast upon Republican crow in preference to Democratic buzzard. Of the two birds they are forced, by fear and long usage, to choose the least objectionable."[17]

Blacks all over the country organized clubs and actively campaigned for the Republican ticket. Late in the campaign, Blaine shifted his emphasis from reconciliation to condemning southern Democratic electoral frauds, making it easier for blacks to support him. In New York City alone, there were twenty-five black Republican organizations. Many prominent black leaders were asked by the Republicans to make speeches. Frederick Douglass, who was particularly active in the Midwest, opened the campaign for Blaine and Logan in Battle Creek, Michigan, then went to Salem, Ohio, to join Blanche K. Bruce for a rally, and from there to Cleveland. In the final days of the campaign, he joined Richard T. Greener in stumping throughout Indiana, a key state. Fortune spoke for the State Central Committee of Connecticut in New Haven and reported that blacks there and in Massachusetts were solid for Blaine. John Langston was asked by several state Republican committees to campaign, but he could not leave his duties as minister in Port-au-Prince. He did, however, admonish blacks to stand by the GOP and not support "a party whose history is black at once with treason to the government and to humanity." Former North Carolina Congressman John Hyman was a leader in organizing southern blacks for the Republican party.[18]

In October, the *Globe* claimed that no black leader of national reputation supported the Democrats and that the press and masses of voters were "measurably solid" for Blaine. Still, there were frequent complaints that while blacks were almost uniformly behind the Republican party, the party was not squarely behind them. Never before, charged the *Globe*, had the Republicans paid so little heed to black voters. The Cleveland *Gazette* urged blacks to enter the contest only shoulder to shoulder with whites and to make sure that they got their just due from the Republicans. Shortly after the Republican convention, the *Globe* called on the party to send speakers south. When few were sent, the *Globe* reported a midwestern paper's bitter complaint:

We are tired of Danvilles and Copiahs. If they must come, let the firey-tongued stump speakers of the north take part in it. We venture to say, however, that it would take a pretty good ox team to pull a Northern stump orator down south. He wants the colored man to vote and die for the old flag, while he stays at home and sacrifices himself upon the altar of a fat office.

Critics were somewhat appeased when in October, after weeks of virtually ignoring the race question, the Republican National Committee opened a black headquarters in Nashville, Tennessee. The *Globe* rejoiced that the Republicans were no longer leaving the southern black man, the most loyal member of the party, to the Bourbons.[19]

Despite disavowals by Republican partisans, the Democratic ticket did have some black support. Cleveland's racial moderation, combined with the party's desire to win the votes of disillusioned northern black Republicans and white Mugwumps, fostered a Democratic campaign largely free of racist rhetoric. Accordingly there was more outspoken northern black support for the Democrats. John Bruce reported the "startling" rumor that blacks in Ohio and other northern states planned to join the Democratic party in large numbers. The Cleveland *Gazette* admitted that the Civil Rights decision had left some blacks in the ranks of the Democrats, but the *Globe* claimed that in Cleveland's home state of New York, black Democrats were "as scarce as hens teeth," and acknowledged only one, John Shaw, as genuine. T. McCants Stewart, Princeton educated and with wide experience as a teacher, preacher, and lawyer, although not formally endorsing Cleveland, praised a growing spirit of independence among blacks and maintained that some Democrats treated them fairly.[20]

There were, however, few black Democratic papers to mitigate the Republican press's influence. Herbert Clark's *Afro-American*, distributed free to Ohio blacks by the Democratic Committee, was possibly alone in supporting the Cleveland ticket consistently. The *Afro-American* often preached that the race should cease supporting Republicans who had failed to prevent political murders in the South. Clark also attacked Logan as the author of discriminatory laws in Illinois. The paper optimistically predicted that "the colored vote will give the Republicans the hoodwink this fall."[21]

Those who supported the Democratic ticket did so in the face of the usual criticism and even ostracism from black Republicans. When Peter Clark of Ohio, father of the editor of the *Afro-American*, spoke for Cleveland, William Scarborough demanded his removal from a teaching position. Although other Republicans defended Clark's right to teach, black Democrats were generally vehemently condemned during the campaign. The *Bee* reminded "would-be Democrats of color" that all they possessed was thanks to efforts of the Republican party and accused them of being motivated by money. The *Globe* was somewhat more tolerant, referring to black independents who bolted the Republican ticket on one occasion as "men of sound practical sense."[22]

Third parties had only limited support in 1884. The nomination of Benjamin Butler stimulated interest in the Greenback-Labor party, but although the *Globe* called on blacks to listen to Butler with respect, only the Indianapolis *World* actually endorsed him. The Prohibition party, in a largely unsuccessful attempt to recruit blacks, suggested Bruce as a possible vice-presidential candidate. Frederick Douglass, when encouraged to join the Prohibitionists, responded that, although he supported the cause, he condemned the party for claiming that the southern question was settled and the Republican mission finished. Douglass also opposed black involvement with labor parties claiming that they were foreign to the peaceable nature of the race. The National Equal Rights party, formed particularly to promote women's suffrage, made a bid for black support by naming Douglass, without his consent, as their vice-presidential candidate. The Huntsville *Gazette* scoffed that "persons who intend to vote for the woman Presidential candidate might be a safe investment for Barnum's circus," while most other blacks, including Douglass, gave the ticket little attention at all. Some despaired of the existing parties altogether and called for the formation of a new party, but that alternative was less frequently mentioned as the campaign gained momentum.[23]

By the closing weeks of the contest, most papers and spokesmen were caught up in the rhetoric and exaggeration usual to a campaign. Many who called themselves independent only a few months before now demanded Republican loyalty and warned of the bleak consequences of Democratic victory. The *Bee* claimed the election of Cleveland would mean a "reminiscence of days of slavery." The Cleveland *Gazette* cried, "What folly! what suicide that we should abandon the part assigned us as trusty freemen," and predicted a terrible future for blacks if the Bourbons took control of the government. Even the *Globe* called the outcome of the gravest importance to blacks as "there is no telling what vandalisms may not be attempted by that iconoclastic school of politicians whose arch-apostle is Jefferson Davis."[24]

While blacks continued to focus on the southern question and black rights, whites gave these issues less attention than in any campaign since the Civil War. Much of the campaign centered on personal allegations, including charges that Cleveland had an illegitimate child and that Blaine had made illegal railroad transactions. The major tangible issue raised was again the tariff. Fortune, despite his support of the pro-tariff Blaine ticket, was one of the few outspoken black supporters of free trade and welcomed the tariff as an issue which men could disagree on without violence. He assumed that the near unanimity of black support for a high protective tariff, despite the fact that it bore heavily on agricultural production which affected most blacks, was because it was Republican doctrine. The *State Journal* agreed that most blacks opposed free trade as Democratic policy but also noted that, ironically, most major industries were owned by Republicans and excluded blacks from their labor. To the majority of blacks, however, the tariff and other issues were of secondary importance. They agreed with the *Globe*'s assertion that "higher than prohibition, higher than civil service reform, higher than the tariff, higher than political place and preferment is the right to life, liberty and the pursuit of happiness which is denied millions of Negroes everywhere in this country, but particularly in the solid South."[25]

The course of disfranchisement had been uneven over the preceding four years, leaving blacks in some areas largely free to vote while in others legal devices such as the poll tax, as well as coercion and terrorism, had effectively eliminated their vote. In South Carolina, for example, where in 1876 over 90 percent of the black population had voted, the percentage, in a gubernatorial contest, had dropped to about 30 percent and over two-thirds of those votes were counted for the Democrats. Mississippi was second to South Carolina in the extent of disfranchisement, but 25 percent of the state's eligible black voters could still support the Republican gubernatorial candidate in 1881. In some southern states a majority of blacks still voted Republican in the early 1880s.[26]

As a result of both this discrepancy and the difference in radical and conservative outlooks, there was considerable disagreement among southern blacks as to how free they were to vote in 1884. William Pledger denied that violence and murder were factors and attributed the reduced black vote in Georgia to failure to register or pay taxes. T. T. Allain, a Louisiana businessman and legislator, claimed that the situation was similar in his state. But many other blacks blamed proscription and terror for reduced voting, and some still advocated immigration to the Midwest, where blacks could vote freely. Robert Smalls predicted bloodshed in South Carolina if something were not done to protect black suffrage there.[27]

Initially there was confusion in the black press as to the outcome of the 1884 election, in part due to a reluctance to acknowledge the first Democratic victory since emancipation. But by mid-November there was no doubt that Cleveland had been elected. Some blacks expressed fear that their situation would badly deteriorate and a few even predicted a return to slavery. There were occasional reports, reminiscent of the slavery era, that blacks were fleeing to isolated areas in the South and to the North. A rumor circulated in Washington, D.C., that a group of blacks planned to assassinate the president-elect. But such extreme reactions were never shared by the majority and were usually short-lived. Cleveland, astonished at such responses, helped alleviate black fears with the promise that he would support the rights of all citizens, a promise that was echoed by Democrats all across the country.[28]

John Lynch was one of the few black leaders who maintained that the Democratic victory might worsen the plight of blacks. Most others worked to assuage such fears, and in several cities they held mass meetings to discuss the impact of the election on black rights. Black ministers in Atlanta invited a number of prominent white Democrats to speak on the consequences of Cleveland's election, a not-altogether-popular decision that left some congregations bitterly divided. Frederick Douglass, in answer to a number of inquiries from apprehensive blacks, wrote "The Outcome of the Recent Election." He admitted that he was not happy with the Democratic victory, a "temporary calamity." But he was not particularly alarmed either, concluding: "The Democratic party may not be a good party but it may be a wise party and wisdom in statesmanship is sometimes better than goodness." In an A.M.E. Church *Review* seminar on the election, published in January 1885, all fourteen of the prominent blacks interviewed rejected extreme reactions to Cleveland's election and most were fairly optimistic that during his administration black rights would be respected. Professor James M. Gregory of Howard University even rationalized that because Cleveland's election had occasioned such fears among blacks, the new president would give them many prominent positions to assuage these fears. Volatile P.B.S. Pinchback now suggested that the solid South might dissolve after Cleveland took office and new, racially egalitarian parties emerge. But he was also concerned that the Democratic victory could serve to retard the race's advances. John Lewis disagreed on the grounds that Democratic policy was closer than Republican to the race's needs and that it would be better to "avoid aggression at home than court deceptive friendship abroad."[29]

A number of black leaders also concluded that the Republican party was largely responsible for its own defeat. The *Freeman* suggested that the party's departure from earlier principles, combined with Blaine's lack of personal honesty and his opposition to race measures, had brought about the Republican debacle. Douglass claimed that the Republicans lost because "they were loud for the protection of things, but silent for the protection of men."[30]

Some blacks were prompted by the election results to evaluate again the race's relationship to political affairs. Political abstinence was more often counseled in 1885 than it had been at any time since emancipation. A group of blacks in Raleigh, North Carolina, issued a call for "masterly inactivity" in politics. Frances E.W. Harper, a former abolitionist and a poet, warned that "men cannot live by politics alone," and suggested disavowing political activity for twenty years while focusing on moral and spiritual development. But for most politically aware blacks this was, as yet, an ill-advised course. Somewhat tentatively, they looked to Cleveland, as they had to his Republican predecessors, as a source of aid and protection.[31]

Despite their guardedly optimistic response, black leaders initially did not have the direct communication with Cleveland that they had enjoyed with Republican presidents. The prevailing mood among them was to accept Democratic victory and win whatever concessions possible. The *State Journal* advised, "Many young colored men will for the first time in their life live under a Democratic administration. The present generation is the hope of the race. They can command greater respect for themselves and their race as intelligent American citizens by accepting philosophically the result of the present political contest than by displaying a vindictiveness, which would only invite unnecessary discord."[32]

Cleveland's inaugural address, in which he stated "There should be no pretext for anxiety touching the protection of the freedmen in their rights or their security," was widely praised by blacks. A. A. Middlebrooks, who had held minor Republican appointments in several southern states, credited the speech with promising more than any Republican president ever had. Some blacks predicted that if Cleveland followed these words with enforcement of their rights, blacks might join the Democratic party in large numbers. In the weeks following the inaugural address, optimism soared to the point of suggesting that Cleveland might appoint a black man to his cabinet and reappoint Douglass U.S. marshall. The Indianapolis *Leader*, while admitting that most blacks voted Republican, claimed that the Democrats had received a larger share of the black vote than ever before and insisted that these votes be rewarded.[33]

During the Cleveland years, the number of blacks espousing Democracy did increase significantly for a variety of reasons. Many who had lost faith in the Republicans now rationalized that Democratic ascendancy would not be as detrimental to their rights as they had long feared. Even the extreme conservative position that southern Democratic hegemony was in the best interest of the race gained some adherents. P. C. Hall supported white Democratic control in the South and suggested that when other blacks adopted this view, they would come "into the full blaze of the sunshine of the undiscovered friendship of the Southern white people." Hall presented his theories in a political tract entitled *A Negro's Opinion in a Little Book on Big Things,* the fourth chapter of which he "gloriously" dedicated to Cleveland. There were also blacks who genuinely believed that participation in two parties was in the race's best interest. Others commonly geared their politics to the best chance for personal gain and now proclaimed themselves Democrats.[34]

The most prominent black Democrat during Cleveland's administration was Charles H. J. Taylor, an editor and politician from Wyandotte, Kansas. Born a slave in Alabama in 1856, Taylor had earned a B.A. from the University of Michigan in 1874 and had then settled in Kansas to practice law and pursue a political career. When his efforts on behalf of the state's Republican party went unrewarded, Taylor shifted to the Democratic party and launched a lifelong crusade to convince blacks that they should divide politically. Other longtime black Democrats now prominent as liaisons with the Democratic administration included Peter Clark, Alexander Powell, George T. Downing, James C. Matthews, and T. McCants Stewart. Shortly after Cleveland's inauguration, Powell hosted a reception for black Democrats where he toasted the Cleveland administration as one that would protect all in their constitutional rights. Peter Clark followed with assurances that if blacks would just divide the vote, much Democratic antagonism would dissipate, for "whenever colored men find themselves in accord with the Democracy in local or national issues they should vote with them and thus disdain much of the malevolence that is born of political rather than race antagonisms." T. McCants Stewart advocated division of the black vote because he believed it unmanly to continue clinging to the Republican party. He exhorted Cleveland to encourage the division by appointing black Democrats and independents to office. George T. Downing claimed black influence on Democratic policy as reason for a division of the black vote.[35]

T. Thomas Fortune, whose paper had been renamed the *Free-*

man, initially insisted that blacks should demand nothing from the Democrats because they had contributed so little to the party's victory. Most black Democrats, however, hoped that they would be rewarded for their political views with an appointment and they were supported by most of the Republican black press. The *Bee* advocated that Cleveland keep black Republicans in office as well as give black Democrats new positions. Chase was often accused of self-interest, but even after his own dismissal from a clerkship, he continued to lobby for the retention of black Republican officeholders. "It is not office with us," he claimed, "but a principle." The Cleveland *Gazette* also rationalized that Cleveland would acknowledge the worth of such leaders as Douglass and Bruce and retain them in office rather than replace them with black Democrats.[36]

A number of black men solicited the president directly, often combining personal appeals with assessments of the positive impact black appointments would have for developing black Democracy. Fortune, who worked for places for friends as well as himself, claimed he had so often spoken publicly for Cleveland that the Republicans had cut off funds to his paper. Particularly hoping to be appointed recorder of deeds (the lucrative and much-sought-after position of Frederick Douglass), Fortune wrote, "It would greatly assist me in the work of liberalizing the political thought of the colored people of the country, which, of course, would benefit the Democratic party in the future." Charles H. J. Taylor, the most frequent solicitor, was more successful. In March 1887, Cleveland named him minister to Liberia, traditionally a black office.[37]

Early in his administration Cleveland assured blacks that he would apply the same appointment criteria to them as he did to whites. It was soon evident, however, that Cleveland was replacing most of the black Republican officeholders with white Democrats. Although this was due more to partisanship than to racism, blacks were soon criticizing the paucity of new black appointments. The Huntsville *Gazette*, for example, complained week after week, "No Turkey as yet to the colored Democrat."[38]

By the end of his first year in office, Cleveland had increased the number of black appointments. The use of civil service examinations, mandated by the Pendleton Act of 1883, increased the number of blacks holding low-level federal jobs in northern states. Some blacks also capitalized on the merit system in the South, but more commonly white Southerners found ways to circumvent the new law. Cleveland, although not directly responsible for the increase in the number of black civil servants, often received credit. He also enhanced his black support by continuing the Republican practice of appointing blacks as ministers to all-black countries. J. E. W. Thompson was named minister to Haiti; Moses Hopkins, C. H. J. Taylor, and Ezekiel E. Smith all served in Liberia. Arthur appointee H. C. C. Astwood was retained in Santo Domingo throughout most of Cleveland's term.[39]

As a result of Cleveland's determination to remove active Republicans, however, several important traditional black positions were lost. Blanche K. Bruce was replaced as register of the treasury by General William Rosecrans. Frederick Douglass was asked to resign his position as recorder of deeds at his own convenience which he did on January 5, 1886. He reasserted his Republican allegiance but also praised President Cleveland for his courteous treatment.[40]

Other blacks, however, were more critical of the president, claiming that he had removed too many black men from office. They particularly focused on Douglass's position, which was coveted by a large number of black and white applicants. The fight to replace Douglass with a black Democrat became, to many blacks all over the country, a test of whether there was any significant difference between Democratic and Republican racial policy.

In March 1886, James Matthews was named to replace Douglass. In 1872, Matthews had supported the liberal Republicans because he believed that "the negro race should divide on the two great parties and make its influence felt in both." Subsequently he had become active in New York Democratic politics. Already well-known by Cleveland, he was a logical appointee. William H. Johnson, a leading black Republican in New York, was one of his few black opponents. Most blacks, both Democratic and Republican, praised Cleveland's choice. The fight that ensued over confirmation brought blacks closer to the Democratic party than they had been at any time since emancipation. Matthews wrote Cleveland that he was receiving congratulations and offers of help from blacks all over the country. Fortune, although frustrated in his own bid for the office, offered to travel to key states for Matthews. Edwin McCabe, emigration leader and auditor of Kansas, offered to work in the Midwest. "Confirm Matthews" became the black political crusade of 1886.[41]

While blacks found reason to praise Cleveland, many white Democrats condemned Matthew's appointment with attacks so vicious that they were labeled "shameful for a civilized country." Blacks were even more angered by Republican opposition led by Senator John J. Ingalls of Kansas. Although Ingalls, who was a member of the Senate Committee on the District of Columbia, had first voted yes for Matthews, he had subsequently determined that it was bad politics for Republican senators to support black Democrats. A petition with five thousand names was presented to Ingalls protesting his changed position. When the Republican-dominated committee rejected the appointment, Cleveland *Gazette* correspondent Walter S. Brown, expressing sentiments shared by many blacks, wrote President Cleveland, "Of all mean and despicable action I ever knew of it made me so angry I could not keep from saying something in reference . . . I have been a republican all my life but as time passes I am becoming more enlightened to the selfish motives by which the republican party are activated toward the colored voter and citizen."[42]

It was hoped that enough Democrats would support the appointment to confirm Matthews, but in late July he was defeated. Black bitterness was directed primarily at Republican opponents. While the most common rationale for opposition was that Matthews did not live in Washington, most blacks insisted that it was a result of blatant racism. It was a serious mistake, many of them asserted, for Republican senators to have voted against a black appointee.[43]

Compared to these Republicans, President Cleveland appeared heroic. As loyalty to the Republicans eroded, blacks all over the country claimed new respect for the president. The Cairo (Ill.) *Gazette* insisted that the appointment put Cleveland in an entirely new light, and the *Freeman* proclaimed "Whatever may be their political bias, the colored people of this country

honor and respect and have confidence in President Cleveland."
Several prominent blacks assured Cleveland that his determination to make this appointment was a great boost to his black
support.[44]

Praise of Cleveland's courage proved justified. Shortly after
the first rejection, he offered Matthews a recess appointment,
prompting another outpouring of black gratitude and support.
The Kansas City *Gate City Press* credited Cleveland with showing
more backbone than any of his predecessors. The Athens *Blade*
determined that "President Cleveland makes a good President
so far as the Negro Democrat goes. He stands by his friends.
We are friendly to such men." Editor Chase of the *Bee* condemned both parties. The Democrats, he maintained, had
proven, despite some recent appointments, that they had no
interest in the black race, while the Republicans had proven
hypocritical in their efforts to prevent blacks from enjoying full
political equality. By November 1886, the controversy had inspired the once tenaciously Republican Chase to declare a black
"Declaration of Independence" from the Republican party.[45]

In December 1886, Cleveland again submitted Matthews's
name to the Senate. The second Matthews fight raged throughout early 1887. Many blacks insisted that the issue was not over
Matthews's competence but over the question of race, and asserted that blacks would hold the Republican Senate responsible
if the appointment was rejected. They were particularly enraged
at Senator Ingalls's claim that no one of their race had the right
to be a Democrat. Although black Republicans had often asserted
the same thing, they found it an intolerable view for a white
Republican. Republicans were warned that such a philosophy
was prompting blacks to throw off their mask of subserviency.[46]

When Matthews was again rejected by the Senate committee,
blacks intensified their fight on his behalf. The *Freeman* insisted
that the reason given for rejection, that Matthews was not a
Washington resident, was never used in other confirmation decisions; that there was not, in fact, any valid reason given for
refusing to confirm him. Scott Wood, chairman of the Virginia
Independent Executive Committee, wrote that most local blacks
were increasingly independent, and championed Cleveland for
his recognition of their race. In early 1887, the *Bee* reported that

almost all black papers were demanding confirmation. If Matthews was finally defeated by Republican votes, the *Bee* asserted, "the negro vote will desert the party of right and justice."[47]

Some blacks did qualify their support or completely oppose the nomination. J. Willis Menard editorialized that "with Matthews as a Democrat we have but little political sympathy, but with Matthews as a colored man, we are in the same boat. . . . We are colored Americans first and partisans afterwards." The Richmond *Planet*, one of the few papers to oppose Matthews consistently, denounced Cleveland as an even worse failure than expected and refused support for any black Democrat who "would wade through the sufferings of our people that far back and glory in being a Democrat."[48]

But the *Planet*'s was a minority view. Most blacks involved in the debate now put race before party. The approaching Senate vote on the recordership occasioned numerous warnings to Republicans that they must vote for Matthews if blacks were to remain loyal. It was time, the *Bee* demanded, that the race become politically aroused to an extent unknown in American politics. When Matthews was again rejected, blacks again directed their criticism at the Republicans. The *Bee* denounced party leaders for driving "the political stiletto into the hearts of thousands of negroes," but found some hope in defeat. "You Senator," Chase wrote Ingalls, "by your bitter and unrelenting persecution of Recorder Matthews have done for the negro that which they have been unable to do for themselves, i.e., enthuse on their race pride."[49]

Cleveland was again widely praised. The Mississippi *Grenada News* declared that the president would stick by the race always. The Chicago *Observor* insisted that blacks should never forget that the only breach between Cleveland and the Senate was a result of Cleveland's defense of a black appointment. The president again proved worthy of this support when, in February, he offered the position to another black man, James Monroe Trotter of Massachusetts, a former Republican postal employee who had supported Cleveland in 1884. The appointment was made, the president wrote T. McCants Stewart, because "I have deemed the question involved in this matter as one arising above politics and as offering a test of good faith and adherence to pledges—nothing more or less." Stewart and Fortune were among those telegraphing congratulations on so fitting an appointment. The choice did anger some black Democrats, especially those from Washington who had expected to be chosen. There was also concern that Trotter was a non-resident, since a Washington appointee would have forced proof as to whether residence or race was the real reason for Senate rejection. But most blacks rallied behind Trotter as they had Matthews. The *Bee* called the appointment "grand and heroic," and proof that Cleveland was far ahead of the Republicans in putting into practice Republican principles. Republican senators were again warned by many papers and spokesmen to vote for confirmation.[50]

In mid-March the *Freeman* could proclaim, "The Republican Senators eat crow—Mr. Trotter confirmed." All but three Republicans voted for Trotter. Turning down a Democratic black appointee for the third time, Republican senators reasoned, could result in the loss of significant black support. Both the *Freeman* and the *Bee* concluded that the Republicans had voted for Trotter to appease black voters. It proved, asserted Chase, that their claim of voting against Matthews because he was a non-resident had been a front for racism. Chase also pointed out the irony of Republicans being forced by a Democratic president to do the race justice and expressed hope that the affair would serve as a warning to the GOP that blacks were in no mood to be trifled with. Fortune claimed that Cleveland had now reached the Republican quota of black appointments which he found remarkable since the Democrats owed blacks nothing.[51]

Following the recorder fight, Cleveland's black support continued to rise. In addition to his tenacious fight for a black recorder, the Democratic president refused federal appointments to two white Mississippians who had blatantly interfered with black rights; he also supported Republican Senator Henry Blair's bill for federal aid to education, which many blacks believed was the only chance for improved black education in the South, and called for reimbursement to victims of the Freedmen's Savings Bank collapse. The Huntsville *Gazette* claimed that the latter ultimately unsuccessful proposal was "the only practical word for the Negro in a President's message for a long time." The *Bee* and the *Freeman* both began to hint at Democratic allegiance. When Trotter was appointed, Chase announced that the *Bee* was no longer partisan but patriotic and that he would do his best to educate blacks to trust the Democratic administration. By the end of the president's first year in office, the *Freeman* was urging blacks to consider affiliation with a transformed Democratic party.[52]

By the mid-eighties, the changing temper articulated by leading black papers was evident all over the country. In December 1886, the Massachusetts Colored League, although not avowedly Democratic, passed resolutions criticizing the Republicans, calling on blacks to reconsider political alliances, noting the trend of Democrats to become more equitable and just and expressing confidence in Cleveland. James Matthews led efforts to organize black Democrats in upstate New York, and T. McCants Stewart, after his conversion to the Democratic party in 1886, joined John Shaw in organizing in the New York City area. In Ohio, where independence had long been popular among blacks, more became specifically Democratic. The Cincinnati William H. Jones Club was Democratic, while the Columbus Equal Rights League still claimed to be an independent organization. League President James Poindexter promoted independence because he feared that in always voting the straight Republican ticket blacks too often voted against their friends. In January 1886, the Independent Voters of Franklin County, Ohio, called for a mass convention of black voters to work for the end to blind partisanship. The Cincinnati *Afro-American*, the state's leading black Democratic paper, was now joined by several others. The National Independent Colored Political Union, organized in Indiana in August 1886, declared, "It is important to our political interests that we assert our independence, and to no longer be willing dupes of the Republican party." Detroit blacks expressed "strong gratification" at Cleveland's "consistent and enlightened" policy concerning black patronage. In 1887, blacks in Louisville, Kentucky, severed ties with all parties to form an independent league, and in Paris, Kentucky, several hundred men formed the Independent Colored Club. The latter resolved: "We will act with the party in the future which will not only pledge itself but prove by its works that it is a friend of the colored race. We are neither Republicans, Democrats, Local Optionists, or Free Turnpikers but are free American citizens."[53]

Even in the South more blacks became independents or Democrats. "O. L." of Chatham, Virginia, looked to a new day in race relations as blacks embraced Democracy because "always in everything except politics 'old master' is the negro's best and more trusted friend." The "colored voters of Arlington, Virginia," wrote that they often found Democrats more tolerant than Republicans and urged blacks to seek allies wherever possible, even among former masters. In April 1887, a black convention was held in Danville, Virginia, to organize the black vote into an independent political power. Henry C. Smith, a clerk in the Sixth Auditors Office in Chattanooga, reported that Tennessee blacks were beginning to understand that they were used by the Republicans, and that "the bloody shirt don't coerce them as it once did." "I will tell you one thing which is as true as the gospell," he wrote, "Mr. Cleveland and the democratic administration is just as popular among the colored people in the south (the colored politicians excepted) as that of any except Lincoln and Grant's administrations."[54]

Although Smith was probably correct that black political leaders, often dependent on patronage, were more reluctant to desert the Republicans, many of them were also becoming more critical. In December 1885, John Lewis asked how intelligent blacks could permanently tie their vote to one party and insisted that they would not be free citizens until they judged political candidates only by their stand on specific issues. In an Emancipation Day speech delivered in January 1886, John Langston, who had resigned his appointment as minister to Haiti and now served as president of the Virginia Normal and Collegiate Institute, claimed that blacks were no longer solidly Republican and that their willingness to vote Democratic was the first step toward solving racial problems.[55]

Black Democrats were even more optimistic. Henry Downing, Democratic recipient of a federal appointment, wrote Cleveland that "the happy course taken by the administration has influenced leaders in my own house like Derrick, McCants Stewart and Greener to look upon the Democratic party with such kindness and is giving birth to a feeling among them of independence

which if fostered, may divorce them from the Republican party."
Stewart, one of the most prominent converts to Democracy, assured Cleveland that "your course, sir, is liberalizing and dividing
the colored vote and your party will be the beneficiary of your
patriotic work."[56]

The most extensive evaluation of the changing partisan views
of blacks was Thomas Fortune's pamphlet *The Negro in Politics*,
published in 1886. Fortune concluded that since 1876 senti-
mental politics had dictated how blacks responded politically,
allowing the Republicans to use their votes with impunity. He
claimed that Republican sentiment had become so deeply
ingrained that black independence was fought not only by Republican politicians but also by the majority of blacks. Although
he believed that blacks had no active political leader who was
not the tool of white politicians, he was hopeful that this was
changing and that the race was thinking more for itself. Fortune
viewed Cleveland's election and his black appointments as indicative of a more positive Democratic policy. Self-sufficiency,
not Republican loyalty, was, to Fortune, the key. "You do not
need to be a Democrat or a Republican to force from politicians
your honest rights," he counseled blacks, "you simply need to
be men, conscious of your own power." Fortune insisted that in
the future blacks vote only for candidates who promised to
protect their rights. He was confident that the race was beginning
to accept his advice "to consult your own interests in the
future."[57]

By late 1886, the *Bee* claimed that independence was the race's
most absorbing political interest. Whereas before 1885 independence had largely referred to separation from the Republican party, it now often implied affiliation with Cleveland
Democracy. In April 1887, the *Freeman* canvassed selected black
papers to ascertain sectional political views. None of the three
southern papers interviewed favored a wholesale break with the
Republican party, but the Pine Bluff (Ark.) *Southwestern Review*
feared that this was happening. The *Freeman*'s survey revealed
that black independence was most extensive in the Midwest. The
Chicago *Observor* called on black Republicans to do as white Republicans did: vote according to interests. The Indianapolis

World agreed that the surest road to full political rights was through a divided vote. But independence was not confined to one section of the country. It was, proclaimed the *Freeman*, the "age of the Negrowump—the voter who is partisan for neither party but for the race."[58]

Despite increased support for Cleveland, however, only a small minority of blacks actually moved beyond talk of independence to committed Democratic allegiance. Sometimes the Democrats were blamed for failing to take advantage of their opportunity, leaving most blacks tied hopelessly to the Republican party. But traditional black antipathy was a major hurdle, prompting even such staunch Democrats as C. H. J. Taylor and James Monroe Trotter to counsel independence more frequently than Democratic conversion. In late 1887, Trotter called for a continuation of the trend "towards courageous independence and self-reliance."[59]

Cleveland's support of Matthews and Trotter dominated the black press for months and made the Democratic president temporarily as popular as any of his Republican predecessors. But Cleveland proved to be a more traditional Democrat when he confronted the far more significant question of how to deal with violations of southern black rights. His passive southern policy advocated home rule which would give the Bourbon Democrats virtually a free hand. Thus, despite considerable admiration for Cleveland, few blacks could seriously consider converting to Democracy, and many continued to condemn the party as vehemently as ever. Some critics made an exception of Cleveland as a man apart from his party; they also distinguished between the northern Democrats and the southern Bourbons. But for most blacks in all sections of the country, atrocities committed by the southern Democrats were too much of a commanding reality to allow conversion to the party at large.

Enthusiasm for both Cleveland and independence diminished as the election of 1888 approached. In July 1887, Chase, while still claiming to be favorably disposed toward Cleveland, accused him of not doing all that he might have for blacks. Throughout 1886, the Cleveland *Gazette*'s qualified support of Cleveland rarely included his party, and by December 1887, Editor Smith had completely rejected the Democrats. He concluded that "there are good and bad in all parties as a rule, but the Democratic party is the quintessence of rottenness."[60]

Black political leaders also began to attack the Democrats more frequently. George W. Williams, frustrated in his bid for office, became one of the most strident critics of Democracy and, unlike many, projected the party's faults onto the president. Williams charged Cleveland with both unfairness in appointment policy and insensitivity to southern violence. He also now condemned blacks who accepted an appointment by such an administration as "Judas Iscariots," who would someday see "that their commissions were signed in the innocent blood of their kinsmen and that their salaries were blood money." In December 1887, John Lynch declared that considering the Mississippi Plan and the general suppression of the black vote, Cleveland had as much right to claim the throne of Great Britain as he did the presidency.[61]

Much of the debate as to whether Cleveland had made Democracy a viable option for blacks was summed up in an exchange between William Scarborough and T. McCants Stewart. Scarborough asked Stewart to defend black support of the Democrats by answering several questions, including: (1) Could blacks conscientiously subscribe to declarations of the Democrats? (2) Was the party not still basically as it had been in 1860? (3) Should Cleveland not be considered in advance of most other Democrats and therefore atypical? (4) Was not support of the northern wing tantamount to supporting the Bourbon southern wing? (5) Could blacks afford to divide their votes before the issue of their civil and political rights had been settled? Stewart responded that the Democrats were significantly different from the slave party of 1860 and were abiding by their last platform which endorsed equality before the law. Stewart agreed that Cleveland was in advance of his party, but he also believed that many other Democrats were following the president's lead and that support of them could break up the solid South. Finally, while he did not favor wholesale exodus from the GOP, he believed that blind adherence to that party must end because in the last two decades black rights had only declined. Stewart was not notably persuasive. The black press was far more critical of his ideas than

Scarborough's, indicative of the continued reluctance to embrace Democracy.[62]

Suggestions of third party allegiance or abnegation of political participation altogether as alternatives to supporting either of the major parties proliferated during the middle years of Cleveland's administration. Throughout 1886 and 1887 there was a wave of black support for the Prohibition party. Fortune, although praising the party as the only one with well-defined principles, at first refused active support because "we have been a guerilla too long now to submit to the party lash." But when Christopher Perry, editor of the Philadelphia *Tribune*, endorsed the Prohibitionists, the *Freeman* was complimentary and finally followed suit, declaring, "Tis a new party with new ideas, and its bound to win. The old parties must skip." The *Freeman* urged labor parties, which had limited black support, to unite with the Prohibitionists in a new reform party. When Fortune gave up the editorship of the *Freeman*, the paper ceased to endorse the temperance party, but Fortune himself continued to be a "Prohibitionist from centre to circumference." John E. Bruce, at this time editor of the Baltimore *Commonwealth*, also became an advocate because he could no longer tolerate "cheap white politicians" and because he had concluded that the Prohibition party was the only one in Maryland that recognized blacks as men and citizens. Bishop Henry M. Turner launched the *Southern Recorder* to work for the Prohibitionists in the South. Rev. A. A. Burleigh also supported prohibition but called for a new "American Party" to work for it. Many other blacks supported the cause but not a new party. The Huntsville *Gazette* estimated that the majority of southern blacks were always found on the side of prohibition but that few were party members.[63]

Throughout the Cleveland years, there continued to be heard proposals that during a Democratic administration blacks should eschew politics. In the summer of 1885, a New York *Times* southern correspondent reported that many black voters had grown indifferent to politics. "Senex" of Charleston, South Carolina, found value in Democratic victory in that it directed the minds of young blacks from political affairs to other fields. Even the New York *Freeman* at one time admonished, "No people ever became great and prosperous by devoting their infant energies to politics" and demanded that education be the race's priority. But a few months later the editor expressed optimism that politics would boom again. Proposals to forego politics were usually ephemeral expressions of pessimism or apathy following political or economic setbacks rather than serious proposals.[64]

Despite the many exhortations that the Cleveland years were a time for blacks to rethink their political allegiance or even to disavow politics altogether, the majority were still at least warily Republican in 1888. Frederick Douglass, the most eminent black political leader, undoubtedly influenced many to remain faithful. Douglass only briefly flirted with independence during the Cleveland years; he more typically lobbied for the GOP. In 1886, he credited Cleveland with being as competent as most Republican presidents but denied that his merit extended to the rest of the party. The difference between the Republicans and the Democrats, Douglass claimed, was still "as palpable as the difference between the character of Moses and that of Pharoah." Finding it unfortunate that some "either thoughtlessly or selfishly or both, chose to deny their obligations to the great Republican party and its leaders," he asserted that "for one I never will forget that every concession of liberty made to the colored people of the United States has come to them through the action of the Republican party, and that all the opposition made to those concessions has come from the Democratic party."[65]

A number of black Cleveland Democrats accepted Douglass's counsel and by late 1887 had reclaimed their Republican allegiance. This reversal was symbolized by the *Freeman* which, reorganized as the *Age*, announced in November 1887: "In politics the *Age* will be strictly Republican, as it sees in that party the greatest promise for the adequate recognition and political advancement of the race." The return of John Shaw to the fold about the same time was also an impetus to black Republicanism in New York, and the trend was similar elsewhere. Augustus Straker reported that in his native South, "the colored people are all Republican at heart."[66]

In November 1887, the New York *Evening Sun* ran a symposium to consider the current political views of black Americans. Stewart, chosen as an advocate of Democracy, reported that he had been convinced by the liberal policy of Cleveland that the Democratic was the best party for the race and country. Dr. T. S. P. Miller, representing the Labor party, concluded that the Republicans had failed in every declaration of principle concerning blacks and that Labor was "a safe and convenient refuge for colored men." It was a proper choice, Miller believed, because blacks were a wage-earning people. Prohibitionist William T. Dixon replied that although he had been a loyal Republican for years, he now believed that "the Republican party, under God, saved by the abolition of slavery the bodies of colored men. The Prohibition will save the souls of all men." Jerome Peterson, who had replaced Fortune as editor of the *Age*, defended traditional Republican allegiance. Although he agreed that the Republicans had virtually deserted their black allies, he insisted that the party now realized that it needed black votes and would work hard to get them. Peterson recognized that some blacks were moving into the Democratic, Labor, and Prohibition parties and acknowledged their right to do so, but was sure that for most, "discretion teaches that it is better to bear the ills we know than to fly to those we know not of."[67]

The symposium prompted another much publicized Stewart dialogue, this time with Frederick Douglass, concerning black support of Democracy. In response to the claim that no race should give all of its votes to one party, Douglass countered that it would be safer to be in one sound ship than in several unseaworthy ones. As for the reputed kindly feelings of the Democrats, Douglass claimed that even if they existed, they would not assure black political rights. He recalled that in Georgia during Reconstruction blacks had voted for their Democratic masters for the legislature only to see that body deprive the race of its vote. Finally, Douglass denied that division of the vote would destroy the solid South by destroying white fear of black domination because he denied that such fear existed. He urged black Democrats to learn that "nothing is gained to the right by surrendering to the wrong." Stewart replied by denying a black debt to the Republicans; slavery, he insisted, had been abolished as a war measure and black suffrage granted only to make the Republican party supreme. Any debt that was owed, he maintained, was ended when blacks were "betrayed and sacrificed by the traitorous Hayes administration." "If our people are not now 'free' to vote for any party," he asked Douglass, "when in heavens name...will the time of our deliverance come?" Stewart summed up his argument for independence with five points: (1) unanimous support for one party had only won contempt from friends and hatred from opponents; (2) blacks, as a poor and weak race, needed all the friends they could get; (3) both industrial and political prejudices were diminishing in parts of the North, suggesting that blacks should cooperate with various parties; (4) Cleveland was fulfilling his promises to blacks, and (5) the South was getting better because as blacks divided their vote so were whites. Douglass countered that present issues made him a Republican, not the dead issues of slavery and war, and that "every shot-gun aimed at the heart of a negro in the South to-day is leveled by the hand of a Democrat." Northern black Democrats, Douglass charged, were trying to do just what Hayes and his friends had agreed to do in 1876: defeat and break up the power of the Republican party in the South and give it to the Democrats. Only when the Democrats assumed the same view of blacks that the Republicans had long held, he concluded, could the race divide without exciting racial prejudice on either side. The Stewart-Douglass exchange was widely discussed in the black press. Fortune, who praised the two men as the most articulate advocates of the two sides, generally agreed with Stewart. He admonished blacks that they should "cease to pin their faith to other people and pin their faith to themselves." "Let them organize as the Irish have done and as I have advised them to do," he continued, "for mutual protection and defense. Let them stop the eternal flow of gab and go to work."[68]

Fortune was determined to make his own words more than "gab." In the spring of 1887, he proposed forming the Afro-American League to unite black organizations. It was one of the most ambitious racial self-help efforts of the late nineteenth century, made necessary, Fortune claimed, because once-sympathetic whites had abandoned blacks to their own battles. Fortune agitated for his league throughout 1887, urging that it was particularly important that blacks organize before the election of 1888 in order to determine who would get the black vote. He could soon list a number of prominent black backers including Booker T. Washington, president of Tuskegee Institute of Alabama, who wrote that thousands of southern blacks were ready to support such an effort. The Raleigh *Outlook* agreed, reporting that conditions in the South were worsening and "if the constitutions under which we live will not protect us, if the political parties which claim to be our friends fail to come to the rescue, there is nothing for us to do then but to recognize such an organization as is mentioned by Mr. Fortune of the New York *Freeman*." Support also came from blacks less directly affected but equally concerned. The Boston *Advocate* praised the proposed league as the start of self-protection of life, liberty, and political freedom.[69]

Although most blacks who responded supported Fortune's proposal, a minority actively opposed it. J. Willis Menard claimed that conditions in the South were improving and that the league would only make things worse. Several other southern editors voiced fear that the organization would antagonize whites and result in bloodshed. The Cairo *Gazette* claimed that behind Fortune and his league was a white man after the black vote. Others opposed it on the grounds that it would mean self-segregation. The most frequently expressed reservation was that the league might dictate political decisions to blacks resulting in the further encroachment of individual initiative. Fortune agreed to promote his organization as an apolitical one, but by late 1887 only a few local leagues had been formed.[70]

As a result of Cleveland's attention to black interests, northern and western blacks especially had begun to work for Democracy on local and state levels. But continued Democratic discrimination and violence in the South limited voluntary black Democratic support there. Moreover, blacks increasingly realized that Cleveland's effectiveness was limited, and that while he had made several dramatic stands on their behalf, he had little interest in launching a major federal offensive to insure racial equality. His fervent laissez-faire, self-help philosophy precluded both massive interference in southern affairs and direct aid to black people. As the election of 1888 approached, most blacks were still convinced that the best chance for restoring the political revolution would come under a Republican administration.

5

Republican Protection or Political Alternatives: The Election of 1888 and the Harrison Administration

The nation's eight million blacks, T. Thomas Fortune claimed in 1888, were more concerned than any other group with choosing the next president. Blacks began considering possible candidates more than two years before the election. There was little doubt that Blaine would again be a serious contender for the Republican nomination, but the sides were sharply drawn over whether blacks should support him. The *Bee* identified Blaine's opposition to election supervision in the South as the major reason he should be opposed and predicted that if the election was between Blaine and Cleveland, the majority of blacks would vote for Cleveland. The *Freeman* concurred, calling Blaine "a demagogue and trickster" whose renomination should be fought on all sides. The St. Louis *Advance*, edited by P. H. Murray, condemned Blaine for his assertion that a black Democrat was a monstrosity and estimated that the majority of blacks supported John Sherman. The Cleveland *Gazette*, one of the few papers supporting Blaine, countered that ninety-nine out of every one hundred black Americans admired the Maine senator. Frederick Douglass did not endorse Blaine directly but predicted that he would be the GOP nominee and called on all blacks to support whomever the party chose. Blaine, however, announced in February 1888 that he was not a candidate. Most blacks expressed relief, although the Jacksonville *Southern Leader* claimed this was a "cunning dodge" by Blaine to keep his candidacy alive.[1]

John Sherman again had considerable support among southern blacks, although many were now more critical of his racial
stands. The Stanton *Virginia Critic* renewed demands for a black
vice-presidential nomination by urging a Sherman-Douglass
ticket. Douglass never encouraged his own inclusion on the ticket
but agreed that the Ohio senator "was the man whose attitude
toward the newly enfranchised Negro citizen of the South best
fitted him for the place." John Langston described Sherman as
the man "to master and manage all those great questions affecting the general welfare, especially the free and just use of
the ballot." The *Bee* and the *Freeman* both considered Sherman
one of several acceptable candidates, although the *Bee* leaned
toward John A. Logan and the *Freeman* endorsed Judge Walter
Q. Gresham. In the weeks just before the convention, both suggested that Roscoe Conkling, from the doubtful state of New
York, might be the best choice. Robert Lincoln, Joseph Foraker,
Chauncey Depew, and William Allison also had black press
support.[2]

The Republican party was again warned that no matter whom
they nominated, the candidate must earn black support. "I am,"
Hamilton Smith wrote Frederick Douglass, "as all negroes ought
to be, a Republican and heartily agree with you, that we have
had enough of sentiment, but now want a standard bearer with
back bone enough to see that the negro is protected in his rights."
The *Freeman* frequently admonished the Republican National
Committee that blacks, especially in the North and West, must
have a voice at the convention. The *Bee* agreed, demanding that
blacks establish at this convention whether they would "be like
dumb beasts or declare their independence."[3]

Despite declining support for Cleveland, blacks were more
interested in the deliberations of the Democratic party than they
had been in any previous presidential election year. Some black
Republicans endorsed Cleveland as the party's best choice.
Shortly before the Democratic convention convened, W. M.
Twine asserted that renominating the president would be a god-
send in that blacks could rest assured that Republican defeat
would not result in their reenslavement. Almost all black Democrats endorsed the president's renomination. George T. Down-

ing insisted that his reelection would bring the greatest possible advancement to the race.[4]

This widespread endorsement of Cleveland's nomination, however, prompted criticism from other staunch Republicans. Theophilus T. Minton of Philadelphia maintained a running battle with admirers of Cleveland, particularly Stewart and Fortune. He argued that Cleveland had done little for blacks, that while he had a great opportunity to break the color line, he had not done so. Others claimed that Cleveland was inhibited by his party. A black South Carolinian summed up the attitude of many Republicans when he insisted, "No honorable colored man, uninfluenced by fear or boodle, is or can be a Democrat, so long as that party fails to protect him in his full rights as a man."[5]

Yet many blacks were still willing to debate this sentiment, even in the emotional atmosphere of an approaching election. The national Colored Press Association Convention, held in Louisville in August 1887, reflected on the changed perception of blacks that had developed over the previous four years. Rather than focus on which Republican candidate blacks should support, the delegates focused on which party they should support. Rev. Allan Allensworth launched the debate by introducing the topic, "Negro Americans' relation to the existing parties" for discussion. Alexander Clark's response that anyone who left the Republican party was a traitor was denounced by several other speakers including P. H. Murray, who claimed that as long as blacks were regarded as the enemies of any party, they would have to fight that party. The delegates opposed the formation of a national political organization of blacks, supporting instead local organizations which could adapt to particular circumstances.[6]

No black man was present as a delegate when the Democratic convention convened in St. Louis in June, but, according to the *Age*, "Negro Democrats were as plentiful in St. Louis as flies in fly time." The Democrats made an effort to capitalize on their improved race relations. The party convention chairman assured them that they had been more honored by Cleveland than by any of his Republican predecessors. As if to underscore the point, C. H. J. Taylor became the first black man asked to deliver a

seconding speech at a Democratic convention. But the Democrats still saw no need to make promises to end southern violence
and voting restrictions, instead assuring blacks that during the
previous four years, "the equality of all our citizens before the
law, without regard to race or section, has been steadfastly
maintained."[7]

President Cleveland was renominated easily, a choice ap-
plauded by both Democratic and Republican blacks. The *Age*,
wavering between Republicanism and independence, described
Cleveland as, "a new school progressive Democrat," and predicted that he would have substantial black support. The partisan
Cairo *Gazette* described the nominee as "the best Democrat in
the country," and "one fit to be placed at the head of affairs of
this great nation." "May God grant you health and prosperity,"
William Gross wired the Democratic nominee, "to execute justice
into all races as you have done in the past." T. McCants Stewart
assured Cleveland of his support and predicted a large black
Democratic vote in November. While still considering himself a
Prohibitionist, Thomas Fortune now claimed that "until colored
men learn to acknowledge the honest friendliness of such Democrats as President Cleveland and stop tagging after such slip-
pery tricksters as Mr. Blaine and Mr. Chandler, and until they
stop whining for recognition as they call it, and put themselves
in position to demand it of whatever party they affiliate with,
they will continue to be the footballs of Republican schemes."
Soon after, Fortune formally endorsed Cleveland. Andrew
Chambers, a North Carolina minister and tenacious southern
black Democrat, not only endorsed the president but also pre-
sumed to advise him on major economic problems. Blacks were
more critical of the vice-presidential nomination of seventy-five-
year-old Allan G. Thurman, a longtime opponent of black rights
who had once blamed the Reconstruction acts for the violence
in the South.[8]

Despite widespread approval of Cleveland as the best choice
the Democrats could make, most blacks were far more interested
in events at the Republican National Convention which opened
in Chicago on June 19. Most of the southern black delegates
attending supported John Sherman. Early in the proceedings
Douglass, following a spontaneous call to address the delegates,

admonished Republicans to "be not deterred from this duty by the cry of a bloody shirt," and called on the party to remain faithful to "those friends with black faces who during the war were eyes to your blind. Shelter to your shelterless, when flying from the lines of the enemy." But Douglass's admonition held little sway with Republicans determined to ignore racial issues and concentrate on economic concerns. The platform did include a bitter denunciation of black disfranchisement but gave far more attention to the tariff. On the eighth ballot the Republicans nominated Benjamin Harrison and subsequently chose Levi P. Morton as his running mate. John Lynch seconded the motion to make the nomination unanimous, using the occasion to demand an end to violence and voting fraud in the South and to advocate a system of public education.[9]

While many blacks considered Harrison an inferior choice, it was not difficult for most of them to support an early advocate of emancipation and a radical Republican. Several papers presented his senatorial efforts on behalf of blacks as proof that he would continue to do all he could for the race. They also noted that in the preconvention months Harrison had been among the small group of Republicans who continued to emphasize the protection of black rights. "Hip, hurrah for the ticket," the sentiment expressed by the Huntsville *Gazette*, was soon echoed all across the country. The Knoxville *World* claimed that "the name of Harrison inspires the colored vote in the South." Another southern paper, however, labeled Harrison "the chief hangman of American Democracy."[10]

The Republican platform of 1888 gave little attention to racial problems beyond proclaiming devotion "to the supreme and sovereign right of every lawful citizen . . . white or black, to cast one free ballot and to have that ballot duly counted," and demanding "free public education for all children." Initially most blacks accepted this as adequate. The Nicodemus (Kans.) *Cyclone* endorsed the platform "in that it is plain, seeks no subterfuge, but takes a bold stand." The *Age* agreed that the suffrage plank was a good one, if only the party could be persuaded to implement it.[11]

The Republican National Committee, which had virtually ignored race at the convention, continued to emphasize economic questions. When the race problem was mentioned, it was generally tied to tariff revision. Harrison never hedged in his support for a free vote and federal aid to education, but he devoted less attention to these issues. Blacks were assured that racial problems would end when southern protectionists were brought into the Republican party. The Harrison and Morton Colored Protective Tariff League in Washington was prominent among the several groups and individuals that, at least initially, accepted economics as the main campaign issue. Black newspapers gave more attention to the tariff question than they had previously given to any issue not strictly racial. In the October edition of the A.M.E. Church *Review*, which focused on the question of protection, black labor leader I. C. Wears recommended tariff policy as a good reason to vote for the Republicans since "it is folly to expect the Democratic party to protect anything." T. McCants Stewart countered that reduction would best serve black interests. To most blacks, however, protection was secondary to proscription. In October, D. M. Lindsay warned that emphasis on the tariff to the exclusion of racial matters had already lost the Republican party black northern supporters and would lose them hundreds more by November. Some white Republicans, particularly William Chandler, came to agree and late in the campaign did make sporadic efforts to interject race questions into the debate.[12]

Although by a considerable majority most blacks (some reluctantly, others more enthusiastically) continued to support the Republican party, there was more support for the Democrats than in any previous election. The Democrats continued to make at least a minimal effort to foster the trend. In July, they subsidized a National Convention of Independent Voters in Indianapolis. The approximately one hundred Democratic and independent black voters divided, sometimes acrimoniously, into an old-Democratic faction headed by C. H. J. Taylor and a new-Democratic faction headed by Thomas Fortune. They finally elected old-Democrat Peter Clark as president with the support of both Taylor and Fortune. Clark admonished the delegates to recognize that federal action as advocated by the Republicans would not solve racial problems. The convention endorsed Cleveland and advocated a reduced tariff. They also issued a call to all black voters "to act as men, each in accordance with his own uncoerced conviction and vote with that party which he may deem likely to promote the interest of himself and [his] race."[13]

The convention initiated a new round of inquiries into the growing independence of black voters. The Springfield *Messenger* found this proof that blacks now leaned toward independence; the Boston *People's Advocate* agreed that unless countermeasures were launched, the convention would prove fatal to the Republicans' black support. The convention also launched a lively debate among blacks as to the efficacy of voting Democratic. Many were less willing to tolerate black Democracy once the campaign began. The Cleveland *Gazette* denounced the convention, insisting that national Democratic leaders had financed it and that its black leaders "are not men to be looked upon, much less trusted as leaders." The *Bee* labeled the convention "the boodle conference," and added that "colored Democrats at Indianapolis don't look natural." Frederick Douglass cautioned blacks not to be misled by the "disreputable and scandalous work of misleading colored men." Democratic papers, on the other hand, were lavish in their praise of the conference. The Indianapolis *Freeman* proclaimed that it "dates the beginning of his [the black man's] real emancipation and records the death of his political serfdom." The Philadelphia *Sentinel* agreed that it was "the public declaration of the end of the political serfdom of the colored men."[14]

Black Democrats, particularly in the North and West, were better organized in this campaign than ever before. In June, Herbert Clark established the National Negro Democratic League, which became the most important black campaign organization. William Gross, president of the New York State Cleveland League, wrote Cleveland that the black vote in New York, New Jersey, and Connecticut could be won by the Democrats. Throughout the campaign he and James Matthews concentrated on refuting Republican claims of Democratic outrages in the South. Kansas and Ohio black Democrats planned a paper and organization in Columbus to educate leaders in various states concerning Democratic principles and history so they in turn could educate the masses. Louis T. Jacobs of Los Angeles printed cards advertising himself as "The Colored Champion Advocate of Democracy of Southern California." In October, Jacobs formed a Cleveland and Thurman Colored Democratic Club which resolved that "Mr. Cleveland's election is the last resort by which the common laboring people are to be rescued from the menacing power of the few who have become tyrannical, insulting and domineering over he many." As far south as Missouri the number of black Democrats was reported to be rapidly increasing.[15]

Black Democratic press coverage was also far more extensive than it had been in past elections. At least ten black newspapers, including the Indianapolis *Freeman*, the St. Paul and Minneapolis *Afro-Independent*, the Philadelphia *Sentinel*, the Topeka *Public Leader*, the Cairo *Gazette*, and the Cincinnati *Afro-American* (which during the campaign was edited by Thomas Fortune) supported the Democrats. The most important Democratic paper, the *Freeman*, edited by E. E. Cooper, admonished its readers with the traditional argument that they could not hope to prosper as the political foes of one-half of the country and the political slaves of the other half. As the campaign progressed, parties and personalities rather than a philosophical debate on independence became the principal concern of the *Freeman*, and it launched a spirited crusade on behalf of the Democratic national ticket. A published letter, with which Cooper emphatically agreed, insisted: "It can't be shown that Benjamin Harrison or any of his ancestors ever did a friendly act, or spoke a kindly word for the Negro race," while challenging "anyone to point to any unfriendly work or deed of Cleveland." Black Republicans, particularly Frederick Douglass, were the special targets of the *Freeman's* wrath. Perhaps the paper's most extreme defense of the Democratic party was its claim that blacks owed their freedom "as much to Davis as to Lincoln, as much to Democrats as to Republicans." The *Afro-Independent* concurred, labeling the Democratic party "the only national party" and admonishing "every Negro . . . to wake from his lethargy of political serfdom for a score of years, and resent the blackguardism of unscrupulous Republican leaders." Stewart, Downing, Trotter, Taylor, and Robert Still were among the prominent black politicians working for the Democrats. Stewart, who led in forming several black Democratic clubs in New York, explained his affiliation as the result of his belief in a division of the black vote, the elimination of the color line in politics, and the reduction of the tariff.[16]

Black Democrats sometimes voiced a complaint familiar to black Republicans—that their party did not adequately support them. Robert Still, a leader of the Democratic Colored State League of Pennsylvania, reported to Cleveland "with extreme regret" that the Democratic party was actually driving many out who had been lured into the party by the president's recognition. All around, Still said, he heard the refrain, "I have confidence in the President but not in his party."[17]

Despite the paucity of white support, black Democratic success was sufficient to force the Philadelphia *Tribune*, a leading black Republican paper, to concede that "it is folly to shut our eyes to this Democratic movement, much as we oppose it." The *Freeman*'s claim that "colored voters are flocking to Cleveland's banner" was wishful thinking, but the number of black Democrats was undoubtedly greater than in the past and than most Republicans were willing to admit.[18]

Many black Republicans were determined to discredit claims of Democratic success and, if possible, to eradicate that success entirely. Black Republican clubs again proliferated; there were over two hundred in New York alone. White Republicans, aware that the election would be close and concerned with the loss of northern black voters, urged black Republicans to keep their ranks faithful. James Clarkson, chairman of the Republican National Committee, complained to Douglass about the widespread organization of black Democrats and urged him to work in as many doubtful states as possible. An official of the New York Republican Campaign Committee flattered Douglass that "a Presidential campaign in this state in which your eloquent voice was not heard would resemble the play of Hamlet without Hamlet." Although advised by the National Committee to concentrate on the tariff, Douglass insisted on discussing racial matters. He called on northern blacks to use their votes as custodians of the rights of southern blacks who, if allowed, would certainly vote Republican. In October, at the urging of Clarkson, a group of prominent black leaders (including Douglass, Pinchback, Lynch, and Smalls) issued an appeal to all blacks, urging them to support the Republican party. John Langston, although busy with his own congressional campaign in Virginia, spoke for the national ticket in several northern cities. In an effort to dispel earlier charges, stemming from his 1886 Emancipation Day speech, that he had bolted the Republican party, he founded Harrison, Morton, and Langston clubs in Virginia. The Republican National Committee, however, refused to endorse his candidacy, which was opposed by the Mahone-dominated Virginia Republican machine, and even persuaded Douglass to campaign against him. As a result, Langston ceased his work for the national party and refused to sign Clarkson's appeal.[19]

Black Republicans could be as virulent as their Democratic counterparts in maligning those of differing political views. Douglass warned that any black man who voted other than Republican "stabs the cause of his people and makes himself, consciously or unconsciously, a traitor and an enemy to his race." The Washington *Bee* scoffed that it was "an atrocious thing to find a Negro Democrat." W. B. Derrick, who made over one hundred speeches for Harrison in the North, condemned blacks who voted Democratic for "blighting the hopes of his people in the oppressed South." Often black Democrats were found guilty by association with southern Bourbons. The Leavenworth *Advocate* scornfully claimed that "Negro Democrats think that they . . . tolerate the murder and slaughter" of fellow blacks. To the increasingly partisan *Age*, "It would seem that the few colored men in the North who are supporting the Democratic party are lending their aid to fasten on their colored brethren in the South the galling chain of oppression more firmly than it is at present."[20]

Most Republican editors refrained from vicious attacks on the president personally and were at times still complimentary. The *Age* praised Cleveland's letter of acceptance in which he called for a guarantee to every black citizen of all citizenship rights, but insisted that such a proposal addressed to the Democratic party at large was "in the style of a recommendation to the wolf to take care of the lamb." The Washington *National Echo* agreed that "even if Cleveland wishes to be fair with the Negro, the party will handicap him." The Topeka *American Citizen*, however, did not hesitate to attack the president directly, asserting that Cleveland's assurances to blacks in his letter of acceptance were proven insincere by the numerous crimes committed against blacks during his administration.[21]

It was vice-presidential candidate Allan G. Thurman, however, who was most frequently attacked by blacks. The *Age* published a number of Thurman's racist statements and claimed that attempts of black Democrats to vindicate this record were "like efforts to overturn a mountain with a needle." J. A. Arneaux labeled the vice-presidential nominee "one of the bitterest Negro haters of the nineteenth century," and reminded his audience that a vote for Cleveland was a vote for this "most dangerous enemy of the race."[22]

But whatever the personal qualities of the candidates, evils committed by the Democratic party were considered by most Republicans as reason enough to defeat the ticket. In August, a conference of eighty-four black leaders met in New York and declared by unanimous vote that, considering the outrages suffered by the race in the South, the time had not arrived when blacks in any part of the country were justified in voting for the Democratic party. Many black Republicans seconded the Cleveland *Gazette*'s assessment that the Democratic party was "the same old devilish Negro-hating party of ante-bellum times" and its warning that "a vote for Cleveland is a vote of approval for this damnable method of cheating the Negroes out of their votes."[23]

The emotions of a heated campaign prompted many black Republicans to suppress their grievances against the Republican party and its candidates. The *Bee* now described Harrison as "the most prominent political subject in the United States." The *American Citizen* insisted that if the political condition of blacks was to improve, "it will be through the broad, just and effective legislation of the GOP, the party of equal rights, political and moral reform." Others, however, while wholeheartedly supporting the Republican ticket, still made it clear that they were supporting what they considered the lesser of two evils. The *Age* maintained that even though the Republicans had not always protected their rights, blacks should support the party as the need for protection was a result of southern Democratic proscription. The Cleveland *Gazette* agreed, saying "We do not claim

that all Republicans are perfect—not at all, but we do affirm that
the Republican party is infinitely superior to the Democratic
party."[24]

On November 6, 1888, Harrison narrowly defeated Cleveland,
although due to inflated southern returns, Cleveland was credited with the majority of the popular votes. Several of Cleveland's
black supporters sent him letters of regret. Walter Brown
claimed to write on behalf of one hundred thousand northern
blacks, "the intelligent among the colored," who had voted for
Cleveland. Brown analyzed Cleveland's defeat as attributable to
the failure of the lower classes, black and white, to understand
the principles of the tariff as advanced by the Democrats. Downing and Gross offered regrets at the demise of an administration
they claimed was the race's best hope.[25]

The majority of blacks, however, were elated with the election
of Harrison and a Republican Congress. Northern blacks, who
gave Harrison a majority of their votes, could justly claim some
credit for the victory because, although they made up less than
4 percent of the population in northern states, their concentra-
tion in urban areas made their vote significant in close elections.
Approximately 23 percent of eligible Southerners, most of them
black, voted for Harrison, a percentage only slightly smaller than
those voting Republican in 1880 and 1884. Three black men—
Henry P. Cheatham of North Carolina, Thomas Miller of South
Carolina, and John Langston of Virginia—were elected to Congress. But in much of the South various methods of disfranchisement continued to erode the black vote. In Florida, for
example, constitutional and legislative disfranchisement together with electoral chicanery and violence enabled the Democrats to establish control in most of the black belt. The
percentage of blacks voting fell from 86 to 64 percent and many
of those votes were counted for the Democrats. In Louisiana
disfranchisement was largely the product of violence. In Iberia
Parish, at least eleven blacks were murdered during one month
of the campaign. As a result of such intimidation, Cleveland
received 1,594 votes there compared to Harrison's 9.[26]

Many black supporters were again initially confident that they
would benefit from a Republican victory by the passage of education and election bills and by significant black appointments.

There were again demands that a black man be appointed to the president's cabinet. J. Willis Menard wrote that "Harrison's election has inspired millions of Negroes in the South with hopes of protection and better enjoyment of their political rights." The Wilmington (N.C.) *Afro-American Presbyterian* reported that a number of Carolina blacks had been planning a massive emigration from the South, but "the result of the late election has inspired them with more confidence and hopefulness, and there is less talk about leaving the country."[27]

Not all blacks, however, were confident that the Republican victory would redound to their benefit. Even inveterate Republican Frederick Douglass questioned whether a Republican party which for twelve years had seemed paralyzed in the face of southern fraud and violence could effect real change. Some blacks quickly became cognizant of the president-elect's intent to pursue a high tariff policy while generally ignoring the problems of black Southerners in an effort to unite the sections and win Republican support in the South. Stewart was quick to point out to black Republicans that Harrison was promising ex-Confederates control of the South. The Chattanooga *Justice* predicted that the new administration would seek to win southern support by dropping its black allies; the San Francisco *Vindicator* agreed that there was nothing in Harrison's words to elicit optimism. The paper concluded that while northern Republicans were possibly less violent than southern Democrats, they were no more just.[28]

Despite the widespread malaise evoked by Harrison's preinaugural statements, the general mood of the black population on inauguration day was optimistic. Charlotte Forten Grimke, a Washington writer who had taught in the South Carolina sea islands during the Civil War, recorded in her diary on "the great day" that "I hope Harrison will fulfill all the great expectations which the country has of him." The editor of the Washington *National Leader*, recalling the black response to Cleveland's election, wrote, "what a contrast between the feelings of the colored citizens four years ago and today."[29]

In his inaugural address, Harrison continued to subordinate the racial question to that of the tariff, but the speech also offered blacks some hope. Although rejecting "a special executive policy for any section of the country," the president maintained that "no power vested in Congress or the Executive to secure or perpetuate it [suffrage] should remain unused upon occasion." A number of Democrats interpreted the speech as opening the way to further proscription of southern blacks, but blacks themselves tended to focus on its more encouraging aspects. The Huntsville *Gazette* described it as an "able, eloquent presentation of all live topics touched on." Even the generally pessimistic *Age* described the address as the "deliverance of a man who intends to administer the laws and maintain the constitution in its entirety, without fear or favor."[30]

The optimism surrounding Harrison's election exemplified the fact that most blacks continued to look to the Republican party as the major champion of their rights. But an increase in black support for the Democratic party in 1888 demonstrated that the GOP was not assured the overwhelming majority of black votes. For the first time since emancipation, blacks had been able to compare a Democratic administration to Republican ones. Some concluded that Cleveland's racial policy was no worse and sometimes even superior to that of his Republican predecessors. As a result, a vocal minority had campaigned for and voted for him. Greater apostasy was precluded, however, by a general conviction that Cleveland's racial sympathy was not shared by the rest of his party, that the southern Bourbons could still capitalize on Democratic ascendancy to further proscribe and terrorize black people.[31]

Although blacks remained overwhelmingly loyal to the Republicans in the 1888 election, they had been further disillusioned by Republican campaign tactics which focused on the tariff while relegating racial issues to secondary importance. Harrison and his Republican advisors were, however, political realists. Republicans had won both houses of Congress but only by slight majorities, and Harrison had lost the popular vote. As a result, Harrison received wide-ranging advice on how to strengthen the party. Some northern Republicans counseled ignoring the southern branch. Others advocated assuring southern support through complete federal control of congressional elections. Harrison was also advised that appointing conservative whites would strengthen southern support. Almost all of Harrison's advisors advocated excluding blacks from office. Soon after Harrison took office, high-tariff leagues sprang up in Alabama and Louisiana and, with his approval, blacks were excluded. The president also privately proposed to ignore black and white Republicans whom he considered incompetent while recognizing southerners who were Republican on the "live issues of the day" but still Democratic for "historical reasons."[32]

Within a month after Harrison's inauguration, the black press was again preoccupied with patronage. Despite few early appointments, many blacks remained optimistic. The New Orleans *Pelican* insisted that the president was using competence as his sole criterion and denounced the rumor that he excluded blacks from consideration as a Democratic falsehood. The Huntsville *Gazette* was disappointed initially with Harrison's patronage policy, but when in April Robert Smalls was appointed collector of customs of the port of Beaufort, South Carolina, the paper was reassured that the president would not ignore blacks. The Leavenworth *Advocate* reported a month later that Kansas blacks had no complaints but were optimistically waiting for the appointment of native John L. Walker as minister to Haiti.[33]

Most blacks, however, were impatient for recognition, and increasingly the president's critics outnumbered his defenders. The *Bee* was prompted to warn readers that "the unseemly haste which some of our contemporaries have in criticizing the President for not appointing colored men of prominence to lucrative positions is . . . as unwise as it is unfair." But the criticism only accelerated. The Chicago *Conservator* protested a month after Harrison took office that "the treatment which President Harrison has thus far accorded the colored people has been very unsatisfactory and far from just." The *Age* complained that the president had not only failed to make appointments but had not even invited black leaders to discuss racial problems. The Leavenworth *Advocate* reviewed black efforts on behalf of the Republican party and concluded "Why he [Harrison] has not appointed . . . irrespective of color we cannot understand." The Cleveland *Gazette* insisted that blacks should not give up on the president until, in mid-April, a delegation of South Carolina blacks reported, following a reception in Washington, that he was more interested in appointing conservative southern whites than blacks. It was now clear, the *Gazette* concluded, that blacks should cease expecting many appointments.[34]

In April, T. B. Stamps, editor of the New Orleans *Standard*, visited Harrison to discuss the question of black appointments. Harrison assured Stamps that "apprehensions are confounded— in due time they [blacks] will receive ample and just recognition." A group from Louisiana also visited the president but reported he had sent them away, insisting that he considered only competence when making appointments. This response compounded the anger of many blacks. Even loyal Republican Frederick Douglass expressed fear that the president had plans to cast the race completely out of the party.[35]

In the late spring and summer of 1889, Harrison appointed, in addition to Smalls, several other perennial black officeholders, including John R. Lynch as fourth auditor of the treasury for the Navy Department; N. Wright Cuney, collector of customs for the port of Galveston, Texas; Dr. James Townsend, recorder of the general land office at Washington; Blanche K. Bruce, recorder of deeds; and Frederick Douglass, minister to Haiti. These appointments at least temporarily assuaged fears of many southern blacks that they would be completely ignored by the president. The [Louisville?] *American Baptist* declared that by naming Douglass "the President has shown . . . his disposition to do justice to our people." Others, however, complained that their venerable leader deserved more, and furthermore that the race was only receiving token places. The *Age* acknowledged the appointments of Lynch and Townsend as good ones but insisted that the administration would have to do much more. The Indianapolis *Freeman* even condemned these appointments on the grounds that such "big leaders of colored Americans" were thralls of the Republican party who hurt the race by defending the president. The Little Rock *Sun*, equally virulent in reporting the appointment of Douglass, insisted that "the Negro race has men who could fill this position with far more credit than Douglass, but we suppose the most prominent tools and sycophants have to be considered first by the powers that be."[36]

President Harrison did name several less prominent blacks to office. Largely through the efforts of Assistant Postmaster General James Clarkson, some received postal jobs. In Louisiana, older black leaders like Pinchback were passed over while two younger men, John Francis Patty and Charles B. Wilson, were named naval officer at New Orleans and surveyor general of Louisiana respectively. The appointment of Cuney as collector of customs of the port of Galveston, one of the most important federal positions in the South, was also the result of Clarkson's efforts. These appointments generated some hope that Harrison was launching a new policy, but this expectation was usually disappointed.[37]

Much of the optimism produced by Harrison's few black appointments was vitiated by his naming lily-white Republicans to positions in the South. Several black leaders pointed with dismay to the appointment of the chairman of the white Republican Convention of Alabama as postmaster of Birmingham. When Harrison rewarded several other lily-white Republicans, the *Age* condemned him for "trying at once to ride the pale horse of the White League and the dark horse of colored Republicans" and admonished readers not to stand for such tactics. Increasingly many blacks would not. Typically, Henry M. Turner was especially harsh in attacking the president, accusing him of "giving as much attention to the wails and dying groans of the Negro South and West as he is to the bark of a dog." Harrison was denounced as "the weakest man that ever sat in the Presidential chair" and one who "will receive the curse of millions at the rate he is now bestirring himself." In November the New Orleans *Weekly Pelican* announced that black discontent was "wide and deep and needs speedy attending to."[38]

By the fall of 1889, this discontent was being channeled into organized pressure and protest. A Republican boss of Georgia advised Harrison to appoint a black postmaster in Athens "in order to hold our forces and keep all elements solid in support of the administration." In Mecklenburg County, North Carolina, blacks burned the president and his cabinet in effigy. Soon after, thousands of angry tarheel blacks attended a mass meeting to protest the administration's patronage policy. The Cleveland *Gazette* asserted that Ohio blacks would no longer be ignored passively; that "unless something is done the dissatisfaction, so general, will cause trouble this fall." The Leavenworth *Advocate*, describing a similar attitude in Kansas, pointed out that not one black Kansan had received a federal or state position and called on all blacks to continue making demands until race discrimination was ended.[39]

Toward the end of his first year in office, Harrison became more responsive to these black demands. His state of the union message included one of the strongest appeals on behalf of blacks delivered by a president in the late nineteenth century. Black pressure had some impact on the president's reappraisal; more influential, however, were two elections of 1889, a congressional canvas in Louisiana and a gubernatorial race in Virginia. In both elections, the Republicans emphasized a high tariff while ignoring civil rights issues; they were soundly defeated. Blacks were quick to claim these results as proof that any Republican policy that ignored the position of blacks would end in defeat.[40]

In the later years of Harrison's administration, black critics focused more on the rise of proscription and violence in the South, but their concern with patronage did not completely end. North Carolinians continued to be particularly vocal. Delegates to a state convention, held in February 1890, complained that their race was given neither jobs nor a voice in party affairs and that "even Congressman Cheatham is ignored." A group in Raleigh issued a "Negroes' Declaration of Independence," proclaiming that "the white Republicans have been traitors to us" and that the blacks, "the backbone of the Republican party, got nothing." Similar sentiment was expressed in Virginia by Joseph T. Wilson who declared before a Richmond convention that blacks were "treated as orphan children" by the Republican party.[41]

Because a majority of Harrison's black appointees were southern, northern spokesmen continued to be particularly vocal in the later years of Harrison's administration. In July 1889, the Philadelphia *Sentinel* warned that although northern Negroes were not yet protesting their neglect, "they are looking on quietly with blood in their eyes." James M. Townsend wrote the president that while Indiana blacks were still loyal Republicans, they would not remain so unless they received some federal positions. Two years later, when few appointments had been made, a white paper reported that "the colored wing of the Republican Party of Indianapolis is in open revolt against Harrison." Blacks in

Ohio were also near open revolt. A Cincinnati group insisted that Harrison's "failure to accord us a decent recognition in the distribution of his official favors is unfair, unjust, and ungrateful. . . . The old game of turkey for the leaders and turkey buzzard for us is played out. . . . Let them win their own victories—if they can—without our help." Fifty-two members of the group issued a statement announcing that "while we are Republicans from principles, yet we can see no reason why we should be expected to fight the battles of the party without sharing in the fruits of its victories any more than others." Similar bitterness was expressed by blacks in Michigan. Adelbert H. Roberts asserted that "when we voted almost solidly for the Republican candidates in 1888 we did it not simply that we might engage in the ratification of the election, but that we might share in the fruits of the victory." The New York *Age*, speaking for discontented blacks in New England and the Middle Atlantic states, pointed out that Cleveland had appointed three blacks of those states to federal offices while Harrison had appointed only one.[42]

The president's patronage policy was naturally most vigorously defended by those leaders who had received lucrative positions. Douglass was occasionally critical but generally maintained that Harrison's chief criterion for selection was fitness for the position. Blanche K. Bruce condemned rumors that Harrison would not make black appointments as a Democratic device designed to provoke discontent among black Republicans. At Harrison's request, he publicly denied charges of former Louisiana carpetbag governor, William Pitt Kellogg, that "President Harrison is in a peck of trouble about the color question." When black discontent in the North intensified, Bruce traveled to Indiana and Ohio to defend the president. John Langston, grateful to the Republican party for awarding him a contested congressional seat, claimed before an Indianapolis crowd that the two thousand federal positions held by blacks were proof that Harrison had not ignored blacks in the matter of patronage. John Lynch denied that patronage was crucial to blacks and demanded that they be "Republicans not from selfish motives but from principles and convictions."[43]

Not all blacks were convinced. Many were as critical of the perennial officeholders who defended the president as they were of the administration. H. C. Smith denounced "that trio of professional office-seekers and holders, Bruce, Lynch, and Douglass." James Townsend, himself a Harrison appointee, wrote the president that while "northern colored men would not detract from such men as Douglass, Smalls, and Lynch," it was incomprehensible in the North why these men were continually appointed while others were overlooked. Within a year, however, Townsend had tempered his criticism and defended Harrison's patronage policy as adequate.[44]

During the Harrison years there were three positions that blacks particularly demanded: governor of the Oklahoma Territory, representative on the world's Columbian Exposition Committee, and judge of the appellate circuit court. A group identifying itself as "representatives of the Afro-American press and the younger element of the Republican party" petitioned Harrison to appoint emigration leader Edwin P. McCabe as governor of Oklahoma, which they estimated was over one-fourth black, as a means to "strengthen our party, energize 8,000,000 people and bless the Nation." The *Age* proposed that Oklahoma be made an exclusively black state, but favored McCabe for governor regardless. Rev. A. B. Gibson, a Milledgeville, Georgia, minister, led the McCabe-for-governor movement in the South.[45]

The possible appointment of a black representative to the Columbian Exposition, to be held in Chicago in 1892, generated even more widespread interest. The Leavenworth *Advocate*'s proclamation that "the Negro must be represented at the fair" was repeated in many other black papers. A committee of the Afro-American Press Association presented Harrison with a petition demanding this position. When no black was appointed to the fair committee, disappointment was intense. The Indianapolis *Freeman*, despite its recent conversion to Republicanism, accused the president of considering only "the cream of Blue-bloodism" in making the world's fair appointments and questioned whether a man with this proclivity could best govern a nation "in which due to non-homogeneity one class isn't ideal."[46]

Equally important to many blacks was the appointment of a black judge to the appellate circuit court created by Congress in 1891. The Afro-American Press Association again lobbied vigorously, suggesting to the president "the propriety and wisdom of selecting a capable Negro jurist to fill a place on the bench of the Federal judiciary." Acquiring the judicial position for a black man was also a particular preoccupation of the Detroit *Plaindealer*. In August 1891, the paper maintained that the most important question for blacks to consider was: "Will President Harrison rise to meet the confidence that Afro-Americans have in him by appointing one of their members to the new court created by the Fifty-First Congress?" The *Plaindealer* assured Harrison that such an appointment would do a great deal to appease discontented northern blacks and specifically advocated Professor D. Augustus Straker, at this time a Detroit lawyer. The Cleveland *Gazette*, another active lobbyist for the judicial appointment, supported John Langston. The *Age* suggested that Langston, Straker, John P. Green, and T. McCants Stewart would all be good choices and advised the president that he "could in no way signalize his administration in more glorious manner" than by the appointment of one of these men. When blacks were again disappointed, the Cleveland *Gazette* reported widespread dismay that the president had "seen fit to ignore the request of 8,000,000 Americans, who furnish the Republican Party its backbone." The *Plaindealer*, although less critical than its determination to gain a judgeship might have suggested, claimed Harrison had let slip an excellent chance to bring all discordant elements back into the Republican party.[47]

Although patronage was the primary concern of many black spokesmen during Harrison's first year in office, they were not unmindful of issues such as inferior educational facilities, disfranchisement, and violence which more profoundly affected the masses. When bills for aid to education and federal protection of voting rights were presented in Congress, many blacks tempered criticism of the president and his party. In the fall of 1889, the usually critical *Plaindealer* counseled blacks to wait before censoring President Harrison's patronage policy as "it is better at the present time for the Afro-American to have earnest friends working for and with him in the cause of American liberty than a few appointments to Federal offices." A year later, Congressman Thomas E. Miller assured his colleagues that "we want offices, but the first and dearest rights the Negro of the

South wants are the rights to pay for his labor, his right to trial by jury, his right to his home, his right to know that the man who lynches him will not the next day be elected by the state to a high and honorable trust."[48]

Miller's remarks reflected the magnitude of violence and discrimination directed toward blacks in the 1880s. Morgan Kousser has concluded that the first high tide of suffrage restriction came between 1888 and 1893. In 1890, Mississippi established the pattern for the rest of the South when it adopted a literacy qualification for suffrage as a means to circumvent the Fifteenth Amendment. In all southern states, fraud, intimidation, and violence complemented legal and constitutional restrictions so successfully that a white southern leader proclaimed in 1889 that "the Negro as a political force has dropped out of serious consideration." This combination of de facto and de jure disfranchisement was fostered by the increasing indifference with which northern Republicans viewed the plight of southern blacks.[49]

Briefly during the Harrison years, however, Republican leaders resolved to intervene in the South again. For the first time since 1875 their party controlled the presidency and both houses of Congress. The first year of the administration had seen the apparent failure of the lily-white policy intended to strengthen the southern branch of the party. Legal disfranchisement, increased violence in the South, and proposals by some southern Democratic congressmen to expel blacks from their region revived a measure of Republican sympathy. The growing inclination of prominent blacks to challenge the Republican party and, in some cases, to declare themselves Democrats or independents also affected Republican interest.[50]

Republican efforts centered on aid to education and protection of the ballot. This did not necessitate a reappraisal of political philosophy for President Harrison or his party since Republican platforms since Reconstruction had called for a free ballot and had supported the Blair bill for federal aid to education. Although during the campaign of 1888 the suffrage issue was downplayed, the party continued to give it token support. Renewed action to protect black rights did, however, demand a reappraisal of Republican political practice. Blacks often felt compelled to remind the president that his support of their vote was not being acted upon. An Alabama convention, meeting shortly before the inauguration, appealed to Harrison to uphold the Thirteenth, Fourteenth, and Fifteenth amendments. In October, John Lynch reminded Harrison that if he would only insist on honest elections, the solid South would become a thing of the past. The *Plaindealer*, reviewing "the spirit of Ku Kluxism in the South," concluded: "He has been President seven months and he has said no word in condemnation of such wrongs."[51]

Since emancipation, there had been a widespread awareness among blacks that education must play a major role in reordering their lives as free men and women. Throughout the eighties, Senator Henry Blair repeatedly introduced his bill for federal aid to education. Because it would guarantee that black schools received a fair share of the funds, it was widely supported by blacks but condemned by most white Southerners and blocked by their representatives in Washington. Southern black leaders constantly lobbied for the bill's passage, often pointing out that this was one way for the Republican party to regain the gratitude of the masses. Charles A. Roxborough, a Louisiana attorney, wrote a lengthy letter to Harrison shortly before the inauguration, reviewing the educational plight of blacks and proposing passage of the Blair bill as the responsibility of the Republican party. A group of Louisiana blacks also wrote, recommending the bill as "the greatest and most powerful lever to elevate our race." Although the Blair bill was of less direct significance to northern blacks, they generally supported it. Democrat Peter Clark agreed with Douglass that education and economic independence were possibly even more important than political rights. The Cleveland *Gazette*, typical of many black northern papers, asserted that "if the bill becomes a law, it will be one of the greatest factors in the solution of the Southern problem because it will go to the root of the matter."[52]

Blacks were generally encouraged, following the president's first annual message to Congress, that federal aid to education as well as federal supervision of elections would become a reality. The president urged Congress to pass an education bill and added that as the need "grows chiefly out of the conditions and needs of the emancipated slaves and his descendents, the relief should be as far as possible . . . applied to the need that suggested it." The president also made a strong appeal for immediate action to end voting fraud and violence. The Lexington (Ky.) *Christian Soldier* labeled the speech "the best ever sent to that legislative body," and the New Orleans *Weekly Pelican* agreed that "no President since Abraham Lincoln has said kinder words for the colored people." Several black papers, however, were more cautious in their appraisal. The Indianapolis *Freeman*, at this time still Democratic, acknowledged that the president spoke in "a brave and statesmanlike manner" but claimed that the speech was in many ways a disappointment. The *Age* believed that the president "lived up to the best traditions of the party" but criticized him for merely proposing amendments to existing laws rather than more sweeping changes in the electoral system.[53]

In January 1890, Senator Blair again introduced his education bill. Debate over its passage raged in Congress and around the country from January to March. This time there was more black criticism than previously. Thomas Fortune, once a leading supporter, now expressed reservations because southern whites might never let the funds reach black schools. H. C. Smith was among those who agreed; he switched his support to a proposal of Ohio Congressman Joseph D. Taylor which would allocate a greater share of federal aid to black schools.[54]

Criticism, however, was overshadowed by a renewed outpouring of black support. John Langston, proclaiming "Our motto is educate," frequently lobbied for the bill's passage. Robert Terrell, an 1884 Harvard graduate, demanded the bill's passage as a way to fight widespread illiteracy, which undermined the republic. Blair introduced into congressional debate several petitions from black groups demanding the bill's passage. One from the Board of Bishops of the African Methodist Episcopal Church beseeched "that the Government which lifted us to the dignity of manhood will complete the work it had so wisely and meritoriously begun by adoption of the measure known as the Blair education bill."[55]

As chances for the bill's success dimmed, black supporters attempted a now-familiar tactic: they attempted to persuade Republicans that it was vital to their partisan interests because blacks would not vote Republican if it failed. Frederick Douglass warned that while neither party could afford to let the bill fail, "least of all can the great Republican party...afford to let it perish or be postponed to a more convenient season." Douglass doubted that the bill would do all that it claimed or would be always faithfully and honestly executed, but he still urged its passage on the grounds that it would ultimately be a blessing to the race.[56]

The Blair bill was defeated by the Senate in March 1890; seventeen out of forty Republicans and twenty out of twenty-eight Democrats voted no. Blacks were tremendously disappointed, particularly with the Republican opposition. Representatives of the Afro-American Press Association wrote Harrison that the failure of the Blair bill, combined with other disappointments, had "produced a profound discouragement and bitter dismay among the Afro-American voters of the entire country." The Detroit *Plaindealer* warned that "the Republican party will be called upon to answer...if another bill be not presented and passed, that embodies the principle of national aid to education." To some, the defeat was another signal to foreswear political activity. Several spokesmen, reflecting on the renewed emphasis defeat brought to self-sufficiency, called on blacks to band together and help themselves. The *Age* urged that "what others will not do for us we must do for ourselves." At conventions in Greensboro, North Carolina, and Richmond, Virginia, blacks, disillusioned with what they considered another betrayal by the Republican party, resolved to abstain from voting entirely.[57]

Congressmen Henry Cheatham and Thomas Miller continued the fight for an education bill. Early in 1891, Cheatham introduced a bill for the establishment and support of common schools, but his proposal was also defeated.[58]

Black disappointment over these defeats was temporarily assuaged in April when Massachusetts Congressman Henry Cabot Lodge introduced a bill allowing federal supervision of elections. The Lodge bill, the first major Republican attempt since 1875 to enforce the Reconstruction amendments, was motivated by political realism combined with the surviving legacy of 1860s Republican idealism. It was a throwback to a time of greater government activism in an era of laissez-faire hegemony. Protest was heard from all over the country but particularly from white Southerners, who dubbed the proposal the "force bill."[59]

Although most blacks gave the Lodge bill their unqualified support, some were critical. Prominent southern opponents included educators Booker T. Washington of Alabama and J. C. Price of North Carolina. Louisiana politician Charles Roxborough, who resigned from the state Republican committee in the summer of 1890 on the grounds that it was dedicated to white supremacy, opposed the Lodge bill as a "danger to the Negro." The Matthew Stanley Quay Club, a Philadelphia organization named for the Pennsylvania senator who advocated the tariff, was one of the few black groups to speak out in opposition to the bill. Most newspapers gave the bill unqualified support, although the Detroit *Plaindealer* feared that because it did not go far enough, the bill could actually increase existing animosities. The Cleveland *Gazette* opposed the provision calling for a signed petition to ensure election supervision, predicting that signing such a document would cost any Southerner, black or white; his life. Despite this concern, however, the *Gazette* wholeheartedly supported the bill and warned that "any failure along this line will militate against the Republican success in 1892."[60]

Supporters, who vastly outnumbered critics, were encouraged when, in July, the bill passed the House with only two negative Republican votes. The Lodge bill faced a much harder battle in the Senate, where enough Republicans—including Mugwumps who had grown disillusioned with black voters, those whose silver interests made them susceptible to Democratic bargains, and those hoping for commercial ties with the South—joined the Democrats in opposition. In August, Senator Quay successfully delayed consideration of electoral regulation until after the vote on a tariff proposal.[61]

The anger that Quay's tactics aroused was mitigated somewhat the following month by the Republican decision to seat two black men, John Langston of Virginia and Thomas Miller of South Carolina, in the House of Representatives. Both men had been involved in contested elections since 1888. The Cleveland *Gazette* wrote that the favorable decision "warmed the spirit of Republicanism in millions of loyal Afro-Americans" and that the party would now only have to pass the Lodge bill to assure success in November.[62]

Congressional elections in November, however, were hardly a Republican success. The party's majority in the Senate dropped from 14 to 8, while the Democrats won an overwhelming majority of 235 to 88 in the House. Republican defeat was largely a result of agrarian discontent and widespread opposition to Republican tariff policy. The election results occasioned a barrage of criticism from blacks who unrealistically blamed it on Republican racial policy. Frederick Douglass assessed the losses as a result of the party's "timid and halting support" of the Blair and Lodge bills. The *Age* asserted that, in view of the election outcome, it was "impossible not to conclude that the seal of condemnation has been placed upon the entire policy of the Republican administration of the past two years." Several southern papers pointed to voting frauds in their states as additional evidence that the supervision of elections was necessary. The Savannah *Tribune* reported that, in Georgia, "it is a shame to see the manner in which colored men were treated at the polls." Although blacks exaggerated the impact of disfranchisement on overall national political realignment, they were correct that it had increased in the preceding two years. In the deep South, Republican voting, which had averaged approximately 13 percent of eligible voters in 1888, had fallen to 7.2 percent.[63]

In his second state of the union message, the president, disturbed by this further erosion of southern Republicanism, urged Congress to pass the election bill, asserting: "Its probable effectiveness is evidenced by the character of the opposition that is made to it." Harrison's words were praised by the black press which now turned its wrath upon Republican opponents, especially Senator Quay. The *Plaindealer* warned that "if he [Quay] defeats the bill again he will cause the Republicans of the country to rebuke the party in 1892, whose campaign leader he is."[64]

Despite such ominous predictions, eight silver Republicans, ready to sacrifice the Lodge bill for their own interests, agreed to vote against election supervision if the Democrats would vote for the increased coinage of silver. Early in January these men teamed together to replace the Lodge bill on the Senate docket with a coinage bill, and chances of the election bill's success dimmed. Despite the impending defeat, black efforts intensified. Throughout January, most papers were preoccupied with lobbying for the bill. The Cleveland *Gazette* devoted an entire editorial page to convincing Republicans that they must pass the bill, asserting that blacks were being "betrayed in the House of supposed friends for silver." All three black congressmen lobbied for the bill. Langston, in a lengthy speech, insisted that voting protection was necessary for all Southerners, white and black. Miller called for "an election law—not a force law—a national law . . . that will compel the people of the South to register the vote of Negroes and the white men alike, and count as they are cast."[65]

After the passage of a silver bill in January 1891, Republican proponents of the Lodge bill again attempted to pass it, but six Republican senators joined the Democrats to set aside the bill for the final time. Black press analysis of Republican responsibility was more temperate than earlier rhetoric indicated. The Indianapolis *Freeman* challenged rumors that blacks would now leave the Republican party as "so much nonsense." The Knoxville *Negro World* insisted that the high standards of the Republicans in the Fifty-first Congress were thwarted only by Democratic treachery. Much black criticism was directed exclusively at Republican opponents. The Detroit *Plaindealer* asserted that "the party is not to blame. It is the schemer and the monopolist representative in the party, the Quays and the Tellers." The Springfield *State Capital* agreed that Harrison was not to blame, but also demanded that Republicans who voted against the bill no longer receive black support. The Afro-American Press Association thanked Harrison "for his earnest interest in this as in the educational measures," but condemned those Republicans "who made a corrupt and vicious and demoralizing bargain with the minority to defeat this righteous measure in the interest of free coinage of silver." The *Age* was one of the few black papers to denounce the president as well as his party, maintaining that "the treachery of the Hayes Administration has been repeated under the Harrison Administration."[66]

The Blair and Lodge bills represented the strongest Republican effort on behalf of blacks since Reconstruction. But the backlash created by opposition to the bills meant further setbacks for black Southerners. These frustrated attempts to solve the "southern question" provoked a counteroffensive from which the white-supremist South emerged even more triumphant than it had in 1877. The threat of federal enforcement of fair elections prompted the renewal of efforts by white southern Democrats to legally disfranchise blacks.[67]

Although many blacks absolved Harrison and the Republican party of responsibility, these defeats furthered black disillusionment with traditional Republican allegiance. In August 1888, the Indianapolis *Freeman* asked its readers to consider the question: "Why should the colored vote divide?" The restoration of Republican power in Washington had only temporarily muted the discussion. With the numerous disappointments of the Harrison years—the insufficient number of federal appointments, the failure of the Blair and Lodge bills, and the increasing violence and disfranchisement in the South—politically oriented blacks again debated independence. Only two months after Harrison's inauguration, the Baltimore *Sun* suggested that the race should divide its vote because "the Negro has nothing more attaching to the Republican party than a reminiscence of emancipation and a record of ruined hopes." In April 1890, the Boston *People's Advocate* noted that while in the past the black voter was justified in voting the straight Republican ticket, present party policy indicated that he should "stop his idol worship and either join some other party which offers better inducements or hold himself aloof from politics." In 1890, J. C. Price, one of the most prominent black leaders to espouse independence, predicted that in the new decade, "it may be safely expected that the Negro will become more independent as a political factor and less certain as a partisan." The Convention of Colored Americans, meeting in Washington in February, was one of several black conventions expressing anew the philosophy of independence. The delegates resolved, "It is our duty to applaud the acts and endorse the utterances of our friends, it matters not where they are or to what party they may belong." By 1891, a white newspaper observed that almost a third of black voters in Columbus, Ohio, were ready to bolt the party, a statistic accurate for other non-southern states as well. The Kansas City *Dispatch*, typical of black press sentiment, predicted: "Now that the Republican party has demonstrated their inability to protect the colored people in their political rights, the Negro will, in the future, ally himself with any party that may seem expedient."[68]

Following a lull in the wake of Harrison's election, political setbacks fostered renewed black interest in the Democratic party. Several conventions of black Democrats were held. Black groups met in northern cities to organize on behalf of Democratic tickets prior to the 1890 elections. The number of black Democratic meetings increased following defeat of the Lodge and Blair bills. C. H. J. Taylor, Thomas Fortune, and T. McCants Stewart continued to be among the most outspoken black Democrats during the Harrison years. In August 1890, Fortune and Stewart founded the Brooklyn Literary Society for the purpose of promoting the Democratic party. Stewart urged New York blacks to switch to the Democratic party because it appointed more blacks to important positions and because "the Democratic party stands in the North and . . . will eventually stand in the South for equal justice for all." Pointing out that lynchings had increased during the Harrison years, Stewart concluded that a Republican president had not in any way benefited the race. Volatile Thomas Fortune, who aligned with the Democratic party in 1891, insisted that Republican high-tariff measures subjected blacks to "industrial slavery" and proclaimed that "upon economic grounds the duty of colored men to stand by the Democracy is imperative." In March 1890, a group in Washington, D.C., formed the National Colored Tariff Reform Association to lobby for black interest on that issue.[69]

Charles H. J. Taylor continued to be the national leader of black Democracy. In 1889, he published *Whites and Blacks*, a book devoted primarily to persuading blacks that their interests were best served by Democratic victory. He charged Republicans with using black voters to win office and then casting them aside. What blacks most needed, Taylor maintained, was to free themselves from subjugation to the Republican party and prejudice toward the Democratic party. Once this was done, political emancipation would be theirs, and Democrats, black and white, would vote their common interests. "The sensible Negroes," he asserted, "are natural Democrats if they only understand themselves." Taylor became such an energetic advocate of black

Democracy in the Midwest that in 1891 the Democratic National Committee asked him to campaign for Democratic congressional candidates in Iowa.[70]

Although the leading black Democratic paper, the Indianapolis *Freeman*, switched in 1891 to Republicanism, several papers continued to endorse the Democratic party. In 1891, the Columbus *Afro-American* became the third Democratic sheet in Ohio and pointed to the founding of additional black Democratic papers as a "splendid omen" for the future. In 1890, Taylor began editing the Topeka *American Citizen*, already one of the leading papers supporting black political independence.[71]

Some southern blacks also remained philosophically or pragmatically committed to the Democratic party. A white journalist suggested in 1889 that Democrats had southern black support through influences of "employer on the laborer, of the creditor on the debtor, of the rich on the poor, of the humane and charitable on the friendless or affected." Although Democratic suasion was rarely humane or charitable, a growing number of middle-class southern blacks did advocate support as an economic expedient and thousands of poor blacks did so to preclude violent retaliation. In 1892, the Democratic candidate for governor in Georgia won the support of most of the state's black leaders for his anti-lynching stand, a situation only rarely repeated elsewhere. Particularly in South Carolina and Mississippi, Republican blacks entered into fusion arrangements with state Democrats in which they traded votes for minor offices. North Carolinian J. C. Price, although never officially proclaiming himself a Democrat, did move beyond independence when he suggested that "the Democrats are the dominant element of the South, and, as far as is consistent with instincts of manhood, the Negro would do well to harmonize with that element." Garland H. White agreed, urging blacks "to unite with the governing class of white people of this section which are Democrats whom we have to depend upon in every emergency." In South Carolina, George Mears, a black Democrat, was elected to the state legislature from 1882 to 1892. In 1891, eight blacks were still listed on the roll of the Statesburg Democratic Club. H. C. C. Astwood was a prominent spokesman for Democracy in Louisiana. M. F. Alexander Easton served as president of the Negro Democratic

Club of Missouri throughout the Harrison years, and J. Milton Turner was also active as a Democratic leader there. John Shufton, an Orlando lawyer, urged black Floridians to join him in switching to Democracy because "no intelligent colored man in the South believes for a moment that it is a disinterested interest that the Republican Party had for the welfare and prosperity of the race."[72]

However, few blacks in the South followed Shufton's advice. Despite the greater tolerance for Democracy that had developed during the Cleveland years, many black Republicans still condemned such political apostasy. Brooklyn minister William H. Dickerson reflected a typical attitude when he wrote: "If there can be found a simon pure Negro Democrat, and especially if he be of Southern extraction and growth, he ought not to be allowed to run at large, but should be caged and placed on exhibition as one of the greatest curiosities of the age." The *Age*, perhaps more rational in its appraisal because of its own flirtation with independence, attacked Dickerson's position as "vicious and calculated to do more harm than good." To the question "Can't a Negro conscientiously be a Democrat?" the *Age* replied: "We can reasonably question his wisdom but not his right, his conscientious right." The Cleveland *Gazette*, less tolerant than the *Age*, responded that "no Afro-American can have the approval of his conscience, unless it is badly seared, in his support of the Democratic party." Old-guard black Republicans, particularly officeholders such as the venerable trio—Douglass, Bruce, and Lynch—were just as vociferous in condemning Democracy and even independence. Lynch asserted that "the busy Afro-American who persists in stirring up strife in the ranks had better cease from their activity."[73]

That black support for the Democratic party was generally ephemeral and dependent upon Democratic incumbency was indicated by the number of black Democrats who joined the Indianapolis *Freeman* in returning to the Republican ranks during the Harrison years. Henry Downing, a lifelong Democrat until 1892, switched to the Republican party because he concluded "there is no place politically in the Democratic ranks for the black man. It fought to fasten the manacles of slavery on him forever, and in the old slave states is now depriving him of the rights conferred upon him."[74]

Toward the end of the Harrison years, there was, for the first time, a realistic alternative to Republican or Democratic allegiance. In the early nineties, thousands of blacks joined the Populist party, and, according to C. Vann Woodward's 1938 account, "never before or since have the two races in the South come as close together as they did during the Populist struggle." How closely aligned poor blacks and whites actually were has been debated ever since Woodward's important work appeared. If support of the Populists offered the prospect of interracial political cooperation, it was not an easy commitment for either group to make. Racial conflict was always a part of the Populist party as well as of its progenitors, the farmers' alliances.[75]

The southern alliance movement was spawned by the general debility of agriculture and nurtured by widespread frustration with the Democratic party's refusal to enact remedies that farmers believed were in their best interests. The black organization, the Colored Farmers' National Alliance and Cooperative Union, was organized by Richard M. Humphrey, a white minister, in Texas in 1886. It quickly spread to other southern states until membership exceeded two hundred thousand by 1890.[76]

Blacks were divided over whether an agrarian organization was the best way to address racial problems. Although the black Republican press was more tolerant of black alliancemen than it was of black Democrats, it often castigated alliance affiliation. The Leavenworth *Advocate*, located in a strong alliance state, condemned the alliance as "a political organization with Democratic tendencies—set on foot by that rebel brigadier Polk of Tennessee." The Selma [Ala.] *Independent* asked: "Is it not plain to every colored man that this Alliance intends to plot the oppression of colored farmers?" The New York *Age* was further removed from alliance activity, and therefore less hostile, but still questioned if the separation of blacks and whites within the alliance was not evidence of its racist policy.[77]

The *Age* was correct that racism pervaded the alliance movement, but there was also cooperation and camaraderie between the Colored Farmers' Alliance and the all-white Southern Farmers' Alliance. In 1889, an Alabama editor assured that the two were "united in their war against the trust." But in many parts of the South, particularly in black-belt counties, white supremacy overruled racial interaction. Another Alabama editor, by insisting that white alliancemen wanted no black support, demonstrated that unity did not always exist. Some blacks, envisioning the Colored Alliance as a vehicle for racial economic self-help, agreed that the two organizations should remain separate.[78]

In addition to the racist barriers to cooperation, black and white alliancemen were also politically divided. Although neither organization officially endorsed a party, most white members were Democrats and most blacks were at least nominally Republicans. Some blacks feared that the alliance was really a subterfuge to lure them into Democratic ranks. Several black papers criticized the Southern Alliance's affiliation with that party. In 1891, a Virginia group specifically denied that they would be tricked into becoming Democrats and resolved "that we, the Colored Farmers' Alliance of the State of Virginia, are beginning to realize that our salvation rests in neither of the old political parties and are no longer slaves to either." Many southern whites, on the other hand, were hostile to the black organization because they feared that it was a plot to revitalize black Republicanism.[79]

Both black and white alliancemen, however, were growing increasingly frustrated with their traditional political homes. In 1890, white alliance endorsement enabled a number of Democrats to win state elections, but most of those elected quickly proved uninterested in alliance reforms. Because the alliances demanded government-sponsored remedies for agrarian problems, conflict with the laissez-faire Democrats loomed as inevitable. Similar black frustration with the Republican party helped erode political division and open the possibility of unity within a new political party.

In December 1890, the Southern and Colored alliances met with the Northern Alliance in Ocala, Florida. Although there was evidence of racial unity at the meeting, there was also considerable conflict, particularly over the Lodge bill. White alliancemen supported black suffrage but repudiated the election bill, ironically on the grounds that it would mean undue government involvement in state affairs. The Colored Alliance, on the other hand, enthusiastically endorsed the bill, a stand praised by much of the black press. This division prompted the president of the Kansas Alliance to despair that "the agitation in the South over the Lodge bill precludes the possibility of an independent movement at this time." There were also disagreements over the Blair bill and specific economic policies.[80]

Blacks and whites found some common ground at Ocala, but ultimately their disagreements proved insurmountable. While blacks supported some immediate alliance goals, they were hostile to any long-range program that would align labor against capital. Capitalists might hire blacks as a cheap labor supply whereas labor had traditionally shunned them. Also, much alliance doctrine was aimed at helping small landowners, a group which included few blacks. Black tenant farmers, in fact, often found their interests squarely at odds with the small landholders for whom they worked. Finally, as Lawrence Goodwyn has explained, the most compelling black problem was not economic but racial. "Before the black man could worry about economic injustice," he writes, "he had to worry about survival."[81]

Despite conflicts which would ultimately preclude a successful Populist coalition, both blacks and whites endorsed the idea of forming a new party and it was officially organized in St. Louis in 1892. Colored Farmers' alliancemen, disillusioned with the lily-white policies of the Republicans, were strong advocates of the Populist party. Since Populism had little chance of success in the South if the races could not unite, some white Populists were willing to challenge the most extreme tenets of white supremacy. Tom Watson, the charismatic and enigmatic Georgia leader, called on laborers of both races to desert the two major parties which had divided them into hostile camps. The Populist party, he insisted, would offer "to White and Black a rallying point which is free from the odium of former discords and strifes." Watson promised blacks freedom to vote, better schools and homes, and an end to violence. He assured whites that cooperation would not involve social integration. Most state Populist organizations gave blacks at least token positions. The election of William Warwick of Virginia as an officer of the 1892 St. Louis convention inspired many other blacks to join or at least consider voting for the new party. The Savannah *Tribune*, while not completely severing its Republican ties, observed these trends and concluded: "A new generation of white men and black men has risen amid a changed environment, stronger in intelligence and individuality, who are less susceptible to the decaying prejudices of a past era."[82]

Yet there was abundant evidence that the subtle nature of prejudice remained with most white Populists, and its most extreme nature with many. Those who were unable to counter the Democratic cry of "white supremacy" often compromised with it. The same white men who elected Warwick to office because it was politically expedient, treated black delegates with condescension. The assertion of a Virginia party member that "this is a white man's country and will always be controlled by the whites" was generally accepted by other white Populists. Robert Saunders, in a study of blacks and Populism in 1892, concludes: "Populist appeals for racial comity were rare, sometimes opportunistic, and seldom evinced any genuine commitment to obtain justice for the Negro in practice." The racism of white Populists was indicated by their common refusal to deal directly with black leaders. Their direct appeals to the masses, however, were often unsuccessful. Although black leaders could not determine how the masses would vote, their leadership was not completely ineffective and Populist recruiters were often more successful when they first converted state and local black leaders.[83]

It is impossible to reconstruct adequately the various black views of Populism. As Goodwyn has pointed out: " 'The Black Response to Populist Approaches' must be inferred; it cannot be documented." A few glimpses, however, do survive. Traditional black leaders, particularly federal officeholders fearful of losing Republican patronage, rarely joined the new party and were often critical. Many of these black leaders, Goodwyn notes, ascertained that the Populists would lose their struggle for hegemony and thus held aloof. Black Democrats and independents, more accustomed to political apostasy, were more likely to join. C. H. J. Taylor, for example, ran for the Kansas legislature on a Populist-Democratic fusion ticket in 1890 and in 1892. Most other blacks who served as leaders in the Populist movement were not nationally known, although some had been politically active at the grass-roots level. Black Populism was especially well organized in Texas, a southern state particularly receptive to third-party movements. Three black Texans—R. H. Hayes, H. J. Hennings, and Melvin Wade—were present at the August 1891 Dallas meeting that initiated the Texas party, and they were able to force greater inclusion of blacks in party affairs. John B. Raynor, who campaigned in the state against black Republican leader Norris Wright Cuney, was the best-known Populist orator and recruiter. P. K. Chase, another active Populist, insisted that "the one and only advantageous political course of the Negro, under present existing affairs, is to support the people's party." J. L. Moore, a county leader of the Colored Farmers' Alliance of Florida, did not wholeheartedly support the Populist party when he wrote, "I for one have fully decided to vote with and work for that party, or those who favor the workingman, let them belong to the Democratic or Republican, or the People's Party." But when he observed that neither the Democrats nor the Republicans could be expected to legislate in the interests of farmers except when it did not conflict with their own interests, he was near an endorsement. In Georgia, the promises of Tom Watson to stand up for black rights won the support of Anton Graves, secretary of the state Republican organization, and of Anthony Wilson, who in 1882 had won a Republican seat in the Georgia Assembly over Watson's objection. Rev. H. S. Doyle became one of the most active Populists in Georgia, delivering sixty-three speeches for Watson in 1892 despite numerous attempts on his life. In Louisiana, Charles A. Roxborough determined that the Republican party was as anti-black as the Democratic and joined the Populist cause. I. Glopsey of Arkansas, a black delegate to the Populist state convention in 1892, saw his resolution "that it is the object of the People's party to elevate the downtrodden irrespective of race or color," written into the party platform.[84]

The most telling evidence of the strength of western black Populism was the considerable effort made by black Republican opponents to curb the race's participation. In Kansas, the Parson's *Weekly Blade* complained that "the most sickening sight that we beheld last Tuesday was a few Negroes who claimed to be leaders of the colored people of this city, distributing People's party tickets." The Lawrence *Historic Times* insisted that no one running on the Populist ticket was worthy of the black vote. Several black Populist papers were briefly published in Kansas to challenge this opposition.[85]

Because Populism was largely a southern and western movement, it received little attention in the northern black press. When the new party was considered, it was usually condemned. The Detroit *Plaindealer,* an exception, did suggest that black farmers of the South might take advantage of the changed political atmosphere, that "there is no reason why Afro-Americans...should not be found in any body of whatever nature, whose particular views are in accord with their own." The Indianapolis *Freeman,* in contrast, insisted that black alliancemen take no part in the burgeoning party movement. When the Populist party was well established, the *Freeman* condemned it as an amalgamation of "Socialists, Greenbackers, Anarchists and Grangers."[86]

Populism was the most significant political movement in the 1890s, but it was not the only alternative for estranged black Republicans. In January 1891, 141 delegates from twenty-three states met in Chicago to organize Thomas Fortune's Afro-American League. J. C. Price was chosen president and Fortune, first secretary. The league was made officially non-partisan, which Fortune hoped would preclude its being absorbed by a white party. Despite this facade, however, the organization was involved in politics from its inception. In time even Fortune hinted that the league might be the genesis of a new black party because neither of the old parties "cares a fig for the Afro-American." Other leaders of the league agreed and wrote President Harrison that both parties were unconcerned with the denial of "the rights and immunities" guaranteed to blacks "by the fundamental law of the land." By 1892, the league had dropped its non-partisan guise entirely to become a black political organization. Conflict with established black political leaders, however, as well as waning interest by those who were initially enthusiastic, tempered its impact. Furthermore, political realities of the late nineteenth century, combined with profound white racism, made the survival of a black political party virtually impossible.[87]

Some blacks continued to advocate abstinence from politics as a philosophical principle, but this was more commonly a course forced on southern blacks by white supremacy. Among those actively advocating disfranchisement were some wealthy southern blacks who wished to protect their property. Plantation owner Isaiah Montgomery, a delegate to the Mississippi Constitutional Convention, voted to restrict black suffrage because of "inferior developments in the line of civilization." He assured the masses of blacks that their sacrifice would serve "to restore confidence, the great missing link between the two races." Wiley Jones, a wealthy black man from Pine Bluff, Arkansas, wrote the same year that he would like to see blacks refrain from voting for at least five years because "too much politics has been the ruin of some of our best prepared young men." John Shufton believed that race problems in the South would end as soon as blacks abandoned politics. The Charleston *New South* agreed that it was "high time" for blacks "to cease following the ignis fatuus of politics."[88]

Non-participation was obviously condemned by most politically active blacks and undoubtedly rejected in sentiment by most eligible voters. Byron Gunner denounced any suggestion that blacks leave politics as "an evil that we should nip in the bud, and out of which we should crush every spark of life." The New York *Age* condemned non-involvement as "political hari-kari of the most reckless and cowardly nature."[89]

The survival of black politics in the wake of the first high tide of disfranchisement was demonstrated by the continued discussion of political independence, Democracy and Populism, and the continued support of the Republican party by the majority. As the election of 1892 approached, many blacks did remain devoted to Republican principles, but Harrison's lily-white patronage policy and the Republican party's inability to pass either the Blair bill or the Lodge bill had further eroded their support. Near the end of Harrison's administration, the Wisconsin *Afro-American* spoke for many blacks when it editorialized: "We have not received the protection, recognition, and justice at the hands of the Republican Party, guaranteed to us by the Constitution of the United States, [but] we are yet unfailing in our devotion to this party and its principles."[90]

6

Republicans, Democrats, Populists, or Economics First: The Election of 1892 and the Second Cleveland Administration

On the surface, the presidential campaign of 1892 was a recapitulation of the one four years earlier, with voters choosing again between Harrison and Cleveland. However, the emergence of the Populist party as a strong third-party movement in the South and West indicated that millions of discontented Americans were challenging the conservative tweedledum and tweedledee politics offered by the Democrats and Republicans. As always, blacks riveted the most attention on the Republican nomination, but they also considered which potential Democratic and Populist candidates would best serve their interests.

Senator Henry Blair, by early 1892 an announced candidate for the Republican nomination, solicited black support through Douglass, but despite Blair's long fight for federal aid to education, he obtained little black assistance. Douglass supported the renomination of President Harrison, whom he credited with efforts to prevent racial violence, for being true to the Blair and Lodge bills, and for a generous patronage policy. John Lynch also supported the president's renomination on the grounds that Harrison had given the country one of the best administrations ever and that no other Republican would be more considerate of blacks. Congressman Henry Cheatham echoed praise that Harrison had done more for the race than any previous president.[1]

President Harrison's main rival for the Republican nomination was Secretary of State James G. Blaine. Blaine again had limited black support. The *Age* described him as an "unsound Republican," and one unfit to be the nominee of the party, but did find him less objectionable than Harrison, whom the editor thought meant well but "from lack of capacity to lead or from the force of circumstances had done exceedingly bad in everything to which he had put his hands." The Langston City *Herald* agreed that Harrison was an unsuccessful president who should be replaced on the 1892 ticket but also opposed Blaine and called for the selection of Robert T. Lincoln. Congressman John Langston opposed Harrison's renomination on the grounds that he had reneged on appointments he had promised blacks during the campaign. As the choice narrowed to Harrison or Blaine, however, most blacks supported the president.[2]

There were again black representatives from most southern states at the Republican convention in Minneapolis. Douglass, Bruce, Hill, and Lynch were prominent black leaders for Harrison. Four delegates—N. Wright Cuney, James Hill, Perry Carson, and J. C. Long—served on the National Committee. Despite a substantial last-minute Blaine drive, the president was easily renominated on the first ballot. Congressman Henry Cheatham seconded Harrison's nomination "on behalf of eight million Negroes." Whitelaw Reid of the New York *Tribune* was chosen as Harrison's running mate. The Republican platform again called for a free ballot for every citizen and denounced "the continued inhuman outrages perpetuated upon American citizens for political reasons in certain Southern states of the union."[3]

Much of the earlier criticism of President Harrison was dropped as most black Republicans again closed ranks behind the ticket. The Huntsville *Gazette* insisted that the choice of Harrison was the best the party could have made. The Topeka *Call* described the platform "as broad as humanity," and found it an invitation to all men to support the Republicans. J. H. Lewis, a friend of Douglass's, urged support because he believed "tis now or never with our cause."[4]

There were again no black delegates at the Democratic convention but blacks were present in Chicago. For the third straight time, Grover Cleveland was chosen as the party's nominee, this time with Adlai Stevenson as his running mate. Although Cleveland's only public statement concerning racial matters in the previous four years had been to praise the Mississippi disfranchisement convention, many blacks still believed that he was the best choice that the Democratic party could make. The Albany (N.Y.) *Calcium Light*, a Democratic paper edited by William H. Johnson, consistently endorsed the ex-president. The *Bee* and the Indianapolis *Freeman* spoke for many black Republicans who considered Cleveland an improvement over his party. The Democratic platform, which attacked the federal elections bill as potentially more harmful for blacks than whites, was more frequently assailed than were the Democratic candidates. The *Plaindealer* found the Democratic position "so rank" that it failed to see how blacks could "so stultify" themselves that they would support it.[5]

Despite considerable black enthusiasm for the creation of a new party, only four black men were delegates at the Populist convention which nominated Gen. James Weaver of Iowa for the presidency and Gen. James Field of Virginia for the vice-presidency. The party's platform appealed to "the plain people" with no mention of race. The Populists generally acceded to the demands of white Southerners on the question of suffrage; although they called for a free ballot, they demanded that it be without federal regulation. Some black papers noted the discrepancy between official support for black suffrage and informal talk of controlling black votes. Generally, however, the largely Republican black press devoted little attention to the third-party convention.[6]

The Populist candidates received the most attention from black papers in the West, which, for the most part, continued to oppose the third party. The Coffeyville *Afro-American* described Weaver as "one of the weak kneed Congress men who refused to stand by the Republican party in 1874 when that party proposed to protest the Negro." The Topeka *Call* joined in trying to convince Kansas blacks that a vote for Weaver would only help the Democrats at Republican expense. The press, however, did not dissuade all black Kansans; many worked for Weaver, and thousands endorsed the third-party candidates.[7]

Southern blacks also continued to be divided over whether Populism was a viable alternative. The degree of support for the new party varied considerably from state to state. Gerald Gaither has concluded that, due largely to the persuasive and charismatic qualities of Tom Watson, blacks in Georgia had the greatest "postive ideological affirmation" with Populism. In Texas, the effective leadership of black Populist John Raynor resulted in considerable black support. When Weaver campaigned in Waycross, Georgia, many blacks were in the crowd, and during a trip to Raleigh, North Carolina, fifty blacks joined an escort for the general. But undercurrents of racism sharply limited Populism's appeal. A majority of politically active southern black leaders supported Harrison where they could. The Populists sometimes tried bypassing established leaders and appealed directly to black alliancemen for support, but this was a tactic that generally failed.[8]

In the Northeast, the Populist party was virtually ignored. The Republicans retained the allegiance of most blacks, but Democratic support was extensive enough to provoke one paper to condemn some black political leaders as traitors. What support for the Democrats that there was generally stemmed from a positive judgment of Cleveland and from antipathy toward Harrison rather than from an in-depth reassessment of the parties. T. McCants Stewart insisted that "Mr. Cleveland is a stronger and more reliable friend of the colored people than Mr. Harrison." William H. Johnson, a Harrison supporter in 1888, switched to Cleveland and impugned other blacks for supporting a man who, he claimed, had used their votes for victory and then ignored their needs for four years. Another important Republican apostate, A.M.E. Bishop John M. Brown, now advised blacks to vote for Cleveland or not at all. The Troy *Daily Press*, which joined Johnson's *Calcium Light* in giving the Democrats black press support in New York, maligned black Republicans for "going back to ancient history to hunt excuses to antagonize the Democracy."[9]

Several conferences and conventions were held during the campaign to stimulate black Democratic support. A small group of black Democrats assembled in Indianapolis in the fall to form the National Colored Men's Protective Association, a meeting described by the Republican-biased Cleveland *Gazette* as a "fizzle." A June meeting in Chicago under the auspices of the Negro

National Democratic Committee was more successful. "We are here today," William H. Johnson announced to the delegates, "because we believe the Republican party has outlived its usefulness at least so far as it relates to the negro, and that it is our duty to cast about for a safer and more sure anchorage. We believe that Grover Cleveland, when President of the United States, gave the best assurances possible that under Democratic rule the Afro-American's best interest, his liberty and happiness were fully conserved."[10]

Most blacks, however, were not convinced, and the Democratic party's campaign rhetoric did little to persuade them. New York *Sun* editor Charles A. Dana, a leading Democratic strategist, insisted on emphasizing the force bill as a Republican measure threatening to bring "the horrors of negro domination" to the South. Cleveland generally accepted Dana's counsel and on several occasions condemned the force bill, although with less racist rhetoric.[11]

It was a campaign strategy, the Detroit *Plaindealer* bemoaned, that was making southern bulldozers "more brazen than ever." Longtime black Democratic leader George T. Downing became especially alarmed at the tone the campaign assumed under Dana's leadership but remained convinced that other Democrats did not share Dana's philosophy. He also concluded, however, that "neither party at present cares for us." Other former Cleveland supporters, notably Henry Downing and Thomas Fortune, found the Democratic strategy so untenable that they endorsed Harrison.[12]

Although Harrison and the Republican party remained vague on racial questions, many blacks still campaigned enthusiastically for the ticket. Frederick Douglass pronounced Republican victory "a matter of life or death" and condemned blacks who supported Democracy. Many Republican meetings were held for or by blacks, and black Harrison and Reid clubs sprang up all over the country. For example, in October, a "Grand Meeting of Colored Republicans in Northern Ohio," which featured speaker John Lynch, was advertised throughout the state. *The Afro-American Campaign Text Book*, which presented the Republican platform and candidates, was promoted nationwide.[13]

While many blacks enthusiastically supported the Republican

party, they were not always willing to set aside accumulated grievances. They warned the Republicans that they could no longer
secure the black vote in November with the cry "the party which
freed him." Blacks again criticized the Republican emphasis on
the tariff and money rather than life and liberty. The Lodge
bill, which white Republicans generally ignored, was the dominant issue in black Republican papers, and they repeatedly denounced Cleveland and his party for its defeat. The Indianapolis
Freeman contended that Cleveland had opposed the bill because
he feared that only through fraudulent elections could a Democratic candidate be elected president. Many black Democrats
accepted the challenge and defended the Lodge bill's defeat.
Delegates at a black conference in Philadelphia agreed that "the
Republican party, in its greedy gain for power, would enforce
a force bill which means the murdering and slaughtering of
thousands of our brethren in the southlands." William Johnson
also condemned the Republican proposal as one which, if passed,
would mean the slaughter of southern blacks.[14]

Many southern blacks countered, however, that the defeat of
the force bill was more likely to result in their slaughter if they
tried to vote at all. In some areas, the Populist challenge, which
sometimes included a fusion arrangement with the Republican
party, fostered Democratic chicanery and violence. Violence and
intimidation were particularly rampant in black-belt counties
where whites were most determined to destroy the potential
black majority. A black Alabamian reported that electoral conditions in his county were such that, unless there was a change,
the majority of blacks would stay home on election day rather
than risk murder. A group from Terrebonne Parish, Louisiana,
although afraid to sign their names, wrote Douglass about the
great suffering of blacks in the South and of the barriers to
voting Republican and begged: "Please try and have some con-
versation with the President in order that god might send him
as he sent Moses to lead the children from the terrible hands of
the enemy." Terrorism was largely at the hands of the Democrats, but Republicans and Populists sometimes resorted to racial
violence as well. General Weaver, who wanted to focus on economic issues when campaigning in the South, lamented that the
only issue there was "who can most hate the Negro."[15]

Cleveland easily defeated both his Republican and Populist opponents; the Democrats also captured both houses of Congress. It was, as described by Lawrence Grossman, "the ultimate triumph of Democratic racial policy." The Democrats had been able to win support by simultaneously exploiting both white fears of federal electoral intervention and black disenchantment with the Republican party. Less than 15 percent of Southerners voted Republican, the first time since the Civil War that the party's share of the popular vote had fallen below 23 percent. The total Democratic percentage of southern votes also fell by over 4 percentage points from 1888 to less than 34 percent. Both parties lost some votes to the Populists, who received over 9 percent of southern votes, and to a drop in overall voter turnout.[16]

The percentage of southern blacks voting, and voting for each of the parties, varied considerably from state to state, depending particularly on how successful Democratic governments had been in enacting restrictive legislation. But legislative restrictions, Democratic violence and corruption, Populist racism, traditional loyalty to the Republicans, and the widespread belief that it was expedient to vote Democratic in order to appease white Southerners, were all factors in disappointing Populist hopes for a large black vote. The Populists received a higher percentage of black votes in the West than in the South. The Topeka *Weekly Call* estimated that forty-five hundred black Kansans, one-third of those eligible, voted Populist. In most southern states in which blacks still voted in large numbers, a higher percentage of their votes were counted for the Democrats than ever before. Despite claims of Texas Populists that "the colored people are coming into the new party in squads and companies," the Democrats had more black votes, many of them a result of bribery. In Georgia, where the Populists had campaigned particularly hard among blacks, over 22 percent of eligible blacks had their votes counted for the Democrats, while the Republicans received 12.1 percent and the Populists only 6.4 percent. In Florida only about 11 percent of eligible blacks voted and most of their votes went to the Democrats. In Mississippi, where 30 percent of eligible blacks had voted in the 1888 presidential election, constitutional disfranchisement was so successful that almost no blacks voted in 1892.[17]

Because blacks were familiar with Cleveland, there was less apprehension as to the consequences of a Democratic victory than there had been eight years earlier. William B. Derrick posed the question "Has the Republican Party a Future?" and answered with a firm "Yes." He was confident that when "reason and sober judgment" again emerged, the party would resume its mission as "the energetic defender of the integrity of the nation." Frederick Douglass issued a circular assuring blacks that they would be "agreeably surprised by the little difference which the change of Administration will make." Although he feared that some whites might temporarily determine that they were freer to mistreat blacks, he doubted that the condition of southern blacks could deteriorate to a worse state of affairs than had existed during Harrison's term in office. J. C. Price was also optimistic about a second term for Cleveland because "I believe that he is a patriot as well as a partisan, and the general interests of the country will be safe in his hands." J. Madison Vance more pessimistically described the victory as a "Waterloo" for the Republicans but also a chance for the Democrats to demonstrate that they were not a menace. Most papers saw no reason for alarm, although the Louisville *Champion* cryptically observed that "it is difficult to try and be merry at your own funeral." The Springfield *State Capital* blamed the results on "Bulldozing Democrats" who had taken hundreds of illegal votes, but also reminded its readers that they had already tolerated the Democrats for four years and could give them another trial.[18]

President Harrison aided these Democratic apologists by naming Howell Edmunds Jackson, a former Confederate officer from Tennessee, to the U.S. Supreme Court shortly before he left office. The Cleveland *Gazette* warned that it was the beginning of a disintegration that could render the party worthless by 1896. But most blacks, looking ahead to a new administration, expressed more disillusionment than anger. The Indianapolis *Freeman*, usually vitriolic in its denunciations of racist appointments, now merely suggested that it "looks a little strange that under any circumstances a Republican President would give such a position to a Democrat." The *Bee* rationalized that the appointment of Judge Jackson would make no difference to blacks since it was a Republican court that had declared the Civil Rights Act of 1875 unconstitutional. The paper, normally very involved in politics, now advised the course commonly heard in times of discouragement—that blacks concern themselves less with political concerns and instead "put money in thy purse and education in thy brains." The Coffyville *Afro-American Advocate* even praised the appointment for removing the Supreme Court from the realm of politics.[19]

For some blacks, Democratic victory was again inducement to assess that party more optimistically. In his inaugural address, Cleveland said little about blacks particularly but urged the country to avoid "the unwholesome progeny of paternalism." Still, many blacks were complimentary. John Langston, when asked by the president what he thought of the speech, assured him that it would receive general approval. T. McCants Stewart wired Cleveland, "Afro-Americans see in yourself and your inaugural address the assurance of national prosperity without sectional, class or racial limitations." The San Francisco *Elevator* saw the speech as a guarantee that blacks would have at least as good a friend in the new president as they had in Harrison. The A.M.E. Zion *Church Quarterly* labeled the speech very liberal on racial problems, at least for a Democrat. A month after the inauguration, the Indianapolis *Freeman* even claimed that "if the Negro gets anything like a fair deal during the next four years the Republicans may as well go out of the business as far as the Negro is concerned."[20]

Cleveland's reelection offered new hope to black Democrats, and many were now lavish in their praise. C. H. J. Taylor exulted that it was "good to be a full fledged Negro Democrat" and called Cleveland "the greatest man in the world." The Macon (Ga.) *Southern Advocate*, a Democratic paper founded just before the election, exemplified several new black papers which pledged support. The St. Paul and Minneapolis *Broad Axe*, edited by A. L. Graves, exclaimed a few days before the inauguration: "Just think of it! After next Saturday it will be a Democratic president, and a Democratic Congress and Senate, a treat the American people have not enjoyed in forty years. The nation will certainly congratulate itself on the change."[21]

The National Democratic League, with Taylor presiding and H. C. C. Astwood chairing the executive committee, was reactivated in the wake of the Democratic victory. Most prominent black Democrats were members, but despite the cautioning example of constant Republican infighting, the Democrats were rarely united in these years. Taylor and Astwood, both highly opinionated and volatile men, usually disagreed on league policy and practice. When Astwood proposed an organizational meeting, Taylor responded that "Negro Democrats should call a halt and await the action of their great commander and honest leader, Grover Cleveland." Undaunted, Astwood still held a meeting to reorganize the state leagues throughout the country and to popularize black Democracy. He also announced plans to launch the *National Democrat* as the official league newspaper.[22]

James Ross headed the National Democratic Association, a league rival. During the week of Astwood's meeting, Ross also held a conference. Both men urged black Democratic unity, but a modus vivendi remained elusive. A Republican paper questioned: "Is this vision of a score or more of able Negroes of standing and influence holding a Democratic powwow at the nation's capital, but the baseless fabric of a dream or was it an actual fact with more of the like to come?" The more pessimistic interpretation was the correct one; disunity continued to hinder the development of organized black Democracy. In early 1894, when President Cleveland complained to Taylor that black Democrats rarely agreed on anything, Taylor responded that past training tended to stifle confidence among blacks. Undoubtedly with himself in mind, Taylor suggested that if the president would announce the black Democrat he had the most confidence in, then unity could develop around that person. Taylor's response was indicative of a major barrier to compromise and group action—personal ambition. It was the dilemma of talented and ambitious black men who had few public arenas other than politics, and it afflicted Democrats and Republicans alike.[23]

In August, Taylor and Astwood presided over a second convention of the National Negro Democratic League in Indianapolis. In his opening remarks, Taylor, who was unanimously reelected president, extolled the virtues of Grover Cleveland. On the second day, the convention delegates endorsed the Democratic platform of 1892 and asserted that affiliation with Democracy was necessary for blacks to obtain full citizenship rights. Most southern problems were blamed on unwise Republican policies that arrayed the races against each other and appealed to the black vote through futile issues. Affiliation with the Democrats, the delegates maintained, would bring better understanding between the races and secure political recognition for blacks. These proceedings were written off by many Republicans as farcical and inconsequential.[24]

A few weeks after the convention, the Republicans were proven correct, at least in regard to the facade of unity. Astwood wrote Taylor that although he intended to remain a Democrat, he could no longer associate with organized black Democracy, a "cesspool of corruption." Other black Democrats, cognizant of the impression that the feud must make on the president, denounced both factions.[25]

In early 1895, another black Democratic conference attempted fusion between the forces of Taylor and Ross but Taylor refused to attend. Ross, who presided, described black Democrats as "a glorious army" and the meeting as "a council of war to take steps working to their safety and their glory." Among Ross's recommendations were: (1) the consolidation of all Afro-American Democratic organizations, (2) the establishment of a newspaper to represent this one great organization, (3) a literary bureau to distribute black Democratic literature, and (4) a sustained effort to keep out imposters. A committee of seven assured the president that black Democrats were "united and harmonious," and though they affirmed their abiding faith in his administration and the principles of the party, they also expressed concern with the damage done black Democracy by the paucity of presidential recognition. This, they acknowledged, was in large measure due to their own division, a situation they intended to change. The demand for office, the committee insisted, was not for personal gain but to demonstrate to black Republicans that the Democratic party was liberal enough to appoint black officeholders. They assured Cleveland that his previous appointments gave him a place in the hearts of blacks second only to Lincoln, but they also hoped that if they unified, even more positions would be forthcoming. The letter was signed by members of the committee, including Ross and Robert Still, and included a note of agreement from Taylor and H. Clay Smith. According to the

Republican black press, no more than a facade of black Democracy had actually been achieved. Ross's fourth proposal, that black Democrats guard against imposters, was indicative of how difficult this unity would be to maintain. There were no clear guidelines to determine who was an imposter, a term which symbolized the intense competition among black Democrats for limited rewards.[26]

The Negro Democratic Congressional League, a third black Democratic organization whose purpose was to "Make the Black Voter a Factor," generally remained aloof from the squabbling. A resolution passed in the summer of 1894 proclaimed: "We endorse the administration of the greatest President this country has ever seen, Grover Cleveland. If the Democratic party would follow his lead without question or hesitation, they would remain in power for the next quarter of a century." The League pointed to Democrats who openly appealed for the black vote as proof that blacks were wanted in the party.[27]

There were also a number of state Democratic organizations formed across the country. Robert G. Still, chairman of the Democratic State League of Pennsylvania, reported that there were fifteen hundred black Democrats in his state. He led a group of them to the Cleveland inauguration. William E. Gross and Rev. P. Hampton White were among the leaders of the Negro Democratic League of New York. Black Democracy in the Empire State was a microcosm of national divisiveness, possibly reflecting the influence of H. C. C. Astwood, who moved to New York during this period.[28]

J. Milton Turner of Missouri was among the most prominent leaders of midwestern Democracy, although when he crossed state lines to recruit in Ohio he stirred up some resentment. Black Democracy was already fairly well organized in Ohio and in other states in the area. In July 1894, the first black Democratic state convention in Missouri was held. In Kansas, Democratic conventions had been held since the first Cleveland administration. By 1893, the Colored Pioneer Democratic Club of Topeka was in its tenth year, giving Taylor grounds for his claim that in his state black Democracy was in ascendancy.[29]

James Ross, following a trip to Atlanta, reported that in certain sections of the South, blacks, especially those he considered "the better elements," were supporting the Democratic party in large numbers. In reality, however, uncoerced and organized southern black Democracy was still rare.[30]

To many blacks, patronage continued to be symbolic of general political equality. Democratic victory hardly diminished the number of requests for appointments, and Cleveland's handling of these requests played a crucial role in fostering black Democracy. Friction continued between those who had only recently endorsed Cleveland and those who felt that no one should apply for office if not "well soaked in democracy [Democracy]." The Indianapolis *Freeman* predicted that black Democrats would once again swarm on Washington to lobby for appointments and counseled Cleveland not to be fooled by the recent converts. Longtime Democrat C. H. J. Taylor warned that while the neophytes should eventually get places, they "will have to stand back until the old pioneers have been served. The best places shall not go to the fellows who stood in the way of Negro Democrats until they found out that they could not prevent the onward march of tariff reform. We want all Democratic Negroes to be admitted to the political smoke-house but the old timers must come first. This is justice and this will happen. Watch and see."[31]

There was also rivalry between northern and southern black Democrats for federal appointments. Northerners often pointed out that because of the impact they could make in close elections, they should be given first consideration. Isaiah Montgomery was among the Southerners who tried to counter their claim. He praised Cleveland for the great progress made in eradicating the color line, "the greatest bane of Southern politics," which, he believed, prompted many northern blacks to vote for him. But while it would seem logical to give this group recognition, Montgomery continued, the Democrats now had a chance to grasp the entire race's confidence by recognizing southern black leaders. The "vast silent majority" of both races, he said, would welcome the change.[32]

Many blacks realized that organization and unity were essential to receiving patronage. The National Negro Democratic League focused on high-level positions. By mid–1893, a Democratic vigilance committee met at the Washington post office daily to watch for lower-level vacancies and to work for the replacement of black Republicans with Democrats.[33]

Black Republicans were also concerned with Cleveland's patronage policy, and many of them laid aside partisan politics to lobby for black Democrats. The Detroit *Plaindealer* promoted Peter Clark as an inoffensive Democrat who deserved a position. The Indianapolis *Freeman* worked for E. E. Cooper, A. E. Manning, and F. N. Hill, three fellow Hoosiers, claiming: "The race knows not three more wide-awake, 'git-up and git,' hungry, anxious Democrats than they."[34]

Both Democrats and Republicans continued to lobby for a position on the world's fair committee. Henry M. Turner protested, "Think of it! The great World's Fair or exposition in Chicago, out of more than the thousand employees gave no recognition to the colored race beyond taking charge of the toilet rooms." The United States Memorial Association of America presented a petition, which included the signature of famed underground railroad conductor Harriet Tubman, supporting the world's fair appointment. The group suggested that a black man named to such a position would serve as "a true warning to all coming administrations to bless and help good citizens, irrespective of sex or cast or previous condition."[35]

Blacks, disappointed in demands for participation in the fair and aware that few other appointments were forthcoming, were soon again freely criticizing Cleveland. Republicans were quick to note during the first week of Cleveland's administration that few black appointments had been made. A month after the inauguration, the Indianapolis *Freeman* quipped: "Its about time 'Grove' was sending in the name of some of his Afro-American henchmen, don't you think?" Taylor constantly defended Cleveland against such criticism and insisted that black Democrats had not been duped. He indirectly acknowledged the charge, however, when he maintained that those who went into the party from principle were not complaining about being ignored. In February, he wrote the president that he did not care about offices, that "all we seek is that justice shall prevail." Taylor, however, continued to be very ambitious. In early March, he wrote Cleveland that before he addressed the Negro State Convention of Nebraska, he needed something "which would cheer the minds and hearts of my anxious brethren." When two months later he still had received no appointment, Taylor wrote again, recalling that blacks were behind the party in the 1892 campaign "in the face of insults and injuries of every kind," and claiming that they now appeared before the country in a false light. Pressure for patronage on the grounds of moral and political obligation was a traditional black Republican tactic now adopted by the Democrats.[36]

Taylor and most other prominent black Democrats were especially interested in Blanche K. Bruce's position of recorder of deeds. The recordership, wrote John Bruce, "is the envy of a score or more of sore-eyed colored Democrats." Taylor, who had considerable support in his own bid for the appointment, assured the president that he could easily get a black man confirmed for this traditionally black post. In Taylor's home state, the Topeka *Call* frequently lobbied for him, and at least one mass meeting was held to endorse his candidacy. But Taylor lost some of his Republican support when he began attacking Republican officeholders, particularly Bruce, for not having the manhood to resign. Peter Clark also applied to Cleveland for a position and asked Douglass to recommend him. The Cleveland *Gazette* predicted that Clark would be appointed recorder and in a statement rather out of character politically, but reflecting the bitterness many younger blacks felt toward traditional officeholders, predicted that he would be a great improvement over Bruce.[37]

Many less prominent black Democrats pushed their own candidacy or that of others for places in the administration. Sidney M. Murphy of Eufaula, Alabama, could offer the unusual credentials of support from the governor and other prominent white Democrats in his state. Prince Robinson, also from Alabama, wrote the president several times concerning his unsuccessful candidacy to be minister to Haiti. "I am a negro, it is true," he wrote, "but I am a straight out Democrat." He always conscientiously worked for the Democrats, Robinson insisted, and as a result often suffered at the hands of the Republicans.[38]

In June, H. Clay Smith was named as U.S. consul to Madagascar, the first important black appointment of Cleveland's second administration. However, no significant appointments followed, while a number of black officeholders lost their positions. In July, Harry C. Smith noted the "President's cabinet, the various secretaries, are making Afro-American department clerks 'walk the plank' these days, and, what is still more aggrevating to democracy's 'colored contingent,' are replacing them with white Democrats, many of whom are 'f'om de south, sah.' " The *Weekly Call* quipped, "Grover Cleveland has been kept so busy preparing his message that he has not the time to look after the Afro-American Democrat. Poor Taylor."[39]

Taylor, still optimistic and defensive, explained that Cleveland had come into office with more problems than most presidents and could, therefore, be excused for his relative slowness in making appointments. "I expect any day to get my summons to come to Washington," he added. "That it will arrive, I am as certain as that I am alive. Mr. Cleveland never forgets his friends." As added insurance, Taylor continued working to discredit Bruce. He was sure, he wrote the president's secretary, that no black man had said more against Cleveland in the last campaign than the present recorder. The National Democratic League asked for the removal of Bruce on the grounds that he had campaigned against Cleveland and the Democratic party in New York, New Jersey, and other states; had contributed money to the Republican campaign fund; and had bragged that he would stay in office until February 1894.[40]

H. C. C. Astwood was generally considered second to Taylor as the most likely recipient of an office. He also denied that there was cause for dissatisfaction among black Democrats and rationalized that other pressing matters prevented Cleveland from making haste. Although Astwood condemned blacks who were now claiming to be Democrats just to receive positions, he suggested that the president might convert black Republicans like Langston and Pinchback who were ignored by their party.[41]

In September, Taylor was appointed minister to Bolivia and Astwood, U.S. consul to Calais. Most blacks were pleased that two important appointments had been made and particularly that they were to traditionally white posts. The Indianapolis *Freeman* offered Taylor "our hearty congratulations and, extending our hand across the chasm of political difference, say—

shake." Bishop Benjamin W. Arnett of Wilberforce University told a Chicago audience that this was greater recognition than blacks had ever received from the Republicans. Many black Democrats agreed that these appointments, combined with that of Smith, vindicated their loyalty. Taylor thanked the president for proving that he regarded blacks as full citizens and not limited in their abilities to hold only "black offices." William Johnson sent a resolution on behalf of the Independent Colored Democratic Organization of Brooklyn, New York, thanking the president for remembering black Democrats and for breaking the color line in the administration of government. The president of the Negro Club of Topeka expressed confidence that if this was an example of future Democratic policy toward blacks, soon the majority would join the party.[42]

Although a few blacks opposed the appointments, particularly that of the controversial Astwood, more joined in the difficult fight for confirmation. The Cleveland *Gazette* was so angered by Democratic resistance to sending blacks to represent the United States in non-black countries that Smith bitterly reiterated "Democracy is an enemy." Other blacks, however, predicted correctly that, as with Matthews eight years before, as much opposition would come from the Republican senators as from Democrats.[43]

When a majority of the Republican senators voted no, both appointments were rejected. One senator acknowledged to Astwood that he could have been confirmed as consul to Haiti or Santo Domingo. Astwood wrote the president that the plight of Taylor and himself was a serious political question affecting eight million Americans. While he still retained confidence in Cleveland, he bemoaned "what a humiliating spectacle Negro Democracy presents today to the country." The Negro National Democratic League, he concluded, would like to work for the party but was discouraged when its foremost leaders were rejected and it felt there was no hope for aid from the president.[44]

Cleveland's black appointments also renewed the conflict between old and new Democrats. Just after the appointments of Astwood and Taylor, John Bruce observed that this recognition had stirred up Republican blacks, "hungry and selfish hypocrites," who were now trying to break into the Democratic party.

Others were more concerned that in Cleveland's second administration few black appointments, Democratic or Republican, had been confirmed. In January 1894, the A.M.E. Zion *Church Quarterly* noted: "Only a few colored men remain who hold prominent Federal positions. The others have pretty nearly all gone. Why is it so? Who can answer? Are there no Afro-American Democrats to take the place of these men as they go out?" There was even a proposal that black Democrats sue the Democratic party for breach of promise. The Indianapolis *Freeman* questioned, "Was it after all but a Cleveland bluff, the nomination of Brer Taylor and Astwood? It certainly begins to look that way. But think of all the good breath we spent praising Grover for his 'noble act.' "[45]

Despite this defeat, Taylor did not give up. He reminded Cleveland that Bruce's position as recorder expired on February 7 and added "*I really desire and need the salary he is now drawing.*" A number of prominent blacks also lobbied for the recordship, but a few days after Bruce resigned, Taylor was nominated. Blacks virtually closed ranks in support of confirmation. The Cleveland *Gazette* insisted that Ohio blacks would have preferred Peter Clark and that the race had no place in the Democratic party anyway, but still congratulated Taylor and joined the bandwagon urging prompt Senate confirmation. Taylor, who actively solicited senators and black leaders for support, reported that most of the latter, except for a few like Bruce and some Democrats who coveted the appointment, were endorsing him. Frederick Douglass used his influence with several senators in Taylor's behalf.[46]

Taylor's confirmation in May 1894 prompted an upsurge of support for Cleveland and the Democratic party reminiscent of the Matthews-Trotter fight. Some black Republicans again declared Cleveland more generous than many Republican presidents. Taylor thanked the president for "making me the greatest Negro in America," and assured him that his sole ambition was "to serve the greatest man who had ever been President and to serve the best interest of my people by taking them out of the Republican party." Taylor continued working to get other black Democrats, particularly Astwood, appointed. But no place was offered Astwood. He angrily announced his return to the Republican fold, providing an individual example of how ephemeral black support for the Democratic party was. Astwood was condemned from all sides for his self-supporting politics. Even former mentor Taylor responded: "Poor foolish Astwood. He has started a newspaper in the interest of the GOP. The man is really half crazy."[47]

Once in office, Taylor began to experience his own conflict with black Republicans. In August, Chase announced in the *Bee*, at first with no explanation, that "Taylor must go," that "the Kansas wind bag" was unfit to serve as recorder or president of the Democratic League. Chase's campaign to prove that Taylor used his office for immoral purposes and personal gain generated a controversy that raged in the black press throughout the fall and winter of 1894–1895. Both men had their defenders, but some only despaired that their confrontation would jeopardize future black appointments. In January 1895, Taylor officially charged Chase with libel and appealed to the White House for aid. Chase's trial resulted in a guilty verdict and three months in jail.[48]

During the period that the Chase-Taylor fight captured front-page headlines, Cleveland did make several important black appointments, including William H. Heard as minister to Haiti. S. T. Mitchell, president of Wilberforce University, was so gratified with the appointments of several Wilberforce associates in the spring of 1895 that he offered Cleveland an honorary degree. The appointment of James Matthews to the recorders court of Albany, although not a federal position, was heralded by many as further proof that blacks could obtain significant positions as Democrats.[49]

Others, however, continued to be critical of a policy identified as lily-whitism on the national level. William H. Hunt wrote Douglass that, although a Republican, he was concerned with the wholesale removal of blacks and asked for help in getting an interview with the president to discuss the situation. James Ross and Calvin Chase focused on the frequent dismissals of black employees from the Bureau of Engraving and Printing. A. A. Mossell, who claimed to have successfully campaigned for Cleveland in his native city of Buffalo, threatened to stop supporting the Democrats if they would not reward the faithful.

Mossell feared that blacks who remained loyal would be characterized as "branded hirelings" and urged Cleveland "to be a loving and impartial shepherd."[50]

In the fall of 1894, President Cleveland wrote T. McCants Stewart: "I have relied upon such men as you, to see the true condition and to appreciate my difficulties and limitations." Stewart responded with a lengthy analysis of the position of blacks in the Cleveland administration, particularly focusing on the removal of government employees. He believed that blacks had indisputably lost ground during Cleveland's second administration because, while only Taylor had received a good position, enough men and women had been removed to cause a scandal. Stewart blamed cabinet officers and department heads but asserted that only the president could restore black office holding. "A class of unprincipled, loud-mouth negroes who have evidently disgusted you," he feared, hurt the chances of the better elements. There were two things that Cleveland could do to put himself next to Lincoln in history, Stewart contended: get proper tariff legislation and break down the color line in the public service by appointing "a new line of Afro-Americans of character, industry and ability."[51]

In the last years of Cleveland's administration, criticism shifted from the president's patronage policy to the general attributes of the Democratic party. A constant theme was that whatever good Cleveland and the northern branch of the party did was canceled by the discrimination and terrorist tactics of the southern branch. For a time, Cleveland enjoyed a better press than his party, but a severe national depression that steadily worsened throughout 1894 eroded his black and white support. After mid–1894, Cleveland was consistently criticized in the black press. When a pro-Democratic paper tried to blame the depression on sources other than the president, the Indianapolis *Freeman* responded: "Get out! Men are starving to-day . . . because the people turned fool 'just for a change, you know,' and elected Grover Cleveland, instead of Benjamin Harrison." Rev. S. B. Wallace questioned whether a government that would not give a man a job deserved that man's support. The Cleveland *Gazette*, pointing to rising unemployment and the kind of protest exemplified by Jacob Coxey's march, ridiculed Cleveland for claiming that recovery was near. The Wichita *People's Friend* concentrated on Democratic economic ineptness throughout the summer of 1894 and concluded that disorder was "directly consequent upon democratic interferences with previous industrial conditions and national prosperity." The acid pen of John Mitchell succinctly summarized the views of many as to the cause of the depression: "Some people suffer from over-eating but most of them are victims of under-eating. Cause: Grover Cleveland is President."[52]

The number of blacks who claimed allegiance to the Democratic party, as well as tolerance for those who remained loyal, dropped sharply. The *Bee*, recalling that at the time of Cleveland's inauguration there appeared to be as many black Democrats as Republicans, proclaimed in the summer of 1895 that "Negro democrats [Democrats] are now things of the past." The Cleveland *Gazette* asserted that those who retained their allegiance were merely after money, and that "the Negro who will act thus is a poor specimen of manhood." The Parsons *Weekly Blade* bluntly stated: "Negro Democracy—a farce."[53]

Some disenchanted black Democrats resisted complete realignment with the Republicans but, reminiscent of the early eighties, advocated political independence. In Columbus, Ohio, the Independent Political Protective Association was formed in the summer of 1893 with over one hundred members. President James Poindexter identified unity of the colored vote as the main objective. In June 1894, there was a call for a national convention led by the Colored Voters League of Pennsylvania, New York, and West Virginia to "elevate the race and protest against the outrages perpetrated upon the colored people of the United States and sow seeds of independent thought and action." There were also a number of local conventions in places as remote as Leadville, Colorado, held to organize independence.[54]

Many black papers again gave at least some credence to the viability of political independence. The *Bee* assumed the label "independent." The Nashville *Citizen*, founded by disgruntled Republicans, counseled nomination of an all-black ticket in local contests. Despite its name, the Providence (R.I.) *Republican Sun* advocated that blacks work for the goodwill of all political parties. The Seattle *Standard* called independence the only salvation of the race, and the *Reformer* demanded: "Let the Negro support the party nearest to him. Do away with the old idea that a Negro cannot be anything but a Republican, Baptist or Methodist. Let them scatter among all parties." Throughout the summer of 1895, the Topeka *Call* urged: "Don't forget the declaration of independence in politics when it is necessary."[55]

Other disillusioned black Democrats bypassed independence and simply declared themselves Republicans. The most notable return to the fold was T. McCants Stewart. When asked in September 1894 to serve on the advisory board to the Afro-American Bureau of the Democratic Congressional Committee, he replied that the "administration has treated colored democrats niggardly, I can not serve." This bitterness soon prompted a complete break with the Democratic party. Stewart explained that he now recognized three classes of black Democrats: those paid to affiliate, office seekers, and those opposed to Republican high tariffs. He placed himself in the third group, claiming that the tariff caused the division of the black vote at times, but that it was no longer a justification for blacks to support the Cleveland administration. Stewart concluded that Cleveland was not the same president he had been from 1885 to 1889. He wrote that while he hated to criticize a man he had once so admired, "it makes my heart sick to think of what we had and to know that we hold only one of the foreign places under the present administration." Stewart revealed that the major catalyst to his switch was northern Democratic refusal to repudiate the southern cry "No Force Bill; No Negro Domination" during the 1892 election. One black Democrat suggested that it would have been more manly of Stewart to continue his efforts to liberalize the Democratic party. Several Republicans questioned how Stewart could have turned Democratic in the first place. But most rejoiced that he was back in the fold. Editor Mitchell of the *Planet* wrote, "We admired him before; we love him now."[56]

Many faithful Republicans became more exuberant in their loyalty. Most of the black papers published in Kansas during the nineties reflected the veracity of the Wichita *People's Friend*'s claim that in Kansas blacks "stand in one grand line of Republicanism." The Topeka *Weekly Call*, the Wichita *People's Friend*, the *Kansas Blackman*, and the Leavenworth *Herald* all remained loyal, although occasionally with qualifications. Rev. W. L. Grant delivered the same sentiments to a crowd of over three thousand at the Parsons fairground in September 1894. Grant praised the Republican party as "our haven of peace and tranquility," and warned that all roads out of the GOP lead to the enemy Democratic party or its orphan, the Populist party.[57]

Such expressions of Republican loyalty were as common in other parts of the country. Harry C. Smith continued to speak through the columns of the *Gazette* for Republicanism in Ohio. Just after the party's defeat in 1892, Smith reported a large and enthusiastic meeting of the Afro-American Republican Club of Ohio. The Indianapolis *Freeman* at times sounded independent but would revert back to such loyal Republican tributes as Editor Knox's proclamation: "I am a Republican, will live a Republican, and God almighty being my helper, will die one." In 1895, there was an upsurge in Republican activity among blacks in Washington, D.C. The Thomas B. Reed Republican Club was organized, and the *Bee* again claimed to be a loyal Republican paper. Chase now proclaimed that "all the negroes ever got or expect to get was and will be from the Republican party." The Richmond *Planet* was typical of many southern black papers in repeatedly avowing Republican allegiance. When the Republicans won the 1894 elections, the Huntsville *Gazette* rejoiced: "The country is safe." But proscription, disfranchisement, and violence made it increasingly dangerous for many southern blacks to declare themselves Republicans or to profess any political sentiments at all. It was starkly clear that southern blacks were not safe regardless of the political party in power.[58]

Disillusionment with Cleveland did not completely stifle criticism of the Republicans. The harshest critics naturally were black Democrats. C. H. J. Taylor wrote of "the Republican party with his trained henchmen, who enslaved the race, politically, ever since Reconstruction, just as effectively as they were in human slavery." Astwood, prior to his return to the Republican fold, blamed the Republicans for building a white man's party in the South and for advocating the force bill which had made blacks targets for hate and violence. Independents and reluctant Republicans were also critical at times. John E. Bruce contended that contemporary Republican leaders were the cause of the party's inadequacies; that, although the party still had purpose, the present leaders were sacrificing it with an approach to human rights that was apathetic and cowardly.[59]

Populism continued to be an important alternative, particularly for many southern and western blacks. The depression prompted some to associate with the new party because it advocated economic change. Although black Republican papers continued to be critical and express doubts about the party's success in recruiting blacks, the Topeka *Weekly Call* acknowledged that a "number of our ardent Afro-American Republicans are developing a fondness for Populism." In the fall of 1894, the *American Citizen* pointed to the formation of a Populist club in Topeka as evidence that Populism was on the increase among western blacks. J. B. Gibbs, the leader of black Populism in Kansas, conducted meetings across the state. New black Populist clubs also appeared in the South. The Union People's party, for example, was formed in Columbus, Georgia, in the summer of 1893. The Democratic editor of the Thomasville *Times* reported in 1894 that blacks in the area were showing considerable interest in Populism, although he assumed that a prohibitive poll tax would preclude their voting for that or any party. Some southern blacks played an important role in the fusion tactics of Populists and Republicans, most successfully in North Carolina in 1894. Others were unhappy with this arrangement, primarily because they feared that the Populist influence on the Republicans would mean opposition to black office holding and restriction of funds for black schools.[60]

The growth of southern black Populism was also retarded by declining racial toleration among white Populists. As Robert Saunders has pointed out, blacks increasingly fell "on the periphery of Populism." Many of the Populist clubs that blacks joined between 1892 and 1896 were exclusively black. Black Populists also had to face the hostility of partisan Republicans who resolved "to wipe the pops from the face of the earth." The Leavenworth *Herald* insisted that the only issue for Kansas in 1894 was redemption of the state from Populism. When the Topeka *Headlight*, the only black Populist paper in the state, failed, the *Herald* rejoiced, only regretting that it had not waited to die in November with the party. The Populists also lost large numbers of potential black votes to the Democratic party which, determined to retain its hegemony in the South, was increasingly successful in exploiting that vote. The result was the tragic irony, recognized by a Louisiana Populist paper in 1894, that "in the river parishes where the Negroes were in the majority the Democrats succeeded in maintaining white supremacy with the Negro votes."[61]

Of major concern to blacks in the early nineties was not only the loss of representation in Congress, but the potential for further political retrogression under a Democratic Congress. George Murray of South Carolina was the only black man in the Fifty-third and Fifty-fourth Congresses. One of the first actions of the Democratic Fifty-third was to repeal the remaining federal election laws. The Indianapolis *Freeman* argued that blacks should not be upset because the election laws had been a farce anyway. The Cleveland *Gazette*, however, claimed that this action put the Democratic Congress outside the boundaries of the Constitution and urged Cleveland not to sign such an unjust measure.[62]

Primarily in response to the depression, 1894 voters returned a Republican Congress to Washington. The *National Baptist World* reported the relief blacks felt that the country could no longer tolerate Democratic blunders and misrule. Relief was muted, however, by the rejection of Henry Cheatham, a North Carolinian who hoped to join Murray as a black congressman. Despite several black petitions in his behalf, the Republican Congress refused Cheatham his seat.[63]

Political and economic discouragement fostered by the Democratic and depression years of the early nineties prompted renewed demands for "race first, politics after." What the race needed, proponents demanded, was unity and property rather than politics. The traditionally political Huntsville *Gazette* now advised southern blacks to "look to your business," and "politics just now will take care of politics." The Topeka *Evening Call* offered similar advice to western blacks when it lamented: "O for a Negro millionaire." This philosophy of economics-before-politics was more often expressed in black papers and by black spokesmen, including Taylor, Stewart, Still, Jere Brown, and J. W. B. Bowen. Brown, politically active in Ohio for years, now expressed hope that the political upheaval of 1892 would drive many of the bright young men of the race into other pursuits. In 1894, Bowen wrote that he regretted that the black man was "dragged from the plow to the legislature to become drunken with the new wine of political power." Several conventions attempted to popularize further the abnegation of politics. Five hundred black Alabamians resolved: "We believe education, property and practical religion will give us every right and privilege enjoyed by other citizens, and therefore, that our interest can be served by bending all our energies to securing them rather than by dwelling on the past or by fault finding and complaining." John Chandler, in "What Must the Negro Do?" popularized the same sentiment in verse:

> Leave the demagogue alone
> Nor waste time with politic crooks
> Be honest, work make bright your home
> Confine yourself to books.[64]

This philosophy, later best articulated by Booker T. Washington, was everywhere being heard, but many blacks still defended the necessity of political participation. The National Federation of Colored Men of the United States, founded in Detroit in December 1895, advocated the continued use of the political process as the best way to fight for the redress of grievances. R. C. O. Benjamin, in a history of blacks published in 1896, insisted that the race remain as an important factor in politics and that the task before them was to understand the responsibilities of citizenship in order that they might enjoy the benefits of political society and good government. Many consistently agreed with Henry M. Turner's charge that "for the Negro to stay out of politics is to level himself with a horse or a cow." Frederick Douglass adamantly opposed any talk of even temporarily denying blacks the vote. "Do not make illiteracy a bar to the ballot," he warned, "but make the ballot a bar to illiteracy."[65]

But it was clear by 1895, as South Carolina followed Florida and Mississippi in calling a constitutional convention to legally disfranchise its black population, that blacks were loosing their fight for political equality. As blacks increasingly confronted election abuses and proscription all across the South, they demanded that the federal government take action. A petition presented on the floor of the House of Representatives lamented that blacks were more denizens than citizens and that in at least three southern states citizenship was a complete farce. At no time, the petitioners insisted, had blacks ceased demanding their rights; to the contrary they were becoming more militant. "Our calm deliberate advice," the petition concluded, "is for every kind of warfare legitimately and courageously in the demand for every right."[66]

But it was an inflated rhetoric that ignored reality. Black Americans had been accustomed to leaders like Douglass who agitated incessantly for full political rights, but their efforts had ultimately failed to stem the tide of disfranchisement and segregation. The political revolution continued to move backward. When in February 1895 blacks eulogized Douglass as "the greatest Negro the world has ever produced and one of the great men of the age," many of them were looking for a very different kind of leader. It was in this climate that Booker T. Washington came to the fore. Seven months after Douglass's death, Washington, speaking at the Atlanta Exposition, proposed that efforts to maintain the black political revolution be curtailed in favor of economic progress. Increasingly disillusioned about the efficacy of the vote, more and more blacks were willing to accept Washington's advice as their most realistic course. White support of Washington's philosophy and leadership helped ensure that his ideas would have widespread impact. His disavowal of federal aid for any segment of the population combined with his philosophy of self-help and economic advancement meshed well with the Social Darwinistic philosophy and the laissez-faire industrial dynamic of America in the 1890s.[67]

The initial response to Washington's speech was largely positive. After the first press coverage, Washington wrote, "the manner in which my Atlanta address has been received in the country has given me the surprise of my life. Of the 300 colored news-papers in the United States I do not know of a single one that has said anything against my address." Fortune and Stewart, although still political activists, joined other black leaders in sending congratulations. Fortune heralded the Alabama educator as the new Douglass.[68]

As Washington's speech received greater scrutiny, however, criticism grew. George N. Smith condemned the comparison of Washington to Douglass, saying it was like comparing "a pigmy to a giant." The *Daily Crusader* labeled the speech another apology for the South made while South Carolinians were busy at their constitutional convention disfranchising the race. L. W. Pulies concluded that Washington's philosophy "was one which conceded the inferiority of the negro." Calvin Chase bemoaned that Washington had "said something that was death to the Afro-American."[69]

During Cleveland's second administration, more blacks considered a variety of political alternatives than at any time before. During the first year, black Democrats were more active and visible than ever. Although the Populists showed less interest in racial unity after 1892, many blacks continued to join the new party. Neither alternative, however, was embraced by the majority. The Cleveland Democrats never extended to blacks the recognition and protection they demanded; the party's southern contingent continued to be identified as the source of proscription and terror. After 1893, as the Democrats were increasingly blamed for the nation's depression, black Democracy rapidly eroded. Despite its early promise, Populism proved too racist and too ineffective to offer recognition or protection. Washington's philosophy deemphasizing politics began to be the most commonly endorsed alternative to active Republicanism, both because of widespread perception of the limited effectiveness of politics and the reality of increasing intimidation and violence. But a large number of black Americans continued to believe that the federal government could still protect their rights and that electing Republicans was the most effective way of assuring that it would. In 1896, they once again put their faith in the outcome of a presidential election.

7

The Setting Sun: The Election of 1896

By 1896, the black political revolution had been effectively nullified by the Bourbon South. In those southern states that had instituted legal means of disfranchisement, the black vote had been reduced to less than 25 percent; in Mississippi it had been virtually eliminated. In states where a significant number of blacks did still vote, belief in the practicality of accommodation or the reality of coercion and violence compelled many to vote Democratic. Only in North Carolina and Texas did a majority of southern blacks still vote Republican.[1]

The rise of Booker T. Washington symbolized the revolution's failure. Northern Republicans embraced Washington's accommodationist stance as an alternative to seemingly futile efforts to protect black suffrage. As Republican leaders who had traditionally at least given lip service to black rights died or were defeated for office, they were replaced by a younger generation to whom, as Morgan Kousser explains, "abolition and Reconstruction seemed irrelevant, merely picturesque or even evil." Despite widespread disfranchisement and violence, abandonment by northern and Republican whites, and the growing adherence of blacks to a philosophy of accommodation, many blacks continued to hope for the election of a president who would restore their rights. To them the election of 1896 was Armageddon—the last chance to save the political revolution of the 1860s.[2]

In South Carolina, where the Democrats had followed Mississippi's lead in enacting constitutional disfranchisement, black political activity briefly proliferated again. The state's Republicans, most of them black, called a special convention because "the very life of suffrage in this State is at stake and other cherished rights and interests are imperiled." Blacks outside the South agreed that the race's desperate situation still demanded united political action. In August 1895, the Omaha *Enterprise* called for a meeting of black leaders prior to the Republican National Convention to organize a common strategy. "You may cry peace, peace," the paper warned, "but there will be no peace, until the united protests of nine millions of Afro-American citizens shall be expressed with no uncertain sound."[3]

Several groups heeded the *Enterprise*'s warning and held meetings to organize precampaign strategy. In September 1895, a committee headed by John G. Jones, George L. Knox, and E. H. Morris bitterly complained that, after thirty years of emancipation, the problems of blacks still included disfranchisement, Jim Crowism, and lynch law; they called for a conference in Detroit to prepare a presentation of black grievances for the Republican convention. The Colored National Convention, meeting in Washington the following month, denounced the Cleveland administration, reaffirmed allegiance to the Republican party, advocated gold and silver, and came within a few votes of endorsing Governor William McKinley of Ohio for the Republican nomination. In April 1896, a group of Virginians headed by John Langston also organized a preconvention meeting to plan strategy for obtaining equal justice at the convention. John Lynch, George Murray, and E. E. Cooper were among the prominent blacks attending the meeting which resolved to fight particularly for a plank against lynching to be included in the Republican platform.[4]

By early 1894, the black press was speculating about the 1896 presidential nominees. When William McKinley, the Republican front-runner, traveled through the South in the spring of 1895, blacks praised him for his courteous treatment. John Lynch frequently campaigned for McKinley and reported that southern blacks were behind him. The Savannah *Tribune* found the Ohio governor to be the choice of a majority in Georgia and the Beaufort *New South* made the same claim in South Carolina. The Ashville (N.C.) *Colored Enterprise* called McKinley the greatest statesman in the country, and in neighboring Tennessee the Colored McKinley Club of Memphis was one of several black groups promoting his candidacy. Former Louisianian H. C. C. Astwood predicted that most of Louisiana's delegates would be for McKinley. The Baltimore *Afro-American* supported McKinley as a man who would protect all citizens and who was right on the tariff issue. In August 1895, the *Bee* came out for McKinley, contending that he was a man with backbone enough to enforce the laws.[5]

McKinley also had black support in the Midwest, particularly in his home state of Ohio. Cleveland's two black papers, the *Gazette* and the *Leader*, both supported him. Editor Smith of the *Gazette* looked forward to a "new deal" in which the "old and useless barnacle" would be set aside and worthy young black leaders from both the North and South recognized. John Green, once an Ohio state senator, knew McKinley personally and assured blacks that the Ohio governor was a "true and tried friend of the colored American." A majority of black Republicans and black newspapers in Kansas and Nebraska agreed. The Leavenworth *Herald* lamented the considerable infighting among blacks supporting different candidates and exhorted them to support McKinley because "this is the year when the people desire a man who will awaken our industries and who believes in protecting not only our industries but that which is more important, American citizenship."[6]

Despite McKinley's considerable popularity, there was black support for other candidates. James Clarkson worked hard to persuade southern blacks, particularly Pinchback, to support Iowa senator William B. Allison, but he found the Louisiana leader solid for House Speaker Thomas Reed. Clarkson was more successful in Texas, where N. Wright Cuney was credited with electing ten Allison delegates. Thomas Fortune sometimes supported Allison and Whitefield McKinley did so consistently. John Langston and Alexander Crummell joined Pinchback in backing Reed. The Indianapolis *Freeman* initially supported President Harrison but efforts to win converts to the Harrison camp met with little success in the South. Before he endorsed Allison,

Fortune supported Levi P. Morton, who continued to have black backers around the country. But despite this support for other candidates, the Indianapolis *Freeman* conceded by mid–1895 that McKinley was the candidate of blacks; that he was perceived as the only man with the courage to go out of his way for a down-trodden race.[7]

Demands for "full justice" at the Republican convention were seriously undermined by the selection of St. Louis as the convention site. Most blacks were unconvinced by promises from St. Louis officials that there would be no discrimination. Even the staunchly Republican Cleveland *Gazette* condemned the choice as the most shameful treatment of blacks in the party's history. Demanding equal accommodations, even if this meant moving the convention to another city, became the preoccupation of the black press. Their predictions proved correct; when black delegates arrived they found the color line sharply drawn by St. Louis hotelkeepers. Some white northern delegates, particularly McKinley supporters, protested and put pressure on the city's leaders to eliminate their blatant Jim Crowism. The Massachusetts delegation refused to accept rooms unless blacks were also welcome. Finally the Indianapolis *Freeman* could proclaim that the "narrow bigoted people" of St. Louis had been taught a lesson—blacks were being given rooms.[8]

At the convention, blacks from New England tended to be for Reed, those from New York for Morton, and the Iowans for Allison. The southern delegation, by far the largest group of blacks present, was nearly solid for McKinley. J. Madison Vance of Louisiana had the honor of seconding the Ohio Senator's nomination. McKinley was easily nominated and chose Garret A. Hobart as his running mate. The Richmond *Planet* claimed that with this ticket and one of the best platforms ever, all people should rally behind the Republicans to save the country from its present sad state. McKinley's racial credentials were reminiscent of his Republican predecessors; as a young man he had opposed slavery and as a congressman he had countenanced federal protection of black voting. But the priorities of McKinley, like those of his party, had changed; for the first time since the Civil War the Republican platform made no mention of black voting.[9]

Despite four years of Democratic rule and increased attention to black Democracy, the Democratic convention was again overshadowed by Republican politics. Press coverage generally focused on Cleveland. The economic depression had eroded his black support, but some faithful Clevelandites promised to support the president if he decided to run again. J. E. W. Thompson claimed Cleveland was the only man in the party who could win and thus maintain the reforms of the past four years. In May 1896, Cyrus D. Bell, editor of the Democratic Omaha *Enterprise*, noted that William Jennings Bryan of Nebraska was emerging as a possible nominee. Bell, who knew Bryan personally, admired the Nebraska candidate but doubted that his financial policy would work.[10]

The Democrats met in Chicago in July. Following a stirring speech for free silver, the most emotional issue of the day, Bryan was nominated with Arthur Sewall as his vice-presidential running mate. The Omaha *Afro-American Sentinel* proudly proposed "three cheers for Bryan, the boy orator of the Platte," but joined the majority of blacks in endorsing McKinley and Hobart.[11]

Although the Leavenworth *Herald* wrote it off as "too dead in this country to create even a ripple," the Populist party was still a viable alternative in 1896. Economic distress had resulted in a 42 percent increase in the Populist vote in 1894. The nomination of a liberal Democrat, however, placed party members in a dilemma. Fearful of splitting the liberal vote between two candidates, the party reluctantly supported Bryan but named their own vice-presidential candidate, Tom Watson, in order to retain party identity. S. D. Walton, one of the two black Georgia delegates at the convention, seconded Watson's nomination on the grounds that Watson had made it possible for blacks to vote freely in Georgia. The nominations of Bryan to head both the Democratic and Populist tickets produced little inducement for blacks to leave the Republican party. Bryan had impressed some middle-class blacks when, as a congressman from Nebraska, he had advocated federal aid to black education, but his support for limiting black political rights convinced many others that his idealistic rhetoric for "letting the people rule" was intended for whites only.[12]

The election of 1896 was the most emotional and divisive

election since before the Civil War. In this "Battle of the Standards" many Americans feared that the country's economic future
was at stake as they chose between the Republican defense of
the gold standard and the Democratic/Populist demand for the
coinage of silver at 16:1. Although blacks as always gave priority
to racial questions, they also stressed economic issues more than
ever before. In April, the Cleveland *Gazette* demanded that protection for American industries become the all-absorbing issue
of the campaign because "upon this issue depends the great and
vital interests of all that is germane to our national prosperity."
But most of the country was far more captivated by the emotional
issue of monetary policy. Black support of McKinley was often
tied to demands for the guarantee of sound money and restored
prosperity. Just before his nomination, the Omaha *Sentinel*
praised McKinley as "the splendid apostle of protection and
reciprocity." The Parsons *Weekly Blade* called for a "vote for
McKinley, Hobart, Protection and Prosperity, and let alone the
free coinage of silver at a rate of 16 to 1." In August, a National
Republican Protective Association was formed by prominent
Washington blacks to educate the masses on campaign issues,
particularly in those states where Democrats were trying to appeal to black voters with the silver issue. Several papers feared
that the campaign for free silver was influencing some blacks,
and warned them that it would only aid the silver mineowners
who would allow blacks neither stock nor labor in their mines.[13]

Although the New York *Times* found blacks virtually solid for
protection and sound money, there were some who supported
the free coinage of silver. Approximately eighty delegates from
eleven states met at the National Negro Democratic Convention
in August and voted opposition to the "monopolies, trusts, combines, and millionaries [sic]" of the Republican party and support
for the coinage of silver. A few days later, black Democrats from
Omaha formed the Colored Bimetallic League, one of several
black Democratic silver clubs scattered across the country. Iowan
George E. Taylor, president of the Colored People's National
Protective Association, was the leading black spokesman for protection and silver coinage. In his "National Appeal to the American Negro: Why We Should Favor the Chicago Platform,"
Taylor claimed that the gold standard was pro-capitalist while

silver money was advantageous to the people. Insisting that nothing in the Republican plank spoke for their rights, Taylor admonished blacks to cease voting Republican just because Lincoln was a Republican and to join forces and share political rewards with the silverites.[14]

Other black Democrats offered more traditional reasons why the race should vote Democratic. The Negro Democratic League campaigned, but was weakened by the resignation of C. H. J. Taylor as president. Alexander E. Manning, sergeant-at-arms at the Democratic convention, was elected to succeed Taylor; he appointed a committee to solicit Bryan's views on racial issues, but it received no meaningful response. In Kansas, William Kelly, one of several prominent black Democratic campaigners in the state, asserted that when blacks consistently voted Republican their political status had only grown worse because they were aligned against their fellow citizens. Now, he urged, they should vote for the candidate of the common people, William Jennings Bryan.[15]

The depression years and patronage disappointments, however, had eroded black Democracy, and Bryan could command less black support than Cleveland had four years earlier. The Minneapolis *World* and the Buffalo *Globe*, two of the few black papers that consistently supported the Democratic ticket, had both folded by late September; the Cleveland *Gazette* gleefully questioned if Democratic free silver had given out too soon. The editor of the Omaha *Enterprise* admitted that he was for the gold standard but assured readers that he would stand by Bryan and the economic position of the party because he was a Democrat. In the South, the Atlanta *Daily Opinion* was possibly alone in consistently campaigning for Bryan and Sewall.[16]

Conflicting contemporary observations make an accurate assessment of Bryan's black support difficult. In contrast to the Weekly *Call*, which claimed that there was virtually no black Democratic support in Kansas, the New York *Times* reported that approximately three thousand out of fifteen thousand black voters in the state were for Bryan. Part of the discrepancy can be explained by the fact that some of Bryan's black supporters considered themselves Populists rather than Democrats.[17]

The Parsons *Weekly Blade* concluded that blacks who followed

the Populists could give no reason for doing so, that the "Po-
pucrats just aren't in it." The Populists did, however, have some
black support although probably less than in the elections of two
and four years before. The dilemma for southern black Populists
was that support of the party's presidential nominee meant support of a Democrat. The Richmond *Planet* described the Populist
endorsement of Bryan as an unholy alliance of the worst elements of both parties. Some blacks were even more critical of
the Populists than the Democrats. The Indianapolis *Freeman*
warned Bryan to shake off Populism, "a breeder of discord and
political heresies." Some southern leaders continued to advocate
at least a fusion arrangement with the Populists, but the majority
supported the Republicans. In North Carolina, an internal struggle for leadership prompted James H. Young, state assemblyman
and editor of the Raleigh *Gazette*, and politician George White
to endorse the Populists, but most of the state's black leadership
supported McKinley. In South Carolina, George Murray was for
free silver yet advocated Republican victory as the best chance
for salvaging black suffrage. In Georgia, William J. White credited the Populists and Tom Watson with having integrated the
ballot box, but Republicans William J. Pledger and H. J. Johnson
worked to counter Watson's black support. John Raynor again
formed black Populist clubs in Texas, but they attracted few
members and were threatened with the revolt of many former
supporters. A black Populist caucus in the state revealed limited
support for the Democratic/Populist platform of free silver.[18]

Many former black Populists and Cleveland Democrats now
supported the Republicans. The black press was virtually united
for McKinley and Hobart. In addition to their general antipathy
toward the Democratic party, some blacks were as fearful of the
Great Commoner's alleged radicalism as many whites were. The
Wilmington (N.C.) *Afro-American Presbyterian* rejoiced that no
black had taken part in the Democratic convention and thus
could not be labeled "lunatic, dervish, communist, anarchist and
the like." The Omaha *Sentinel* warned that blacks could not afford to be identified with Bryan as he sought to incite trouble
between employers and employees.[19]

Blacks also drew upon traditional anti-Democratic arguments
to oppose Bryan. The Raleigh *Gazette* warned black Southerners

that Democrats were again trying to assure their party's victory by prohibiting black participation in the election through violence and fraud. William H. Anderson listed four reasons he thought blacks should fight Bryan's election: (1) Bryan lacked the moral stamina for supporting the rights of all citizens, (2) he evaded the racial question which was indirectly a justification of southern discrimination, (3) he sought to flatter northern blacks more than those from the South, and (4) although he condemned lynching, he implied that blacks were guilty of the crimes that they were accused of.[20]

Flowery praise of the Republican party was again common. The Richmond *Planet* proclaimed: "Major William McKinley is the only Moses in the desert of socialism, anarchism and communism." H. C. Smith simply concluded: "We should support his candidacy BECAUSE HE IS OUR FRIEND." But flattery was still combined with admonitions to the party to do justice to black citizens. The New Orleans *Weekly Vindicator* warned that "the republican party needs the colored vote, not only at the South, but more necessarily in the east and west, and it has got to be respected and husbanded, and he who spurns or rejects it is both a bigot and a fool." Many black Republican campaigners were concerned that the money question was given too much attention to the exclusion of racial problems. Black poet Paul Lawrence Dunbar dramatized their concern in his poem, "The Real Question":

> Well you folks kin keep on shoutin' wif yo' gold or silvah cry.
> But I tell you people hams is sceerce an' fowls is roostin' high,
> An' hit ain't de so't o' money dat is pesterin' my min'
> But de question o want answered 's how to git at any kin![21]

Although Republican campaign manager Mark Hanna raised a record amount to finance McKinley's campaign and flooded the country with literature and speakers, he devoted very little time or money to the organization of blacks, except in the border states. By midway through the campaign, many black politicians were chafing under the Republican party's lack of attention. For the first time since emancipation, the familiar voice of Frederick Douglass was not heard, but many perennial black orators still stumped for the GOP. They warned the Republicans frequently, however, that blacks would leave the party in droves if something was not done on their behalf. Some of the discontent was dissipated by the creation of a black department of the National Republican Committee, located in Chicago and directed by Ferdinand L. Barnett and Richard Greener. Their appointments were widely heralded as recognition of a new leadership among blacks, but warnings were also common that they could succeed only if given proper aid. A limited number of black spokesmen were financed by the committee, but most continued working for the party by using their own resources or those of some black organization. Blanche K. Bruce became the first black man to deliver a speech under the auspices of the National Republican Committee when he campaigned in New Jersey. Richard Greener and John Langston campaigned in the South with committee backing. Despite the support of these noted black leaders, however, the committee gave less responsibility to black spokesmen than usual. Greener was critical that, although they permitted him to discuss financial issues, they commissioned most black orators simply to "woop 'em up" by waving the bloody shirt and appealing to emotion rather than dealing in depth with issues or becoming deeply involved in planning the campaign.[22]

Because most of McKinley's campaign was conducted from the porch of his home, blacks joined other Republicans in traveling there to hear him speak. Approximately one hundred Canton blacks welcomed their hometown's nominee on July 3. In August, H. C. Smith led five hundred blacks from Cleveland, Akron, and the surrounding area to visit McKinley and declare their great admiration. Bishop Arnett, spokesman for three hundred delegates from the A.M.E. Church who visited McKinley, declared, "I have shaken hands with every President from Lincoln down, and I want the honor of conferring the Presidential succession on you." Eight million black people, he added, looked on McKinley as the "star of hope." Other black groups from the surrounding area visited McKinley, but few from farther away could afford the trip. The activities of thousands of loyal black Republicans centered on the McKinley clubs that sprang up all across the nation.[23]

Faithful black papers and spokesmen, generally optimistic that the 1896 election would return the Republicans to Washington and that this would have a positive impact on restoring their rights, worked hard for the ticket in the final weeks. "Democracy has always been the bitterest enemy," warned the Cleveland *Gazette*. "Vote against all of its many candidates." Only ingrates, scorned the Parsons *Weekly Blade*, would now desert "the immortal party of Lincoln."[24]

In November 1896, McKinley was easily elected. The Indianapolis *Freeman* rejoiced that the country had thus been saved, and the *Weekly Blade* pointed out that, where permitted, blacks had "stood up loyally for the nation's honor." Where blacks were free to vote, they had voted overwhelmingly Republican. But in much of the South they were not free. In South Carolina, for example, where twenty years before 96 percent of eligible blacks had voted, in 1896 only 11 percent went to the polls.[25]

When shortly after his election McKinley thanked blacks for their part in this triumph of Republican principles, he inspired renewed hope that political rights might be restored and that they might be granted places in the new president's administration. There was even talk once again of a black man being named to the cabinet. But some blacks were more cognizant of the racist reality of American society in 1896. Alexander Crummell wrote shortly after the election that McKinley was "(negatively) a friend of the Negro" and, therefore, would do nothing toward promoting black participation in the public service. McKinley's inaugural address gave Crummell little reason to rethink his assessment. Although the new president made general reference to "free and fair elections" and condemned lynchings, he also discarded the Republican inaugural tradition of specifically demanding that black rights be respected. Instead, in this and later policy statements, he emphasized reconciliation and assumed a paternalistic stance toward blacks, an approach to southern racial problems that meshed well with Booker T. Washington's philosophy. His views also accorded well with those of most of white America. Several months before McKinley took office, the Supreme Court gave judicial sanction to segregation when, in the *Plessy* v. *Ferguson* decision, it declared "separate but equal" treatment constitutional. The decision marked the triumph of racism over the Reconstruction amendments. The Indianapolis *Freeman* expressed well the black response:

The decision will have a demoralizing effect. It will do much towards destroying the faith that Negroes have in the institutions that white men control. At the reception of this news the Negroes of this country will ponder well his situation. It may not be the setting sun of his hopes but such decisions are drastic upon his reasoning powers. What will be done? What must be done to fortify and make impregnable his position in this country, is a burning question.... It is the darkest hour before dawn. Victory, somehow, will be snatched from the teeth of seeming defeat. The oaken crown shall be perched on him who seemed all vanquished. In due time, in this most unequal contest, the odds will be casted on the proper side.[26]

8

The Cancer of Disappointed Hopes: Conclusion

In 1891, English essayist James Bryce, in his generally astute observation of American life, reported that most blacks did not resent being denied the right to vote. Much of nineteenth-century white America agreed. The thesis of black apathy in the face of political discrimination has become entrenched in much subsequent historiography. In an early history of disfranchisement, a member of the Mississippi convention of 1890 wrote: "Suffrage had come to them [blacks] unsolicited; it departed from them unregretted." Few twentieth-century historians would agree, but a number have described growing political apathy following increased discrimination and violence. C. Vann Woodward, in his monumental study *Origins of the New South*, argues that with "the Negro himself apathetic, resistance to disfranchisement from within the South reached a low point by 1898." Gerald Gaither's study of blacks and Populism agrees that, by the 1890s, only a "small group of blacks" advocated continued political participation. Undoubtedly for thousands of poor blacks, the day-to-day struggle for survival did preclude concern with political activity. Some became disillusioned, believing that political participation was either a meaningless gesture or an invitation to violence. They sold their votes or did not vote at all. But many blacks continued to fight to maintain rights won during Reconstruction.[1]

Determination to preserve the perquisites of citizenship united black Americans across class, sectional, and political lines. The removal of the last federal troops in 1877 was one of a series of events symbolizing the reversal of the Reconstruction revolution. Over the next two decades blacks confronted one setback after another as they struggled in vain to maintain what they could of their political position. It was not, wrote Frederick Douglass, "a Negro problem, not a race problem, but a national problem; whether the American people will ultimately administer equal justice to all the varieties of the human race in this Republic." But black political retrogression was rarely perceived by white Americans as their problem; even that sector of white society most sensitive to black rights and aspirations lost concern with the abrogation of those rights. It was, therefore, left largely to blacks themselves to fight a retrogression that left them denizens, not citizens.[2]

Much of the effort to maintain and restore citizenship rights focused on the race's relationship to political parties, particularly to the Republican party. For some, identification with the Republicans went far beyond mere toleration. Because they credited the party of Lincoln with their emancipation, some blacks embraced it with much the same fervor that they did their religion. In 1890, a semiliterate black man from Messena, Georgia, wrote Douglass, "I wonts to see the light done here in Georgia I am a Negro man an is an Republican man."[3]

For such individuals, psychological dependency on the Republican party acquired during the war and Reconstruction was difficult to cast off even after the party had largely abandoned the cause of black rights. But many of even the least educated blacks increasingly realized that the Republicans did not always deserve such allegiance. An example of this ambivalence toward the Republican party's devotion to their cause was expressed by a poor Mississippian shortly after the Republican defeat in 1892. He wrote Douglass of his concern that blacks were not allowed to vote in the election and that the Republicans were not doing enough to protect them. "I think you old Republicans shud look ind that," he urged "to see whether a negro has every right or not."[4]

Many black leaders, rather than leave the party, attempted to persuade it to act as the agent of black freedom; they reminded the Republicans that they had a moral duty to protect blacks who were consistently loyal to them. Initially this approach primarily meant lobbying for federal laws to protect black people and for federal enforcement of those laws, but by the 1880s and 1890s, black leaders focused equal attention on political appointments as symbolic recognition of racial equality. Relations with the Republicans during this period grew increasingly strained as blacks concluded the party was failing to meet either obligation.

Despite their close identification with the party, black Republicans were a group apart. Racial identity always transcended political labels. Unlike other groups in late-nineteenth-century America, black political activity was overwhelmingly influenced by race rather than by class, religion, or other socioeconomic factors. In 1883, the Washington *Grit* succinctly explained the political nature of many blacks: "Politically, we are Republicans, pure and simple. But when the rights or interests of the colored race are involved, we become more Negro than anything else." In their anomalous position, blacks functioned in many ways as an independent lobby. Black methods, goals, leadership, and, to some extent, organization were distinct from the Republican party at large. The two groups were united by tenuous bonds. By 1896, few blacks were as loyal to the Republicans as many had been in the late 1860s.[5]

As a result, they constantly searched for political alternatives. Although many condemned the Democratic party as the architect of disfranchisement, a small minority counseled affiliation. To some southern blacks, forced to live in the midst of Democratic rule, accommodation seemed the only choice. Some northern blacks determined that the Democratic position on such issues as the tariff was more in accord with their needs. Others saw the Democratic party as a vehicle for agitation. In their search for a way to reform the Republican party, they believed that threats or even actual support of the Democrats might work. When the focus of discontent was on Republican ingratitude and desertion, Democratic terrorism was sometimes downplayed. When Grover Cleveland, the only Democratic president of the era, proved no more racist than Republican chief executives had been, a minority of blacks concluded that the Democratic party—

at least its northern "Cleveland" branch—could be supported on its own merits.

But most blacks, although disillusioned with the Republicans, could not countenance support of the Democrats. Consequently, numerous third parties, notably the Populist party, were promoted as alternatives. Although the Populist party too was imbued with racism, it briefly offered some hope of political cooperation between poor whites and blacks of the South and West. But Populism was short-lived; its collapse led to further deterioration of black rights.

The opprobrium associated with the name Democratic and the futility of third-party support led some blacks to advise the ill-defined course of "independence," but they were rarely able to transform their rhetoric into a practical political program. Another alternative, particularly urged after major political setbacks, was to refrain from political activity altogether. Some who advocated this course were accommodationists, motivated by a desire to appease whites and end racial conflict. Others concluded that political participation had failed and that they would have to fight for their rights outside of the party framework. However, the demands of both conservatives and militants that political activity be abandoned were usually condemned until 1896 when the economics-before-politics philosophy of Booker T. Washington began to gain ascendancy.

Regardless of the specific political course advocated, many blacks continued to espouse racial unification and self-help. Conventions were frequently called and organizations formed in an attempt to bring black people together. The Afro-American League, the major all-black political organization of the period, failed, however, to prevent the further erosion of black rights and lasted only a short time. Effective black unity was always difficult to achieve. Often black leaders were as suspicious and contemptuous of one another as they were of whites. In addition, the race did not have the financial resources necessary to make formal unification successful or to fight white opposition.

The hopelessness of their situation was reflected in the ideological inconsistency of many blacks, an inconsistency reflected in most black newspapers and by most leaders. They searched in vain for the most efficacious political course including Republicanism, Democracy, Populism, other third parties, independence, and the disavowal of politics. Rarely did any black spokesman maintain a dogmatic political ideology; the insurmountable obstacles to perceived ends did not allow it. The limited extant evidence suggests that the masses of blacks followed the fluctuations of their leaders. Vincent DeSantis perceptively describes the political reality of black people at the end of this period: "Depressed by Republican policies since the end of Reconstruction, torn between loyalty for and resentment against the party of emancipation, and severely restricted in their privileges of voting, southern Negroes presented a picture of helplessness and confusion."[6]

Blacks had searched persistently for the best political course to pursue because they were determined to be American citizens. But by 1896 the fight for political equality appeared lost. The Supreme Court decreed separation the law of the land. Florida, Mississippi, and South Carolina led in constitutional disfranchisement of blacks; other southern states effectively followed suit through legislative action. In all of the South, coercion and terror assured Jim Crow's ascendancy. The number of lynchings increased and became the symbol of unassailable white power. A growing number of blacks adopted accommodation as the only alternative to violence, and that philosophy replaced agitation as the dominant black political response. Blacks, who had in 1876 successfully elected black senators and congressmen and who had aspired to have black men nominated for the vice-presidency and named to the cabinet, could not vote at all in 1896. The old question of what political party would best serve the interests of black people became moot as the solidly Democratic South allowed them no participation at all. It was a time of despair for all black people. Just after McKinley's election, the Indianapolis *Freeman* lamented: "Way down in the heart of many who have assayed forth in many political battles, the cancer of disappointed hopes has been eating away the heart's core."[7]

In the early years of the twentieth century, the black political revolution was in full retreat. The high hopes of black Americans for political equality had been dashed in the decades after the end of Reconstruction, but the ideals of the revolution survived to be passed on from one generation of blacks to the next. The legacy of nineteenth-century blacks to future generations can sometimes be traced in individual cases. James Monroe Trotter, who demanded equality for his generation in the 1880s, set an example for his son William Monroe Trotter, a leading agitator for black rights in the twentieth century. W.E.B. Du Bois, influenced by Fortune for whom he briefly worked, was transformed from a conservative young man who opposed the Lodge bill to the leading opponent of accommodation. A. Phillip Randolph, a black labor leader in the twentieth century, recalled that his father's stories of Reconstruction days in Florida inspired him to challenge the barriers to black political and occupational participation which his generation confronted. The influence was generally less direct, but all black people in the twentieth century can trace the genesis of their political advances to the demands for equality that were first articulated years before.

Notes

Preface

1. J. Morgan Kousser, *The Shaping of Southern Politics: Suffrage Restriction and the Establishment of the One-Party South, 1880–1910* (New Haven: Yale University Press, 1974), 11.
2. Willie Lee Rose, *Slavery and Freedom* (New York: Oxford University Press, 1982), 98, 110.
3. Nell I. Painter, *Exodusters: Black Migration to Kansas After Reconstruction* (New York: Alfred A. Knopf, 1976), 17–34; Lewis Suggs, *The Black Press in the South, 1865–1979* (Westport, Conn.: Greenwood Press, 1983), x; Leon F. Litwack, *Been in the Storm So Long* (New York: Alfred A. Knopf, 1979), 526; Rose, *Slavery and Freedom*, 103.

1. A Revolution Goes Backward

1. Leon F. Litwack, *Been in the Storm So Long: The Aftermath of Slavery* (New York: Alfred A. Knopf, 1979), 122, 532, 547; James M. McPherson, *The Negro's Civil War* (New York: Alfred A. Knopf, 1965), 271–276, 291; Nell Irvin Painter, *Exodusters: Black Migration to Kansas After Reconstruction* (New York: Alfred A. Knopf, 1976), 30.
2. Joel Williamson, *After Slavery: The Negro in South Carolina During Reconstruction, 1861–1877* (Chapel Hill: University of North Carolina Press, 1965), 373; Painter, *Exodusters*, 11; Litwack, *Been in the Storm*, 507, 531.
3. Litwack, *Been in the Storm*, 524–529.
4. Ibid., 515.

5. Paul Kleppner, *The Third Electoral System, 1853–1892* (Chapel Hill: University of North Carolina Press, 1979), 90–96; William Gillette, *Retreat from Reconstruction, 1869–1879* (Baton Rouge: Louisiana State University Press, 1979), 19; LaWanda and John H. Cox, "Negro Suffrage and Republican Politics: The Problem of Motivation in Reconstruction Historiography," *Journal of Southern History,* XXXIII (August 1967), 303–330; Litwack, *Been in the Storm,* 538.

6. Williamson, *After Slavery,* 336–337; Thomas Holt, *Black Over White: Negro Political Leadership in South Carolina During Reconstruction* (Urbana: University of Illinois Press, 1977), 12; J. Morgan Kousser, *The Shaping of Southern Politics: Suffrage Restriction and the Establishment of the One-Party South, 1880–1910* (New Haven: Yale University Press, 1974), 14.

7. W. F. Nowlin, *The Negro in American National Politics* (Boston: The Stratford Company, 1931), 338; U.S. Congress, House, *Congressional Globe,* 42d Cong., 2d sess., 1872, 1443; Lawrence Grossman, *The Democratic Party and the Negro: Northern and National Politics, 1868–1892* (Urbana: University of Illinois Press, 1976), 2; Earl Thorpe, *The Mind of the Negro: An Intellectual History of the Negro People of the United States* (Baton Rouge, La.: Ortlieb Press, 1961); Seth Scheiner, *Negro Mecca: A History of the Negro in New York City, 1865–1920* (New York: New York University Press, 1965), 174; Williamson, *After Slavery,* 339.

8. Martin E. Dann, ed., *The Black Press, 1827–1890: The Quest for National Identity* (New York: G. P. Putnam's Sons, 1971), 52.

9. Gillette, *Retreat from Reconstruction,* 13; William S. McFeeley, *Grant: A Biography* (New York: W. W. Norton, 1982), 238–239; Kenneth Stampp, *The Era of Reconstruction, 1865–1877* (New York: Vintage, 1965), 186–192; Grossman, *The Democratic Party,* 42–43.

10. Gillette, *Retreat from Reconstruction,* 259–279.

11. Ibid., 162, 261, 302.

12. Elsie M. Lewis, "The Political Mind of the Negro, 1865–1900," *Journal of Southern History,* XXI (May 1955), 195–197; U.S. Congress, House, *Congressional Record,* 43d Cong., 1st sess., 4786; August Meier, *Negro Thought in America, 1880–1915* (Ann Arbor: University of Michigan Press, 1964), 26–27.

13. Grossman, *The Democratic Party,* 8, 38–39, 60.

14. Meier, *Negro Thought,* 27; C. Vann Woodward, *Origins of the New South, 1877–1913* (Baton Rouge: Louisiana State University Press, 1951), 218; Litwack, *Been in the Storm,* 521.

15. Williamson, *After Slavery,* 343; Painter, *Exodusters,* 13–14.

16. Kousser, *The Shaping of Southern Politics,* 14; John Mercer Langston, "The Late Colored Convention," Cincinnati *Commercial,* n.d., John Mercer Langston Papers, Fisk Univ.

17. William Dudley Foulke, *Life of Oliver P. Morton* (Indianapolis-Kansas City: The Bowen Merrill Company, 1899), II, 104–106; Washington *People's Advocate*, April 22, 1876; Robert Factor, *The Black Response to America: Men, Ideals and Organization from Frederick Douglass to the NAACP* (Reading, Mass.: Addison-Wesley Publishing Company, 1970), 71.

18. *Proceedings of the Republican National Convention* (Concord, N.H., 1876), 67–68; Keith Ian Polakoff, *The Politics of Inertia: The Election of 1876 and the End of Reconstruction* (Baton Rouge: Louisiana State University Press, 1973), 16.

19. Gillette, *Retreat from Reconstruction*, 214, 304.

20. Kenneth E. Davidson, *The Presidency of Rutherford B. Hayes* (Westport, Conn.: Greenwood Press, 1972), 28; *Proceedings of the Republican National Convention of 1876*, 75; Washington *People's Advocate*, June 10, 24, 1876; Blanche K. Bruce to Rutherford B. Hayes, June 25, 1876, Rutherford B. Hayes Papers, Hayes Presidential Center, Fremont, Ohio.

21. George Sinkler, *The Racial Attitudes of American Presidents from Abraham Lincoln to Theodore Roosevelt* (New York: Doubleday and Company, 1971), 161–173; Davidson, *The Presidency of Rutherford B. Hayes*, 10–16; C. Vann Woodward, *Reunion and Reaction: The Compromise of 1877 and the End of Reconstruction* (Boston: Little, Brown and Company, 1951), 23–24; Polakoff, *The Politics of Inertia*, 115.

22. Grossman, *The Democratic Party*, 51; Washington *People's Advocate*, July 22, 1876.

23. Pinckney B. S. Pinchback to Henry C. Warmouth, March 6, 1876, Henry C. Warmouth Papers, Southern Historical Collection, University of North Carolina; *Proceedings of the Republican National Convention of 1876*, 24, 27, 67–68, 75; Isaac Smith to Hayes, August 22, 1876, Hayes Papers.

24. Frederick Douglass to Zachariah Chandler, August 19, 1876, Zachariah Chandler Papers, Library of Congress; James Haskins, *Pinckney Benton Stewart Pinchback* (New York: Macmillan, 1973), 225; George W. Williams to Frederick Douglass, May 3, 1876, Frederick Douglass Papers, Library of Congress; John Hope Franklin, *George Washington Williams: A Biography* (Chicago: University of Chicago Press, 1985), 43.

25. Grossman, *The Democratic Party*, 52–54; Magnus L. Robinson, Benjamin F. Coke, and R. Branmun Robinson to *Gazette*, September 20, 1876, John Mercer Langston Papers, Howard University; Langston, "The Late Colored Convention," Langston Papers, Fisk University.

26. Grossman, *The Democratic Party*, 52–53; William I. Hair, *Bourbonism and Agrarian Protest: Louisiana Politics, 1877–1900* (Baton Rouge:

Louisiana State University Press, 1971), 4; Lawrence D. Rice, *The Negro In Texas, 1874–1900* (Baton Rouge: Louisiana State University Press, 1971) 41; Williamson, *After Slavery*, 409.

27. Hair, *Bourbonism and Agrarian Protest*, 4–5; Washington *People's Advocate*, August 26, 1876; Robert Denis to Hayes, October 4, 1876, Peter Ford to Hayes, December 15, 1876, Hayes Papers; Leslie Fishel, "The North and the Negro, 1865–1900: A Study in Race Discrimination," (Ph.D. diss., Harvard University, 1953), 142.

28. New York *Times*, July 19, August 31, September 24, October 21, 1876; Peggy Lamson, *The Glorious Failure: Black Congressman Robert Brown Elliott and the Reconstruction in South Carolina* (New York: W. W. Norton, 1973), 251–255; Glenn O. Phillips, "The Response of a West Indian Activist: D. A. Straker, 1842–1908," *Journal of Negro History*, LXVI (Summer 1981), 132; Stampp, *The Era of Reconstruction*, 203; Painter, *Exodusters*, 39; Gillette, *Retreat from Reconstruction*, 307–310.

29. Washington *People's Advocate*, July 29, August 12, 1876; Frenice Logan, *The Negro in North Carolina, 1877–1894* (Chapel Hill: University of North Carolina Press, 1964), 21; A. A. Taylor, *The Negro in Tennessee, 1865–1880* (Washington, D.C.: Associated Publishers, 1941), 259; Williamson, *After Slavery*, 343–344; Kousser, *The Shaping of Southern Politics*, 92; Polakoff, *The Politics of Inertia*, 250.

30. Robert D. Marcus, *Grand Old Party: Political Structure in the Gilded Age, 1880–1896* (New York: Oxford University Press, 1971), 6.

31. John Langston to Hayes, November 9, 1876, Hayes Papers; Program, "Centennial Thanksgiving Services," St. Paul A.M.E. Church, Urbana, Ohio, November 30, 1876, Daniel Murray Collection, Library of Congress; Lee Scott Theisen, "A 'Fair Count' in Florida: General Lew Wallace and the Contested Presidential Election of 1876," *Hayes Historical Journal*, II (Spring 1978), 24.

32. Leo McElroy to Hayes, November 11, 1876, Grandison Harris to Hayes, January 8, 1877, Hayes Papers; Matt Sullivan to Blanche K. Bruce, November 22, 1876, W. W. Dedrick to Bruce, November 14, 1876, Blanche K. Bruce Papers, Howard University; John Roy Lynch, *Reminiscences of an Active Life: The Autobiography of John Roy Lynch* (Chicago: University of Chicago Press, 1970), 194–195.

33. Woodward, *Reunion and Reaction*, 46–64; Pinchback, untitled speech, n.d., Pinckney Benton Stewart Pinchback Papers, Howard University.

34. Woodward, *Reunion and Reaction*, 214; New York *Times*, March 6, 1877, March 11, 1878; Vadalia (La.) Concordia *Eagle*, March 3, 1877; Vincent P. DeSantis, *Republicans Face the Southern Question: The New Departure Years, 1877–1897* (Baltimore: Johns Hopkins Press, 1959), 65; Letters to Hayes, Hayes Papers.

35. H. Wayne Morgan, *From Hayes to McKinley, National Party Politics, 1877–1896* (Syracuse: Syracuse University Press, 1969), 19–22; De-Santis, *Republicans Face the Southern Question*, 66–103; Stanley P. Hirshon, *Farewell to the Bloody Shirt: Northern Republicans and the Southern Negro, 1877–1893* (Bloomington: Indiana University Press, 1962), 62–63; Woodward, *Reunion and Reaction*, 13, 24–28, 35, 211.

36. John Langston, "The Other Phase of Reconstruction," April 17, 1877, Langston Papers, Fisk University; Richard T. Greener to Hayes, March 8, 1877, J. Willis Menard to Hayes, August 8, 1877, Hayes Papers.

37. Woodward, *Reunion and Reaction*, 227; W. D. Derrick et al. to Hayes, March 20, 1877, Huntsville, Alabama, black citizens to Hayes, n.d., Hayes Papers; Tallahassee *Weekly Floridian*, July 24, 1877.

38. Charles R. Williams, ed., *Dairy and Letters of Rutherford Birchard Hayes* (Columbus: Ohio State Archaeological and Historical Society, 1922–1926), III, 417. Hayes wrote, "My course is a firm assertion and maintence of the rights of the colored people of the South according to the Thirteenth, Fourteenth and Fifteenth Amendments coupled with a readiness to recognize all Southern people, without regard to past political conduct, who will now go with me heartily and in good faith in support of these principles."; John Bagwell to Hayes, May 14, December 5, 1878, Hayes Papers; DeSantis, *Republicans Face the Southern Question*, 122–132; David Gerber, *Black Ohio and the Color Line, 1860–1915* (Urbana: University of Illinois Press, 1976), 223–224. Gerber describes the reaction of black Ohioans to Hayes's policy as ranging "from full support to outrage" (223).

39. George W. Williams to Hayes, December 5, 1878, George Hull to Hayes, November 12, 1879, Hayes Papers; Dr. Hiram Revels to *Western Christian Recorder*, n.d., Hiram Revels Papers, Schomberg Collection, New York Public Library; New Orleans *Weekly Louisianian*, April 5, 1879; C. C. Antoine to John Sherman, March 31, 1879, John Sherman Papers, Library of Congress.

40. DeSantis, *Republicans Face the Southern Question*, 123; Gerber, *Black Ohio*, 224; Robert Harlan to John Sherman, August 20, 1877, Sherman Papers; Abraham Barber to Hayes, December 5, 1878, John Freeman to Hayes, July 18, 1876, Hayes Papers; New York *Times*, August 23, 1877.

41. New York *Times*, December 17, 1877; Hair, *Bourbonism and Agrarian Protest*, 19; Okon Edet Uya, *From Slavery to Public Service: Robert Smalls, 1839–1915* (New York: Oxford University Press, 1971), 82; D. Augustus Straker to Douglass, March 24, 1877, Douglass Papers; John R. Lynch to Blanche K. Bruce, October 27, 1877, Bruce Papers; Lynch, *Reminiscences*, 202; Williams, *Dairy and Letters*, II, 501.

42. Benjamin Johnson to Hayes, December 15, 1878, Hayes Papers; Luther W. Redus to Bruce, January 4, 1878, H. M. Foley to Bruce, December 31, 1878, Bruce Papers; New York *Times*, August 23, 1877.

43. H.C.C. Astwood et al. to Hayes, December 28, 1878, Hayes Papers; Charles Vincent, *Black Legislators in Louisiana During Reconstruction* (Baton Rouge: Louisiana State University Press, 1976), 217.

44. Meier, *Negro Thought*, 27; New Orleans *Weekly Louisianian*, December 14, 21, 1878; Washington *People's Advocate*, June 21, 1879; George B. Tindall, *South Carolina Negroes, 1877–1900* (Columbia: University of South Carolina Press, 1952), 36; Samuel Bennett to W. H. Wallace, March 15, 1878, W. H. Wallace Papers, Southern Manuscript Collection, University of North Carolina.

45. P.B.S. Pinchback to Bruce, December 14, 1878, Blanche K. Bruce Papers.

46. Rice, *The Negro in Texas*, 55–60; William Hestor to Bruce, April 6, 1879, Bruce Papers; George T. Downing to Douglass, March 19, 1877, Douglass Papers; Painter, *Exodusters*, 39, Gerald Gaither, *Blacks and the Populist Revolt: Ballots and Bigotry in the "New South"* (University: University of Alabama Press, 1977), 26; George T. Downing to Douglass, March 19, 1877, Douglass Papers.

47. Richard T. Greener to Hayes, March 8, 1877, Hayes Papers; Henry H. Garnet to Douglass, March 19, 1877, Douglass Papers; T. B. Hood to Douglass, March 19, 1877, Archibald Grimke Papers, Howard University; Benjamin Hall to Douglass, March 19, 1877, Douglass Papers, Harvard University; Washington *People's Advocate*, July 19, August 2, 16, 1879; New Orleans *Weekly Louisianian*, March 1, 1879.

48. Peter Klingman, *Josiah Walls: Florida's Black Congressman of Reconstruction* (Gainesville: University Presses of Florida, 1976), 118; Kousser, *The Shaping of Southern Politics*, 24; DeSantis, *Republicans Face the Southern Question*, 91–92; Robert Elliott to John Sherman, November 21, 1879; N. Wright Cuney to Sherman, July 30, 1879, Collector of Customs Applications, Treasury Records, Record Group 56, National Archives; New Orleans *Weekly Louisianian*, September 27, 1879; Edwin Belcher to Sherman, October 7, 1879, June 29, 1880, Sherman Papers; Ruth Currie McDaniel, "Black Power in Georgia: William Pledger and the Takeover of the Republican Party," *Georgia Historical Quarterly*, LXII (Fall 1978), 232; J. M. Bynum to Bruce, November 21, 1877, Hayes Papers.

49. Executive Committee of the National Conference to Leading Colored Men, n.d., Pinchback Papers.

50. Henry Scroggins to Bruce, December 18, 1878, Blanche K. Bruce Papers.

51. Painter, *Exodusters*, 87.

52. Ibid., 138, 87, 92; D. D. Bell to Bruce, January 11, 1878.

53. Billy D. Higgins, "Negro Thought and the Exodus of 1879," *Phylon*, XXII (Spring 1971), 39–40; S. H. Harrin, Henry Ford and B. C. Thomason to Hayes, June 8, 1877, Hayes Papers; L. W. Ballard to Bruce, November 2, 1877, Bruce Papers.

54. Painter, *Exodusters*, 159; Hirshon, *Farewell to the Bloody Shirt*, 64–66.

55. Thomas Conway to Hayes, May 16, 1879, Hayes Papers; Higgins, "Negro Thought," 42–44; Robert G. Athearn, *In Search of Canaan: Black Migration to Kansas, 1879–1880* (Lawrence: University of Kansas Press, 1978), 144–145; Painter, *Exodusters*, 211.

56. Ibid., 243; New Orleans *Weekly Louisianian*, May 1879; Hirshon, *Farewell to the Bloody Shirt*, 72; William Toll, "Free Men, Freedmen, and Race: Black Social Theory in the Gilded Age," *Journal of Southern History*, XLIV (November 1978), 573–574; Higgins, "Negro Thought," 42–50; Athearn, *In Search of Canaan*, 135.

57. Hirshon, *Farewell to the Bloody Shirt*, 72; Richard T. Greener to James A. Garfield, Garfield Papers, Library of Congress; John Smyth et al. to Hayes, 1878, Hayes Papers; Painter, *Exodusters*, 225–227.

58. W. H. Mann to Hayes, January 23, 1880, Phillip Little et al. to Hayes, October 13, 1878, Thomas Farner to Hayes, January 28, 1879, Edward W. Bailey to Hayes, May 28, 1879, Hayes Papers; A. H. Johnson to Sherman, August 1879, Sherman Papers; Athearn, *In Search of Canaan*, 117.

59. T. Thomas Fortune, "Whose Problem is This?," A.M.E. Church *Review*, II (October 1894), 253; T. Thomas Fortune, *The Negro in Politics* (New York, 1886), 26.

60. William S. Scarborough, *Our Political Status* (Xenia, Ohio, 1884), 8; Frederick Douglass, "Causes of Republican Defeat," 1885, Douglass Papers; Cleveland *Gazette*, February 4, 1983; Omaha *Enterprise*, May 16, 1896.

61. W. D. Sherman, Jr. [?] to John Sherman, May 10, 1880, Sherman Papers.

2. Still Necessarily a Republican

1. New Orleans *Weekly Louisianian*, February 15, March 6, 1880; Williamson, *After Slavery*, 362.

2. Justus D. Doenecke, *The Presidency of James A. Garfield and Chester A. Arthur* (Lawrence: Regents Press of Kansas, 1981), 17–21; Morgan, *From Hayes to McKinley*, 62–63.

3. Haskins, *Pinckney Benton Stewart Pinchback*, 245; Pinchback to Bruce, December 14, 1878, Blanche K. Bruce Papers; New Orleans *Weekly Louisianian*, May 8, 15, 22, 1880; DeSantis, *Republicans Face the Southern Question*, 132.

4. Letters to John Sherman, 1879, 1880, especially C. C. Antoine to Sherman, March 31, 1879, Robert Elliott to Sherman, November 21, 1879, J. H. Rainey to Sherman, February 10, 1880, Sherman Papers; Franklin, *George W. Williams*, 95; Loren Schweninger, *James T. Rapier and Reconstruction* (Chicago: University of Chicago Press, 1978), 166; James Hill to Bruce, January 16, 1880, Blanche K. Bruce Papers; Lynch, *Reminiscences of an Active Life*, 211–212; Washington People's Advocate, June 19, 1880.

5. Doenecke, *The Presidency of James A. Garfield*, 14.

6. New Orleans *Weekly Louisianian*, May 15, June 30, 1880; George Henry to Bruce, May 6, 1880, Blanche K. Bruce Papers; Samuel Denny Smith, *The Negro in Congress, 1870–1901* (Chapel Hill: University of North Carolina Press, 1940), 38; Bruce to Garfield, April 27, 1880, Garfield Papers.

7. Franklin, *George W. Williams*, 96; *Proceedings of the Republican National Convention of 1880* (Chicago: John B. Jeffrey Printing and Publishing House, 1881), 2–33, 187, 289; Sadie Daniel St. Clair, "The Public Career of Blanche K. Bruce" (Ph.D. diss., New York University, 1947), 160. The votes were from Louisiana, Illinois, Michigan, and Mississippi; Douglass and Greener to George F. Hoar, June 22, 1880, Douglass Papers, Harvard University; John E. Bruce, *Short Biographical Sketches of Eminent Negro Men and Women* (Yonkers, N.Y.: Gazette Press, 1910), 64.

8. Doenecke, *The Presidency of James A. Garfield*, 22–25, 47–48; Hair, *Bourbonism and Agrarian Protest*, 174.

9. New Orleans *Weekly Louisianian*, June 12, 19, 1880; Letters in the Garfield Papers; G. W. Williams to Sherman, June 17, 1880, Sherman Papers. Much later Douglass acknowledged that he was disappointed because he considered Garfield a relatively weak man who would not be as effective as Grant in ending southern bloodshed. Frederick Douglass, *Life and Times of Frederick Douglass* (Boston: DeWolfe, Fiske, and Company, 1895), 523. For years after the election at least two black men, Mifflin Gibbs and Ferdinand Harris, attended the "306" reunions, gatherings of the 306 delegates who voted for Grant to the end. Mifflin Gibbs, *Shadow and Light: An Autobiography* (New York: Arno Press, 1968), 215.

10. Grossman, *The Democratic Party*, 56; Morgan, *From Hayes to McKinley*, 83; New Orleans *Weekly Louisianian*, July 3, 1880; Washington *People's Advocate*, July 10, 1880.

11. Garfield Papers, particularly John E. Bruce to Garfield, September 24, 1880; New York *Times*, September 20, 1880.

12. John E. Bruce to Garfield, October 4, 1880, Garfield Papers (November 4 was the correct date); Topeka *Tribune*, June 24, July 8, 15, September 9, 16, 1880.

13. Allan Peskin, *Garfield* (Kent, Ohio: Kent State University Press, 1978), 500; Trenton *Sentinel*, August 14, 1880; Topeka *Tribune*, August 5, 1880.

14. Trenton *Sentinel*, July 17, 1880; New York *Times*, July 16, 22, 31, August 26, 1880.

15. Topeka *Tribune*, July 22, 1880; Washington *People's Advocate*, August 28, 1880; New York *Times*, August 6, October 26, 1880.

16. Robert Smalls to Garfield, June 11, 1880, Garfield Papers; New York *Times*, September 17, 1880.

17. Grossman, *The Democratic Party*, 56; Taylor, *The Negro in Tennessee*, 259–261.

18. Washington *People's Advocate*, July 31, August 28, September 25, 1880; Trenton *Sentinel*, September 11, 1880; Unidentified newspaper clipping, October 15, 1800, Langston Papers, Howard University (the correct date was 1880).

19. Grossman, *The Democratic Party*, 81–99.

20. J. H. Smith to James Hill, July 7, 1880, Blanche K. Bruce Papers.

21. Kousser, *The Shaping of Southern Politics*, 14–15; Peskin, *Garfield*, 512.

22. Morgan, *From Hayes to McKinley*, 120–121.

23. Fisk Jubilee Singers to Garfield, November 1880, Richard T. Greener to Garfield, November 3, 1880, J. H. Rainey to Garfield, November 8, 1880, Garfield Papers.

24. Washington *People's Advocate*, November 20, 1880; Trenton *Sentinel*, November 6, December 11, 1880, January 29, 1881; New York *Times*, December 3, 16, 1880; W. A. Pledger to Garfield, December 3, 1880, John Lynch to Garfield, December 11, 1880, James Hill to Garfield, January 8, 1881, Mississippi Representatives to Garfield, February 7, 1881, Garfield Papers; "The Spoils of Office," unidentified newspaper clipping, n.d., Langston Papers, Fisk University; J. C. Napier to Garfield, March 27, 1881, J. C. Napier Papers, Fisk University.

25. DeSantis, *Republicans Face the Southern Question*, 140–141; Trenton *Sentinel*, February 26, 1881; James D. Richardson, *A Compilation of the Messages and Papers of the Presidents, 1789–1902*, Vol. VIII (New York: Bureau of National Literature and Art, 1903), 8.

26. Lamson, *The Glorious Failure*, 281; New Orleans *Weekly Louisianian*, January 8, April 16, 1881; Hirshon, *Farewell to the Bloody Shirt*,

92–93; Doenecke, *The Presidency of James A. Garfield*, 49; New York *Times*, January 18, 1881.

27. John E. Bruce to Garfield, March 17, 1881, Garfield Papers; Letters in folder "Peters to Pollock" Presidential Appointments, 1833–1945, Applications, Mississippi, Collector of Internal Revenue, Department of Treasury, Record Group 56, National Archives; Washington *People's Advocate*, November 6, 1880.

28. James Poindexter to Garfield, December 24, 1880, George W. Williams to John Sherman, February 22, 1881, Frederick Douglass to Garfield, December 18, 1880, Garfield Papers.

29. New Orleans *Weekly Louisianian*, May 21, 1881; Trenton *Sentinel*, April 23, May 7, 1881; Washington *People's Advocate*, May 21, 1881; Huntsville *Gazette*, June 25, 1881.

30. Doenecke, *The Presidency of James A. Garfield*, 47–53; Hirshon, *Farewell to the Bloody Shirt*, 96–97; Nelson Morehouse Blake, *William Mahone of Virginia: Soldier and Political Insurgent* (Richmond, Va.: Garrett and Massie, 1935), 262–263; Huntsville *Gazette*, June 25, August 27, 1881.

31. Garfield Papers, July through September, 1881, particularly Richard D. Cross to Bruce, July 4, 1881. Apparently Bruce sent the letter to Garfield.

32. Garfield Papers, summer of 1881; Douglass, *Life and Times*, 478.

3. Between Scylla and Charybdis

1. New Orleans *Weekly Louisianian*, October 29, November 12, December 10, 1881; Huntsville *Gazette*, December 10, 24, 1881. Unfortunately Arthur destroyed most of his presidential papers, thus eliminating a major source for understanding black attitudes toward his administration.

2. Doenecke, *The Presidency of James A. Garfield*, 124–125; Hirshon, *Farewell to the Bloody Shirt*, 100–101.

3. DeSantis, *Republicans Face the Southern Question*, 151–153.

4. Hirshon, *Farewell to the Bloody Shirt*, 116; Cleveland *Gazette*, September 6, 1883; Washington *Bee*, June 23, 1883; New York *Globe*, April 21, 1883.

5. Hirshon, *Farewell to the Bloody Shirt*, 107–113; DeSantis, *Republicans Face the Southern Question*, 172–173; McDaniel, "Black Power in Georgia," 236–237.

6. Arkansas *Weekly Mansion*, July 21, 1883; Hirshon, *Farewell to the Bloody Shirt*, 116; DeSantis, *Republicans Face the Southern Question*, 173; Ralph Wardlow, *Negro Suffrage in Georgia, 1867–1930, Phelps-Stokes Fel-*

lowship Studies, no. 11, *Bulletin of the University of Georgia*, XXXIII (September 1932), 48.

7. Hirshon, *Farewell to the Bloody Shirt*, 119–120.

8. Washington *People's Advocate*, December 17, 1881; Huntsville *Gazette*, December 17, 1881, April 28, 1883; New Orleans *Weekly Louisianian*, February 18, April 29, May 20, 1882.

9. New York *Globe*, April 21, 1883; New York *Freeman*, April 16, 1887.

10. Grossman, *The Democratic Party*, 74–80; Trenton *Sentinel*, May 27, September 16, 1882; New York *Times*, September 5, October 19, 1882. Butler had been a radical Republican but in 1880 became a Democrat.

11. Grossman, *The Democratic Party*, 81; New York *Times*, July 7, August 26, 1882; New York *Globe*, September 8, 1883; Gerber, *Black Ohio*, 231–233.

12. Olin Burton Adams, "The Negro and the Agrarian Movement in Georgia, 1874–1908" (Ph.D. diss., Florida State University, 1973), 37; New York *Times*, August 7, 8, September 22, 1883.

13. Howard Brotz, ed., *Negro Social and Political Thought, 1850–1920* (New York: Basic Books, 1966), 406.

14. Philip Foner, ed., *The Life and Writings of Frederick Douglass* (New York: International Publishers, 1945), 355.

15. Washington *Bee*, June 24, 1882, January 6, February 10, 17, 24, 1883; Cleveland *Gazette*, September 15, 1883; New York *Times*, May 15, August 14, 1883.

16. New York *Globe*, April 21, August 18, 1883.

17. Washington *Bee*, January 27, 1883; George Pierce to Douglass, April 21, 1883, George T. Downing to Douglass, May 10, 1883, Douglass Papers, Library of Congress; New York *Globe*, May 12, 1883.

18. New York *Globe*, May 12, 26, August 18, 1883; Kousser, *The Shaping of Southern Politics*, 130.

19. New York *Globe*, May 26, 1883.

20. Ibid., March 3, August 18, 1883.

21. "Proceedings of the State Convention of Colored Men of South Carolina," pamphlet, Langston Papers, Fisk University.

22. John E. Bruce, "The Sixth Resolution," 1883, John E. Bruce Papers, Schomberg Collection, N.Y.; Washington *Bee*, May 12, 19, 26, 1883; New York *Times*, August 18, 1883.

23. Washington *Bee*, June 30, September 8, 1883; Herschel V. Sashin to Douglass, September 17, 1883, Douglass Papers, Library of Congress; New York *Times*, September 9, 1883.

24. New York *Times*, September 25, 26, 29, 1883; New York *Globe*, October 15, 1883.

25. Foner, *The Life and Writings*, 390; Washington *Bee*, December 22, 1883.

26. New York *Globe*, September 29, 1883.

27. Washington *Bee*, November 24, 1883; Arkansas *Weekly Mansion*, November 18, 1883; New York *Times*, October 30, 1883; Vincent P. DeSantis, "Negro Dissatisfaction with the Republican Party in the South," *Journal of Negro History*, XXXVI (April 1951), 156.

28. Arkansas *Weekly Mansion*, November 18, 1883; New York *Globe*, October 20, 1883; Washington *People's Advocate*, October 20, 1883; Washington *Bee*, November 10, 1883.

29. Schiener, *Negro Mecca*, 179; Foner, *The Life and Writings*, 423; Cleveland *Gazette*, October 27, 1883; LaWanda and John Cox, eds., *Reconstruction, the Negro and the New South* (Columbia: University of South Carolina Press, 1973), 145; Herbert Aptheker, ed., *A Documentary History of the Negro People of the United States*, II (New York: Citadel Press, 1951), 658–659; John Langston, *The Civil Rights Law* (New York, 1884), 3–30, Langston Papers, Fisk University.

30. E. Merton Coulter, *Negro Legislators in Georgia* (Athens: Georgia Historical Quarterly, 1968), 34; A.M.E. Church *Review*, I (1885), 247.

31. Peter Gilbert, ed., *The Selected Writings of John Edward Bruce: Militant Black Journalist* (New York: Arno Press, 1971), 21–22; New York *Globe*, November 20, 1883; T. Thomas Fortune, *Black and White: Land, Labor and Politics in the South* (New York: Ford, Howard and Hulbert, 1884), 118–127.

32. Cleveland *Gazette*, November 3, December 22, 1883; Arkansas *Weekly Mansion*, December 22, 1883; New York *Globe*, September 1, 1883.

33. Gilbert, *The Selected Writings*, 23.

34. New York *Globe*, August 18, September 1, 1883.

4. The Age of the Negrowump

1. *Congressional Record*, 48th Cong., 1st sess., 1884, Joint Resolution no. 92; Kousser, *The Shaping of Southern Politics*, 14; Savannah *Echo*, January 20, 1884; Foner, *The Life and Writings*, 359.

2. New York *Globe*, January 19, 1884; New York *Times*, January 17, 1884.

3. J.R.L. Diggs to Douglass, July 23, 1883, Douglass Papers, Library of Congress; New York *Globe*, May 26, 1883, March 8, April 19, 1884; Washington *Bee*, February 24, 1883, April 5, 1884.

4. *Proceedings of the State Conference of Colored Men of Florida* (Gainesville, September 8, 1883), Douglass Papers, Library of Congress; Hunts-

ville *Gazette*, May 24, 1884; Washington *Bee*, September 8, 1883; Washington *People's Advocate*, January 19, March 15, 1884; New York *Globe*, August 25, 1883, March 1, 1884.

5. Washington *Bee*, July 7, September 8, 1883, February 23, 1884; Washington *People's Advocate*, July 14, 1883; Harrisburg *State Journal*, January 28, 1884; Arkansas *Mansion*, August 11, 1883.

6. James Pickett Jones, *John A. Logan: Stalwart Republican From Illinois* (Tallahassee: University Presses of Florida, 1982), 175–176; Washington *People's Advocate*, February 23, March 15, 1884; Washington *Bee*, January 12, February 16, May 17, 1884; New York *Globe*, April 19, 1884.

7. Washington *Bee*, May 10, 1884; Harrisburg *State Journal*, May 3, 1884; Hirshon, *Farewell to the Bloody Shirt*, 124.

8. New York *Globe*, February 9, May 10, 1884; Washington *Bee*, May 26, 1883; Huntsville *Gazette*, October 20, 1883.

9. New York *Globe*, March 28, 1884; Cleveland *Gazette*, February 6, April 5, May 3, 1884.

10. New York *Times*, April 29, 30, 1884; Cleveland *Gazette*, May 3, 1884.

11. Harrisburg *State Journal*, April 12, 19, 1884.

12. Morgan, *From Hayes to McKinley*, 202; *Proceedings of the Republican National Convention of 1884* (Chicago: Rand, McNally and Co., 1884), 6–17; Cleveland *Gazette*, March 8, 1884; New York *Globe*, May 3, June 7, 14, 1884.

13. Cleveland *Gazette*, July 5, 1884; Harrisburg *State Journal*, June 14, 1884; Hirshon, *Farewell to the Bloody Shirt*, 126–130.

14. Washington *Bee*, June 7, 28, August 30, 1884; Cleveland *Gazette*, July 26, 1884; New York *Globe*, July 5, 1884.

15. New York *Globe*, June 21, July 19, September 13, 1884; Gilbert, *The Selected Writings*, 5; B. F. Jones to John Bruce, August 22, 1884, John E. Bruce Papers.

16. New York *Globe*, June 21, July 19, 1884; Cleveland *Gazette*, September 13, 1884; Kirk Porter and D. Bruce Johnson, eds., *National Party Platforms* (New York: Macmillan, 1956), 65–68.

17. Washington *Bee*, June 21, 1884; New York *Globe*, July 5, 1884.

18. Hirshon, *Farewell to the Bloody Shirt*, 126; Schiener, *Negro Mecca*, 183; New York *Globe*, August 2, October 18, 25, 1884; Cleveland *Gazette*, October 25, 1884; Washington *Bee*, September 20, 1884.

19. Chicago *Conservator* quoted in New York *Globe*, June 28, July 26, August 2, September 27, October 4, 11, 1884; Cleveland *Gazette*, July 26, 1884.

20. Grossman, *The Democratic Party*, 107–108; John E. Bruce, "The Democratic Party and the Negro," September 4, 1884, John E. Bruce

Papers; Cleveland *Gazette*, July 12, 1884; New York *Globe*, July 19, September 13, 1884.

21. *Afro-American* quoted in Washington *Bee*, October 4, 1884; Washington *Bee*, October 8, 1884; Cleveland *Gazette*, November 1, 1884; Harrisburg *State Journal*, September 27, 1884.

22. William Scarborough, *Our Political Status* (Xenia, Ohio, 1884), 10; New York *Globe*, June 28, July 5, 1884; Washington *Bee*, September 27, October 4, 1884.

23. New York *Globe*, February 9, April 5, August 23, 1884; St. Clair, "The Public Career of Blanche K. Bruce," 187; Julia Williams to Douglass, August 6, September 29, 1884, Douglass to no addressee, August 29, 1884, Douglass Papers, Library of Congress; Washington *People's Advocate*, May 5, 1883; Factor, *The Black Response to America*, 55; Huntsville *Gazette*, September 20, 1884; Washington *Bee*, March 8, 1884.

24. Washington *Bee*, August 30, 1884; Cleveland *Gazette*, October 11, 1884; New York *Globe*, October 25, 1884.

25. Morgan, *From Hayes to McKinley*, 223–224; New York *Globe*, December 15, 1883, January 12, September 13, 1884; Harrisburg *State Journal*, August 2, 1884.

26. Kousser, *The Shaping of Southern Politics*, 28.

27. New York *Times*, November 27, 1884; T. T. Allain to E.G.W. Butler, April 23, 1885, Grover Cleveland Papers, Library of Congress; Cleveland *Gazette*, December 13, 1884.

28. Grossman, *The Democratic Party*, 109; Morgan, *From Hayes to McKinley*, 231.

29. Cleveland *Gazette*, November 22, December 13, 1884; Rice, *The Negro in Texas*, 84; New York *Times*, November 19, 21, 1884; William W. Rogers, *Thomas County, 1865–1900* (Tallahassee: Florida State University Press, 1973), 80; Eugene J. Watts, "Black Political Progress in Atlanta, 1865–1895," *Journal of Negro History*, LIX (1974), 270; Frederick Douglass, "The Outcome of the Recent Election," (1884), Douglass Papers, Library of Congress; Huntsville *Gazette*, November 8, 1884; New York *Freeman*, November 29, 1884; "The Democratic Return to Power—Its Effect?" A.M.E. Church *Review*, I (1885), 213–250. Those interviewed were Frederick Douglass, William Scarborough, P.B.S. Pinchback, Thomas Fortune, John Green, Frances E. W. Harper, William Hannibal Thomas, George T. Downing, C. S. Smith, Peter Clark, William Still, John D. Lewis, H. M. Turner, and Thomas H. Jackson; Pinchback to "My Dear Doctor," November 24, 1884, Pinchback Papers.

30. New York *Freeman*, November 29, 1884; Frederick Douglass, *Three Addresses on the Relations Subsisting between the White and Colored People of the United States* (Washington, D.C., 1885), no. II, 24–41, Douglass Papers, Library of Congress.

31. New York *Times*, November 26, 1884; "The Democratic Return to Power," 24.

32. Harrisburg *State Journal*, November 22, 1884.

33. Richardson, *A Compilation*, VIII, 302; A. A. Middlebrooks to Cleveland, March 27, 1885, Cleveland Papers; Washington *Bee*, November 22, December 13, 1884; Cleveland *Gazette*, March 7, 1884; New York *Freeman*, November 22, 1884. Years later, John Lynch insisted that the number of blacks voting for Cleveland in New York was far in excess of the plurality with which he carried that crucial state. Lynch, *Reminiscences of an Active Life*, 135.

34. New York *Freeman*, January 24, 1885.

35. Randall Woods, "C.H.J. Taylor and the Movement for Black Political Independence, 1882–1896," *Journal of Negro History* LXVII (Summer 1982), 123–124; Washington *Bee*, November 22, 1884, March 14, 1885; New York *Freeman*, December 6, 20, 1884, April 4, June 6, September 12, 1885.

36. New York *Freeman*, May 2, July 11, August 15, 1885; Washington *Bee*, January 24, March 28, May 16, 30, 1885; Cleveland *Gazette*, April 11, 1885.

37. C.H.J. Taylor letters to Cleveland, 1885, T. Thomas Fortune to Daniel Lamont, November 23, 1887 (Lamont was Cleveland's secretary), Fortune to P. A. Collins, March 3, 1886, Cleveland Papers. George T. Downing also wrote to Collins, a representative from Pennsylvania, seeking assistance in securing the appointment.

38. Grossman, *The Democratic Party*, 125–126; C. S. Smith to John H. Oberly, March 24, 1885, Cleveland Papers; Huntsville *Gazette*, April 4, 1885.

39. Grossman, *The Democratic Party*, 127.

40. Ibid., 122; Douglass to William Bird, April 6, 1886, Douglass Papers, Harvard University; George F. Hoar to Douglass, March 11, 1886, Douglass to Hoar, March 12, 1886, Douglass Papers, Library of Congress; Washington *Bee*, February 20, 1886; Douglass, *The Life and Times*, 556–558.

41. Grossman, *The Democratic Party*, 129–131; J. C. Matthews to Lamont, March 1886, Cleveland Papers.

42. Washington *Bee*, March 13, 20, 1886; New York *Times*, August 1, 1886, Walter S. Brown to Cleveland, July 3, 1886, Cleveland Papers.

43. Washington *Bee*, August 14, 1886.

44. New York *Freeman*, March 20, August 14, 1886; Letters to Cleveland through the summer and fall of 1886, Cleveland Papers.

45. New York *Freeman*, August 21, 28, 1886; Washington *Bee*, August 28, September 4, 11, November 13, 1886.

46. Grossman, *The Democratic Party*, 132–133; Washington *Bee*, December 18, 1886.

47. New York *Freeman*, December 25, 1886; Washington *Bee*, January 22, 1887.

48. J. Willis Menard to Cleveland, January 22, 1887, Cleveland Papers; New York *Freeman*, August 21, 1886.

49. Washington *Bee*, January 29, February 5, 19, 1887.

50. New York *Freeman*, March 5, 1887; Fortune to Cleveland, March 1, 1887; T. McCants Stewart to Cleveland, March 1, 1887, Cleveland Papers; New York *Times*, March 2, 1887; Cleveland *Gazette*, March 5, 1887; Washington *Bee*, March 5, 1887.

51. Grossman, *The Democratic Party*, 137–141; New York *Freeman*, March 12, 19, 1887; Washington *Bee*, January 1, March 19, 1887. Although Cleveland had not filled as many lesser positions with blacks as his Republican predecessors, he had named black men to most of the traditionally black offices such as the recordership and the Liberian post.

52. Grossman, *The Democratic Party*, 114–120; Huntsville *Gazette*, December 11, 1886; Washington *Bee*, April 18, 1885. Chase was embarrassed when, while on a visit to Cleveland, he was confronted with a campaign issue of the *Bee* in which he had advocated violence as a way to defeat the Democrats. Chase acknowledged the validity of the president's criticism and then praised him for not being hypocritical about it as he believed Republican presidents would have been; New York *Times*, April 12, 1885; New York *Freeman*, October 17, November 7, 1885.

53. Meier, *Negro Thought in America*, 85–86; New York *Freeman*, October 17, December 12, 1885; June 19, 1886, February 5, 1887; Cleveland *Gazette*, August 1, September 19, 1885, April 2, 1887; J. Wingo to Cleveland, January 29, 1886, Detroit Colored Citizens to Cleveland, March 28, 1887, Cleveland Papers; Washington *Bee*, August 28, 1886.

54. New York *Freeman*, October 24, 1885; Washington *Bee*, November 26, 1886, September 3, 1887; Rice, *The Negro in Texas*, 42.

55. New York *Freeman*, December 19, 1885; New York *Times*, January 2, February 27, 1886.

56. Henry Downing to Cleveland, March 28, 1887, Stewart to Cleveland, December 31, 1886, Cleveland Papers.

57. T. Thomas Fortune, *The Negro in Politics* (New York, 1886).

58. Washington *Bee*, October 16, November 13, 1886; New York *Freeman*, April 16, 1887.

59. New York *Freeman*, March 28, 1886, April 16, 1887; New York *Age*, November 5, 1887.

60. Washington *Bee*, July 2, 1887; Cleveland *Gazette*, December 3, 1887.

61. New York *Freeman*, May 21, 1887; New York *Age*, December 24, 1887.

62. Cleveland *Gazette*, September 25, 1886; New York *Freeman*, November 27, 1886.

63. New York *Freeman*, June 26, July 24, October 2, 1886, November 6, 1886, August 27, September 3, October 1, 1887; New York *Age*, October 22, November 12, 26, 1887; A. A. Burleigh, "Prohibition and the Race Problem," A.M.E. Church *Review*, III (1887), 292; Huntsville *Gazette*, August 6, 1887.

64. Tindall, *South Carolina Negroes, 1877–1900*, 247; New York *Times*, August 30, 1885; New York *Freeman*, April 11, September 5, December 12, 1885.

65. Douglass, "Three Addresses," no. III, 45–68, Douglass to Cornelius Bliss, October 5, 1887, Douglass Papers, Library of Congress.

66. New York *Age*, October 29, November 12, 1887.

67. Ibid., November 5, 1887.

68. Ibid., November 12, 19, 26, 1887.

69. New York *Freeman*, May 26, June 18, 25, July 2, 9, 23, September 10, 1887; New York *Age*, December 25, 1887.

70. New York *Age*, December 25, 1887.

5. Republican Protection or Political Alternatives

1. New York *Age*, January 28, February 25, 1888; Washington *Bee*, May 22, October 23, 1886, July 16, 1887; New York *Freeman*, June 19, 1886; New York *Times*, August 10, 1887; Cleveland *Gazette*, September 18, 1886; Foner, *The Life and Writings*, 44.

2. DeSantis, *Republicans Face the Southern Question*, 189; Washington *Bee*, September 11, 1886; New York *Age*, January 7, July 2, 1887, March 3, May 12, 1888; Edward White, "The Republican Party in National Politics, 1888–1891" (Ph.D. diss., University of Wisconsin, 1941), 1–6.

3. Hamilton Smith to Douglass, April 17, 1888, Douglass Papers, Library of Congress; New York *Freeman*, May 29, 1886; Washington *Bee*, June 19, 1886; New York *Age*, March 3, 1888.

4. New York *Age*, February 11, 1888; Andrew J. Chambers to Cleveland, March 2, 1887, Cleveland Papers.

5. New York *Age*, February 4, 11, 18, 25, 1888; New York *Freeman*, June 12, 1886; Tindall, *South Carolina Negroes, 1877–1900*, 42.

6. New York *Times*, August 11, 1887; New York *Age*, August 13, 1887.

7. Topeka *American Citizen*, June 15, 1888; New York *Age*, June 16, 1888; Porter, *Party Platforms*, 77.

8. New York *Age*, June 16, 1888; William E. Gross to Cleveland, June 6, 1888; T. McCants Stewart to "Dear Sir," May 17, 1888, Cleveland Papers; Emma Lou Thornbrough, *T. Thomas Fortune, Militant Journalist* (Chicago: University of Chicago Press, 1972), 93; Grossman, *The Democratic Party*, 27–28.

9. *Proceedings of the Republican Party Convention of 1888* (Chicago: Rand, McNally & Co., 1888); Henry Stoddard, *As I Knew Them: Presidents and Politics From Grant to Coolidge* (New York: Harper, 1927), 162; White, "The Republican Party," 105–108; Porter, *Party Platforms*, 79–83.

10. Harry J. Sievers, *Benjamin Harrison, Hoosier Statesman: From the Civil War to the White House, 1865–1888* (New York: University Publications, 1959), 144, 231; DeSantis, *Republicans Face the Southern Question*, 222; Hirshon, *Farewell to the Bloody Shirt*, 165; New Orleans *Weekly Pelican*, December 1, 1888; Nowlin, *The Negro in American National Politics*, 83; Huntsville *Gazette*, June 20, 1888; New York *Age*, July 7, 1888.

11. Porter, *Party Platforms*, 80; Nicodemus *Cyclone*, June 29, 1888; New York *Age*, June 30, 1888.

12. Hirshon, *Farewell to the Bloody Shirt*, 162–167; Morgan, *From Hayes to McKinley*, 310; Harrison and Morton Colored Protective Tariff League to Douglass, September 21, 1888, D. M. Lindsey to Douglass, October 7, 1888, Douglass Papers, Library of Congress; I. C. Wears, "Tariff Talk," A.M.E. Church *Review*, V (October 1888), 80–82; T. McCants Stewart, "Tariff Reduction—The Problem of the Hour," A.M.E. Church *Review*, V (October 1888), 83–95.

13. Woods, "C.H.J. Taylor," 128; Indianapolis *Freeman*, July 28, 1888; Cleveland *Gazette*, July 28, 1888; New York *Age*, July 28, 1888. Estimates as to the number of delegates attending varied. The *Freeman*'s estimate of one-hundred was the highest.

14. Indianapolis *Freeman*, August 18, 1888; Washington *Bee*, August 4, 1888; Topeka *American Citizen*, August 24, 1888; New York *Age*, August 4, 1888; Hampton *Southern Workman*, August 1888.

15. Cleveland *Gazette*, August 4, 1888; William E. Gross to Cleveland, July 2, 1888, Louis T. Jacobs to Cleveland, October 10, 1888, Cleveland Papers.

16. Fishel, "The North and the Negro," 477; Indianapolis *Freeman*, July 28, September 15, November 3, 1888; St. Paul and Minneapolis *Afro-Independent*, September 22, 1888; Schiener, *Negro Mecca*, 183; Stewart to Cleveland, September 9, 1888, Cleveland Papers.

17. George T. Downing to Cleveland, June 29, 1888, Robert Still to Cleveland, April 14, 1894, Cleveland Papers.

18. New York *Age*, October 13, 1888; Indianapolis *Freeman*, September 8, 1888; Unidentified newspaper clipping, July 21, 1888, Benjamin Harrison Papers, Library of Congress.

19. Schiener, *Negro Mecca*, 183; Morgan, *From Hayes to McKinley*, 307; James Clarkson to Douglass, August 21, September 7, 1888, J. N. Knapp to Douglass, August 20, 1888, Frederick Douglass, "Address to the Colored Citizens of the United States" (1888), Douglass Papers, Library of Congress; Nowlin, *The Negro in American National Politics*, 84; De-Santis, *Republicans Face the Southern Question*, 192; John Mercer Langston, *From the Virginia Plantation to the National Capital or the First and Only Negro Representative in Congress From the Old Dominion* (Hartford: American Publishing Company, 1894), 45.

20. Douglass, "Address to the Colored Citizens"; Schiener, *Negro Mecca*, 184–185; Washington *Bee*, August 11, 1883; Leavenworth *Herald*, September 22, 1888; New York *Age*, September 8, 1888.

21. New York *Age*, September 15, October 20, 1888; Topeka *American Citizen*, July 30, September 14, 1888.

22. New York *Age*, September 22, 1888; Cleveland *Gazette*, August 4, 1888.

23. William E. Gross to Cleveland, September 8, 1888, Cleveland Papers; Cleveland *Gazette*, September 8, 1888.

24. Washington *Bee*, August 4, 1888; Topeka *American Citizen*, November 2, 1888; New York *Age*, September 29, 1888; Cleveland *Gazette*, October 27, 1888.

25. Walter Brown to Cleveland, November 10, 1888, G. T. Downing to Cleveland, November 9, 1888, W. E. Gross to Cleveland, November 9, 1888, Cleveland Papers.

26. Kousser, *The Shaping of Southern Politics*, 12, 99; Hirshon, *Farewell to the Bloody Shirt*, 181; U.S. Bureau of the Census, *Eleventh Census of the United States: 1890*, I, 45.

27. Washington *Bee*, November 17, 1888, February 29, 1889; Howard Brotz, ed., *Negro Social and Political Thought, 1850–1920* (New York: Basic Books, 1966), 321; Hampton *Southern Workman*, January, 1889.

28. Frederick Douglass, speech fragment, Douglass Papers, Library of Congress; Hirshon, *Farewell to the Bloody Shirt*, 170; New York *Age*, December 1, 1888, January 5, 1889; San Francisco *Vindicator*, February 10, 1889.

29. Charlotte Forten Grimke Diary, March 4, 1889, Francis Grimke Papers, Howard Univ., Washington, D.C.; Washington *National Leader*, March 9, 1889.

30. Davis Newton Lott, ed., *The Inaugural Addresses of the American Presidents from Washington to Kennedy* (New York: Holt, Rinehart and

Winston, 1961), 157–161; Hirshon, *Farewell to the Bloody Shirt*, 178; Huntsville *Gazette*, March 9, 1889; New York *Age*, March 9, 1889.

31. DeSantis, *Republicans Face the Southern Question*, 187.

32. Vincent P. DeSantis, "Benjamin Harrison and the Republican Party in the South, 1889–1893," *Indiana Magazine of History*, LI (1955), 279–283; Hirshon, *Farewell to the Bloody Shirt*, 165.

33. Letter in the Douglass Papers, Library of Congress; New Orleans *Weekly Pelican*, April 27, 1889; Huntsville *Gazette*, April 27, 1889. The appointment of *Gazette* editor Charles Hendley as receiver of public money in Huntsville undoubtedly influenced the paper's shift of opinion; Leavenworth *Advocate*, May 4, 1889.

34. Washington *Bee*, April 13, 1889; Indianapolis *Freeman*, April 6, 1889; New York *Age*, April 6, 1889; Leavenworth *Advocate*, April 13, 1889; Cleveland *Gazette*, April 13, 1889.

35. Cleveland *Gazette*, April 27, 1889; New York *Age*, April 13, 1889; Chicago *Tribune*, April 27, 1889, newspaper clipping, Harrison Papers.

36. Galveston *Freeman's Journal*, August 17, 1889; New York *Age*, May 25, July 13, 20, 1889; Indianapolis *Freeman*, May 18, 1889.

37. Harry J. Sievers, *Benjamin Harrison, Hoosier President: The White House and After* (Indianapolis: Bobbs-Merrill, 1968), 81–82. According to Sievers, Clarkson claimed to have "put some thousand Negroes in rural post offices," and "appointed hundreds more as letter carriers and railway clerks;" DeSantis, "Benjamin Harrison and the Republican Party," 295; DeSantis, *Republicans Face the Southern Question*, 223–224.

38. Hirshon, *Farewell to the Bloody Shirt*, 165. New York *Age*, June 22, 1889; Cleveland *Gazette*, August 10, October 5, 1889; New Orleans *Weekly Pelican*, November 16, 1889.

39. Washington *Bee*, March 30, 1889; A. E. Buck to E. W. Halford, January 26, 1890, Harrison Papers (Halford was Harrison's secretary); Hirshon, *Farewell to the Bloody Shirt*, 185; Cleveland *Gazette*, July 27, 1889; Leavenworth *Advocate*, July 15, 1889.

40. Rayford W. Logan, *The Betrayal of the Negro: From Rutherford B. Hayes to Woodrow Wilson* (New York: Macmillan, 1965), 65; Hirshon, *Farewell to the Bloody Shirt*, 182–185; New York *Age*, November 9, 1889.

41. A. W. Shafer to Harrison, February 13, 1890, Harrison Papers; Woodward, *Origins of the New South*, 220.

42. Philadelphia *Sentinel*, July 27, 1889, newspaper clipping, J. M. Townsend to Harrison, July 31, 1889, *Daily Journal*, June 21, 1891, newspaper clipping, unidentified newspaper clipping, 1891, Cincinnati *Enquirer*, July 1, 1891, newspaper clipping, Harrison Papers; Cleveland *Gazette*, July 4, 1891; Detroit *Plaindealer*, November 7, 1890; New York

Age, February 28, 1891, Harrison appointed John S. Durham of Pennsylvania as consul to Santo Domingo. Frederick Douglass, minister to Haiti, had lived in New York much of his life but at the time of his appointment was a resident of Washington, D.C.

43. Huntsville *Gazette*, June 29, 1889; George Sinkler, *The Racial Attitudes of American Presidents from Abraham Lincoln to Theodore Roosevelt* (New York: Doubleday and Company, 1971), 250–252; New Orleans *Weekly Pelican*, April 27, 1889; Washington *Sunday Herald and Weekly National Intelligencer*, November 10, 1889, Cincinnati *Commercial Gazette*, July 18, September 5, 1891, newspaper clippings, Harrison Papers; New York *Age*, August 29, 1891.

44. Cleveland *Gazette*, October 24, 1891; J. M. Townsend to E. J. Halford, July 31, 1889, *Daily Journal*, September 25, 1891, newspaper clipping, Harrison Papers.

45. Afro-American Press to Harrison, April, 1890, Harrison Papers; New York *Age*, March 15, 1890; Aptheker, *A Documentary History*, II, 648–649.

46. Leavenworth *Advocate*, issues throughout 1890; New York *World*, March 25, 1891, newspaper clipping, Harrison Papers; Indianapolis *Freeman*, November 27, 1890.

47. Springfield *State Capital*, March 25, 1891; Detroit *Plaindealer*, issues throughout 1891, especially January 25, March 18, August 21, 1891; Cleveland *Gazette*, issues throughout 1891, especially January 19, March 19, 1891; New York *Age*, March 14, 1891.

48. Detroit *Plaindealer*, October 25, 1889; U.S. *Congressional Record*, 51st Cong., 2d sess., 1891, 1216.

49. Kousser, *The Shaping of Southern Politics*, 238; John Hope Franklin, *From Slavery to Freedom: A History of Negro Americans* (New York: Vintage Books, 1969), 334. Franklin quotes Henry Grady.

50. Hirshon, *Farewell to the Bloody Shirt*, 190–192; Logan, *The Betrayal of the Negro*, 62.

51. DeSantis, *Republicans Face the Southern Question*, 195; Colored Citizens of Alabama to Harrison, March 21, 1889, Harrison Papers; Detroit *Plaindealer*, October 4, 1889.

52. Charles A. Roxborough to Harrison, February 21, 1889, Colored Citizens of Louisiana to Harrison, April 1, 1889, Harrison Papers; Huntsville *Gazette*, issues throughout the fall of 1889, especially October 25, 1889; Peter Clark to Douglass, May 13, 1889, Douglass Papers, Library of Congress; Indianapolis *Freeman*, March 9, 1889; Cleveland *Gazette*, November 30, 1889.

53. Richardson, *A Compilation of the Messages and Papers of the Presidents, 1789–1902*, IX (New York: Bureau of National Literature and

Art, 1903), 32–58; Detroit *Plaindealer*, December 13, 1889; New York *Age*, December 7, 1889.

54. U.S. *Congressional Record*, 51st Cong., 1st sess., 1890, 2517; Daniel Crofts, "The Black Response to the Blair Education Bill," *Journal of Southern History*, XXXVII (February 1971), 56–57; Cleveland *Gazette*, January 25, 1890.

55. John M. Langston, *The Demands of the Hour* (Washington, D.C., 1891), 14, Langston Papers, Fisk University; Robert Terrell, undated, untitled speech, Robert Terrell Papers, Library of Congress; U.S. *Congressional Record*, 51st Cong., 1st sess., 1890, 1068–1069.

56. Foner, *The Life and Writings*, 459; Douglass to editor, *National Republican*, fragment, 1890, Douglass Papers, Library of Congress.

57. Hirshon, *Farewell to the Bloody Shirt*, 199–200; Representatives of the Afro-American Press Association to Harrison, April, 1890, Harrison Papers; Detroit *Plaindealer*, April 4, 1890; New York *Age*, March 29, April 5, 1890; New York *Times*, April 20, 1890.

58. Croft, "The Black Response," 61; U.S. *Congressional Record*, 51st Cong., 2d sess., 1891, 2830.

59. Ibid., 1st sess., 1891, 6538; Morgan, *From Hayes to McKinley*, 340.

60. Louis R. Harlan, *Booker T. Washington: The Making of a Black Leader, 1856–1901* (New York: Oxford University Press, 1972), 164; Gerald H. Gaither, *Blacks and the Populist Revolt, Ballots and Bigotry in the "New South"* (University: University of Alabama Press, 1977), 31; Charles A. Roxborough, "An Open Letter from Charles A. Roxborough Resigning from the Republican Committee, With Reasons Therefore," July 31, 1891, Charles A. Roxborough Papers, Louisiana State University; Detroit *Plaindealer*, August 8, 1890; Cleveland *Gazette*, March 1, July 19, 1890. One of the Lodge bill's most adamant black critics was William E. B. Du Bois, a recent Harvard graduate. "When you have the right sort of Black voter," he asserted, "you will need no election laws." The New York *Age* accurately predicted that Du Bois's sentiments were "simply the opinions of a very young man who will think and talk differently a few years hence," New York *Age*. June 13, 1890.

61. Hirshon, *Farewell to the Bloody Shirt*, 215–216.

62. Minneapolis *Observor*, September 13, 1890; Cleveland *Gazette*, September 27, 1890.

63. Hirshon, *Farewell to the Bloody Shirt*, 231; Frederick Douglass, "The Cause of the Republican Defeat," *Frank Leslie's Illustrated Newspaper*, CXXI (November 29, 1890), 302; New York *Age*, November 8, 22, 1890; Huntsville *Gazette*, November 22, 1890; Kousser, *The Shaping of Southern Politics*, 213.

64. Fred L. Israel, *The State of the Union Messages of the Presidents*,

1790–1966 (New York: Bowker, 1966), 1674; Washington *Bee*, January 3, 1891; Indianapolis *Freeman*, December 6, 1890; New York *Age*, December 12, 1890; Detroit *Plaindealer*, December 20, 1890.

65. Fred Welborn, "The Influence of the Silver Republican Senators, 1889–1891," *Mississippi Valley Historical Review*, XIV (1928), 476–477; Cleveland *Gazette*, January 10, 1891; U.S. *Congressional Record*, 51st Cong., 2d sess., 1890, 1479–1482, 2695.

66. DeSantis, *Republicans Face the Southern Question*, 213–214; Welborn, "The Influence of the Silver Republicans," 480; Indianapolis *Freeman*, January 17, 1891; Knoxville *Negro World*, February 28, 1891; Detroit *Plaindealer*, January 23, 1891. Henry Teller was a Republican senator from Colorado; Springfield *State Capital*, May 2, 1891; Cleveland *Gazette*, April 4, 1891; New York *Age*, January 31, 1891.

67. Logan, *The Betrayal of the Negro*, 85; Kousser, *The Shaping of Southern Politics*, 238.

68. Indianapolis *Freeman*, August 18, 1888; Hampton *Southern Workman*, May, 1889; Detroit *Plaindealer*, August 8, 1890; Kansas City *Dispatch* quoted in Cleveland *Gazette*, February 14, 1891; Cleveland *Gazette*, February 28, 1891; New York *Herald*, August 6, 1891, newspaper clipping, *Daily Journal*, September 25, 1891, newspaper clipping, Harrison Papers; Topeka *Call*, August 9, 1891; J. C. Price, "The Negro in the Last Decade of the Century," *Independent*, XLI (1891), 5; Senate Miscellaneous Documents, 51st Cong., 2d sess., no. 82; Robert Smalls, "Election Methods in the South," *North American Review*, CLI (1890), 299.

69. Cleveland *Gazette*, August 30, 1890, August 22, 1891, March 28, 1892; Martinsburg *Pioneer Press*, September 6, 1890; New York *Age*, November 7, 1891, November 21, 1982; Woods, "C.H.J. Taylor," 128. Stewart exaggerated the increase in lynchings. According to Rayford Logan (*Betrayal of the Negro*, p. 85), there were 170 lynchings in 1889 compared to 184, 138, 120, and 137 for each year of Cleveland's administration.

70. Charles H. J. Taylor, *Whites and Blacks* (Atlanta: James P. Harrison, 1889), 17–42; Woods, "C.H.J. Taylor," 130.

71. New York *Age*, October 10, 1891; Woods, "C.H.J. Taylor," 129.

72. E. L. Godkin, "The Republican Party and the Negro," *Forum*, VII (1889), 249; Gaither, *Blacks and the Populist Revolt*, 91; Meier, *Negro Thought in America*, 27; W. J. Walls, *Joseph Charles Price: Educator and Race Leader* (Boston: Christopher, 1943), 393; Frenice Logan, *The Negro in North Carolina, 1877–1894* (Chapel Hill: University of North Carolina 1964), 21–22; Tindall, *South Carolina Negroes*, 66–67; August Meier, "The Negro and the Democratic Party, 1875–1915," *Phylon*, XVII (1956), 170–181; New York *Times*, June 22, August 22, 1891; Irving

Dilliard, "James Milton Turner, A Little Known Benefactor of His People," *Journal of Negro History*, XIX (1934), 409.

73. Ernest M. Collins, "Cincinnati Negroes and Presidential Politics," *Journal of Negro History*, XLI (1956), 131; New York *Age*, July 25, September 12, October 24, 1891, November 5, 1892; Meier, *Negro Thought in America*, 33; Cleveland *Gazette*, August 29, 1891; Wisconsin *Afro-American*, October 29, 1892.

74. Meier, *Negro Thought in America*, 34; Wisconsin *Afro-American*, October 8, 1892.

75. C. Vann Woodward, *Tom Watson: Agrarian Rebel* (New York: Macmillan, 1938), 222.

76. Woodward, *Origins of the New South*, 192; Gaither, *Blacks and the Populist Revolt*, 12.

77. Robert McMath, Jr., *Populist Vanguard: A History of the Southern Farmers' Alliance* (Chapel Hill: University of North Carolina Press, 1975), 44, 52–53; Lawrence Goodwyn, *Democratic Promise: The Populist Movement in America* (New York: Oxford University Press, 1976), 656; Leavenworth *Advocate*, October 18, 1890. Leonidas Polk, president of the Southern Farmers' Alliance, was from North Carolina; William H. Chafe, "The Negro and Populism: A Kansas Case Study," *Journal of Southern History*, XXXIV (1968), 408; Topeka *American Citizen*, August 3, 1888; New York *Age*, August 2, 1890.

78. William W. Rogers, "The Negro Alliance in Alabama," *Journal of Negro History*, XLV (1960), 41–42.

79. William Edward Spriggs, "The Virginia Colored Farmers' Alliance: A Case Study of Race and Class Identity," *Journal of Negro History*, LXIV (Summer 1979), 197; Gaither, *Blacks and the Populist Revolt*, 10.

80. Woodward, *Origins of the New South*, 255; Gaither, *Blacks and the Populist Revolt*, 21.

81. Chafe, "The Negro and Populism," 413–415; Herbert Shapiro, "The Populist and the Negro: A Reconsideration," in *The Making of Black America: Essays in Negro Life and History*, ed. August Meier and Elliott Rudwick, vol. II (New York: Atheneum, 1969), 32; Goodwyn, *Democratic Promise*, 282.

82. Goodwyn, *Democratic Promise*, 294; Gaither, *Blacks and the Populist Revolt*, 36–37; Kousser, *The Shaping of Southern Politics*, 34; Tom Watson, "The Negro Question in the South," *Arena*, VI (1892), 540–550; Woodward, *Origins of the New South*, 26; Shapiro, "The Populist and the Negro," 31; Robert B. Carl, "Race Relations in the Agrarian Revolt: The Georgia Experience, 1889–1896," *Atlanta Historical Bulletin* (Winter 1977), 56.

83. Shapiro, "The Populist and the Negro," 31; Woodward, *Origins*

of the New South, 258; Gaither, *Blacks and the Populist Revolt*, 40; Robert M. Saunders, "The Southern Populist and the Negro in 1892," *University of Virginia Essays in History*, XII (Charlottesville: University of Virginia Press, 1966–67), 25.

84. Goodwyn, *Democratic Promise*, 277, 282–285; Chafe, "The Negro and Populism," 415; Kousser, *The Shaping of Southern Politics*, 36; Jack Abramowitz, "John B. Raynor—A Grass-roots Leader," *Journal of Negro History*, XXXVI (1951), 164–166; Rice, *The Negro in Texas*, 79; Gaither, *Blacks and the Populist Revolt*, 118; Jack Abramowitz, "The Negro in the Populist Movement," *Journal of Negro History*, XXXVIII (1953), 267–269, 274; Melton Meltzer, ed., *In Their Own Words: A History of the American Negro, 1865–1916* (New York: Thomas Crowell, 1965), 109; Hair, *Bourbonism and Agrarian Protest*, 223.

85. Lawrence *Historic Times*, October 3, 1891.

86. Detroit *Plaindealer*, December 19, 1890; Indianapolis *Freeman*, January 17, 1891, July 16, 1892.

87. Emma Lou Thornbrough, "The National Afro-American League, 1887–1908," *Journal of Southern History*, XXVII (1961), 495–499; Woodward, *Origins of the New South*, 220; the Afro-American League to Harrison, January 22, 1890, Harrison Papers; Fishel, "The North and the Negro," 486; Michael L. Goldstein, "Preface to the Rise of Booker T. Washington: A View From New York City of the Demise of Independent Black Politics," *Journal of Negro History*, LXII (January 1977), 83–85.

88. Isaiah Montgomery, untitled speech, 1890, Montgomery Family Papers, Library of Congress; Detroit *Plaindealer*, September 12, 1890; C.H.J. Taylor, *Whites and Blacks*, 27; "Progress Among the Negro," *Nation*, XLVIII (June 6, 1889), 461.

89. Cleveland *Gazette*, August 9, 1890; New York *Age*, November 23, 1890.

90. Wisconsin *Afro-American*, August 20, 1892.

6. Republicans, Democrats, Populists, or Economics First

1. Henry Blair to Douglass, February 25, 1892, Frederick Douglass, "A Plea for the Renomination of General Harrison," undated manuscript, Douglass Papers, Library of Congress; Unidentified newspaper clipping, June 1, 1892, Harrison Papers; Springfield *State Capital*, May 28, 1892; New York *Age*, August 29, 1891.

2. New York *Age*, December 6, 1890; Langston *City Herald*, June 11, 1892; Coffeyville *Afro-American Advocate*, May 13, 1892; Cleveland

Gazette, May 21, 1892; Springfield *State Capital*, May 2, 1891; Lawrence *Historic Times*, August 29, 1891.

3. *Proceedings of the Republican National Convention of 1892* (Minneapolis: Charles W. Johnson, 1903); Nowlin, *The Negro in American National Politics*, 67, 76; George Knoles, *The Presidential Campaign and Election of 1892* (Stanford: Stanford University Press, 1942), 49–53; Porter, *National Party Platforms*, 165–169; Douglass, Bruce, and Hill were present but not delegates at the convention.

4. Huntsville *Gazette*, June 25, 1892; Topeka *Call*, June 25, 1892; Langston *City Herald*, July 2, 1892; J. H. Lewis to Douglass, 1888, Douglass Papers, Library of Congress.

5. Grossman, *The Democratic Party*, 158; Knoles, *The Presidential Campaign*, 194; Langston *City Herald*, May 28, 1892; Washington *Bee*, July 21, 1892; Indianapolis *Freeman*, July 2, 1892; Porter, *National Party Platforms*, 159–164; Detroit *Plaindealer*, July 22, 1892.

6. Porter, *National Party Platforms*, 165–169; Knoles, *The Presidential Campaign*, 194; Abramowitz, "The Negro in the Populist Movement," 278; Gaither, *Blacks and the Populist Revolt*, 41–42.

7. Coffeyville *Afro-American*, October 9, November 4, 1892. Weaver did not leave the Republican party until 1877. See Fred Emory Haynes, *James Baird Weaver* (Iowa City: State Historical Society of Iowa, 1919); Topeka *Call*, October 9, 1892; Abramowitz, "The Negro in the Populist Movement," 263.

8. Gaither, *Blacks and the Populist Revolt*, 95; Abramowitz, "The Negro in the Populist Movement," 263; Saunders, "The Southern Populist," 22–24; Kousser, *The Shaping of Southern Politics*, 216.

9. Coffeyville *Afro-American*, July 1, 1892; Indianapolis *Freeman*, August 6, 1892; Richmond *Southern News*, October 15, 1892; Langston *City Herald*, May 14, 1892; New York *Age*, January 9, 1892; Chicago *Eagle*, September 17, 1892; Grossman, *The Democratic Party*, 166.

10. Cleveland *Gazette*, October 1, 29, 1892; New York *Times*, June 22, 1892.

11. Grossman, *The Democratic Party*, 158–160.

12. Hirshon, *Farewell to the Bloody Shirt*, 238–239; Grossman, *The Democratic Party*, 158–165; Detroit *Plaindealer*, July 1, 1892; Brooklyn *Eagle*, November 3, 1892.

13. Newspaper clipping, September 28, 1892, speech fragment, numerous invitations to speak, Douglass Papers, Library of Congress; Cleveland *Gazette*, October 8, 15, 1892. Most black Republican papers advertised the *Afro-American Campaign Text Book* weekly throughout the campaign.

14. Coffeyville *Afro-American Advocate*, September 22, 1892; Cleve-

land *Gazette*, July 23, October 1, 29, 1892; Detroit *Plaindealer*, May 20, 1892; Indianapolis *Freeman*, July 23, 1892; Springfield *State Capital*, July 5, 1892.

15. Hair, *Bourbonism and Agrarian Protest*, 260; W. D. Floyd to Booker T. Washington, July 18, 1892, Booker T. Washington Papers, Library of Congress; Citizens of Terrebonne County, Louisiana, to Douglass, June 14, 1892, Douglass Papers, Library of Congress; Morgan, *From Hayes to McKinley*, 431.

16. Grossman, *The Democratic Party*, 156; Kousser, *The Shaping of Southern Politics*, 12.

17. Kousser, *The Shaping of Southern Politics*, 102, 144, 215; Chafe, "The Negro and Populism," 418; Rice, *The Negro in Texas*, 70; Roscoe C. Martin, *The People's Party in Texas: A Study in Third Party Politics, University of Texas Bulletin*, no. 2208 (February 22, 1930), 96; Carl, "Race Relations in the Agrarian Revolt," 56–58.

18. William B. Derrick, "Has the Republican Party a Future?—Yes," A.M.E. Church *Review*, X (1893), 220–223; Frederick Douglass, "Douglass on the Late Election," November 1982, Douglass Papers, Library of Congress; New York *Times*, November 22, 1892; Walls, *Joseph Charles Price*, 393; Washington *Bee*, November 12, 1892; J. Madison Vance to H.C.C. Astwood, November 11, 1892, Cleveland Papers. Astwood mailed Vance's letter to Cleveland; New York *Age*, November 19, 1892; Springfield *State Capital*, November 12, 1892.

19. Cleveland *Gazette*, February 11, 1893; Indianapolis *Freeman*, February 11, 1893; Washington *Bee*, February 11, 1893; Coffeyville *Afro-American*, February 12, 1893.

20. Lott, The *Inaugural Addresses*, 165; T. McCants Stewart to Cleveland, March 6, 1893, John Langston to Cleveland, March 15, 1893, Cleveland Papers; San Francisco *Elevator*, March 8, 1893; A.M.E. *Zion Church Quarterly* (April 1893), 388, 404; Indianapolis *Freeman*, April 22, 1893.

21. C.H.J. Taylor to Thurber, July 13, 1894, Andrew Chambers to Cleveland, July 27, 1895, Cleveland Papers; Springfield *State Capital*, December 3, 1892; St. Paul and Minneapolis *Broad Axe*, March 2, 1893.

22. C.H.J. Taylor to John E. Bruce, August 26, 1893, John E. Bruce Papers. Taylor's letter was written on Negro National Democratic League stationery which included information on officers. Peter Clark, J. C. Matthews, and J. Milton Turner were among the members of the Executive Committee. J.E.W. Thompson headed the Committee on Correspondence and T. McCants Stewart and Robert Still served on it. The Rules Committee was headed by P. H. White of New York and the Committee on Headquarters by Smith Wormley of Washington, D.C.;

Kansas City *American Citizen*, August 11, 1893; Washington *Bee*, August 12, 1893.

23. Washington *Bee*, April 5, August 26, September 9, December 2, 1893; Indianapolis *Freeman*, September 2, 1893; Taylor to Thurber, February 22, 1894, Cleveland Papers.

24. New York *Times*, August 15, 16, 1894; Washington *Bee*, August 25, 1894; Cleveland *Gazette*, August 25, 1894.

25. Wichita *People's Friend*, September 14, 1894; New York *Times*, September 4, 1894.

26. Washington *Bee*, January 12, 1895; H. G. Hill et al. to Cleveland, January 10, 1895, Cleveland Papers.

27. New York *Times*, August 9, 1894.

28. Robert Still to Cleveland, November 10, 1892, Cleveland Papers; Kansas City *American Citizen*, March 10, 1893; New York *Times*, June 11, 12, September 4, 1894; Indianapolis *Freeman*, September 22, 1894.

29. Cleveland *Gazette*, September 9, 1893; Kansas City *American Citizen*, May 26, 1893, July 13, 1894.

30. Washington *Bee*, October 13, 1894.

31. Washington *Bee*, March 4, 1893; Indianapolis *Freeman*, June 14, 1893; Kansas City *American Citizen*, February 10, 1893.

32. Isaiah Montgomery to Cleveland, May 5, 1893, Cleveland Papers.

33. Cleveland *Gazette*, June 3, 1894; Washington *Bee*, April 22, 1895.

34. Washington *Bee*, December 2, 1893; Indianapolis *Freeman*, June 14, 1893.

35. Henry M. Turner, "Speech Before the National Council of Colored Men" (Cincinnati, Ohio, November 29, 1893), Henry M. Turner Papers; Elizabeth Haroday to Cleveland, March 24, 1893, Cleveland Papers.

36. Indianapolis *Freeman*, April 8, 1893; Kansas City *American Citizen*, April 12, May 5, May 12, 1893; Taylor to Thurber, March 23, 1893, Cleveland Papers; New York *Times*, May 15, 1893.

37. Cleveland *Gazette*, March 18, June 3, 1893; Topeka *Call*, issues through the spring of 1893; Detroit *Plaindealer*, February 24, 1893; Kansas City *American Citizen*, May 12, 1893; Washington *Bee*, April 15, May 20, 1893; Peter Clark to Douglass, May 7, 1893, Douglass Papers, Library of Congress.

38. Thomas G. Jones to Cleveland, June 6, 1893, Prince Robinson to L. W. Tarpin, March 24, 1893, Robinson to Cleveland, March 27, June 8, 1893, August 1, 17, 1895, Robinson to Olney, June 12, 26, 1895, Cleveland Papers. Tarpin was Cleveland's secretary and Olney his secretary of state.

39. Cleveland *Gazette*, July 8, 1893; Topeka *Weekly Call*, August 19, 1893.

40. Kansas City *American Citizen*, issues throughout the summer of 1893; Washington *Bee*, June 24, 1893; Taylor to Thurber, August 8, 1893, Cleveland Papers; Negro National Democratic League to Cleveland, August 29, 1893, Cleveland Papers.

41. Washington *Bee*, July 22, 1893.

42. Indianapolis *Freeman*, September 16, October 14, 1893; Benjamin W. Arnett, "The Address of Bishop Benjamin William Arnett of Wilberforce, Ohio, at Chicago, Illinois," September 22, 1893, Daniel Murray Collection, Library of Congress; Washington *Bee*, October 7, 1893; Taylor to Cleveland, September 8, 1893, William Johnson to Cleveland, September 27, 1893, Cleveland Papers; Topeka *Weekly Call*, September 30, 1893.

43. J. Lewis to Charles R. Douglass, September 30, 1893, Douglass Papers, Library of Congress; Cleveland *Gazette*, October 28, November 4, 1893; Indianapolis *Freeman*, September 23, 1893.

44. Astwood to Cleveland, November 7, 1893, Astwood to Thurber, November 13, 1893, Cleveland Papers; Indianapolis *Freeman*, November 11, 1893.

45. Cleveland *Gazette*, September 30, 1893; A.M.E. Zion *Church Quarterly*, IV (1894); Parsons *Weekly Blade*, March 17, 1894; Indianapolis *Freeman*, January 13, 1894.

46. Taylor to Cleveland, March 10, 1894, Taylor to Thurber, February 8, April 7, 16, 1894, Cleveland Papers; New York *Times*, March 18, May 24, 1894; Washington *Bee*, April 7, 1894; Cleveland *Gazette*, April 7, 1894. On January 28, 1893, however, the *Gazette* said that Taylor was "most deserving" of this position. Taylor to Douglass, April 11, 29, May 24, 1894, G. F. Hoar to Douglass, May 16, 1894, Douglass Papers, Library of Congress. One of the senators that Douglass contacted on Taylor's behalf was George F. Hoar of Massachusetts. Hoar replied, "I expect to support Mr. Taylor unless something new should be developed. But I should advise you as a friend never to go on the bond, for $10,000 for a colored man who supports the Democratic party. If he do it to get office, he is not to be trusted morally. If he do it from honest conviction, he hasn't sense enough to be trusted for $10,000."

47. Indianapolis *Freeman*, June 2, 1894; Cleveland *Gazette*, September 29, 1894; Taylor to Cleveland, July 23, 1894; Taylor to Thurber, August 9, October 11, 1894, Cleveland Papers.

48. Washington *Bee*, August 11, 1894; January 26, 1895; Leavenworth *Herald*, December 1, 1894; Indianapolis *Freeman*, March 30, 1895.

49. S. T. Mitchell to Cleveland, May 21, 1895, Cleveland Papers. Cleveland turned down the degree, explaining that he had also recently turned down one from Harvard because he did not want to accept a degree that he had not earned; Richmond *Planet*, November 16, 1895.

50. W. H. Hunt to Douglass, February 6, 1894, Douglass Papers, Library of Congress; Washington *Bee*, May 3, December 23, 1893; A. A. Mossell to Cleveland, April 12, 1894, Cleveland Papers.

51. Stewart to Cleveland, September 19, 1894, Cleveland Papers. Stewart included a copy of Cleveland's letter to him.

52. Taylor to John Bruce, November 18, 1895, John E. Bruce Papers; Parsons *Weekly Blade*, September 8, 1894; Richmond *Planet*, March 9, April 27, 1895; Indianapolis *Freeman*, April 21, 1894; Caesar A. A. Taylor, "Cleveland's Administration," A.M.E. Church *Review*, II (1894), 172–177; S. B. Wallace, *What the National Government is Doing for Our Colored Boys—Two Sermons Delivered at the Israel A.M.E. Church* (Washington, D.C., August 10-September 9, 1894), Murray Collection; Cleveland *Gazette*, May 19, 1894; Wichita *People's Friend*, July 13, 1894; Richmond *Planet*, August 3, 1895.

53. Washington *Bee*, August 17, 24, 1895; Cleveland *Gazette*, October 5, 1895; Quoted in the Topeka *Weekly Call*, September 22, 1894.

54. Cleveland *Gazette*, June 10, 1893; Indianapolis *Freeman*, April 22, 1893, April 21, 1894, November 18, 1895; Wichita *People's Friend*, June 29, 1894.

55. Washington *Bee*, October 28, 1895; Seattle *Standard* quoted in Indianapolis *Freeman*, June 10, 1893; *Reformer* quoted in Indianapolis *Freeman*, June 17, 1893; Indianapolis *Freeman*, October 14, 1893; Kansas City *American Citizen*, January 25, 1893; Topeka *Weekly Call*, June 29, 1895; New York *Times*, August 23, 1895.

56. Topeka *Weekly Call*, September 22, 1894; Cleveland *Gazette*, October 26, 1895; Indianapolis *Freeman*, October 26, November 9, 1895; Springfield *State Capital*, November 10, 1895; Leavenworth *Herald*, November 2, 1895; Richmond *Planet*, November 2, 1895.

57. Wichita *People's Friend*, July 6, September 21, 1894; Topeka *Weekly Call*, May 19, 1894; August 25, 1895; Wichita *National Baptist World*, October 19, 1894; Topeka *Kansas Blackman*, April 27, 1894; Leavenworth *Herald*, February 6, 1894.

58. Cleveland *Gazette*, January 28, 1893; Indianapolis *Freeman*, August 18, October 27, 1894; New York *Times*, July 9, 1895; Washington *Bee*, September 28, November 23, 1895; Richmond *Planet*, issues throughout Cleveland's second term; Huntsville *Gazette*, November 10, 1894.

59. Taylor et al. (the National Negro Democratic League) to Cleveland, May 10, 1893, Astwood to James M. Vance, January 2, 1893, Cleveland Papers; Cleveland *Gazette*, March 4, April 29, 1893.

60. Topeka *Weekly Call*, April 22, 1893; Kansas City *American Citizen*, September 7, 1894; Adams, "The Negro and the Agrarian Movement,"

93; Rogers, *Thomas County*, 90–91; William Mabry, *The Negro in North Carolina Since Reconstruction* (Durham, N. C.: Duke University Press, 1940), 36.

61. Saunders, "The Southern Populist," 241–253; Wichita *People's Friend*, July 13, 27, 1894; Leavenworth *Herald*, October 6, 1894; Woodward, *Origins of the New South*, 276.

62. Baltimore *Afro-American*, April 29, 1893; Smith, *The Negro in Congress*, 6; Indianapolis *Freeman*, October 28, 1893; Cleveland *Gazette*, November 6, 1893.

63. Wichita *National Baptist World*, November 23, 1894; George W. Murray to Whitefield McKinley, November 18, 1894, Carter G. Woodson Collection, Library of Congress; Smith, *The Negro in Congress*, 108, 124.

64. Washington *Bee*, August 10, 1895; Huntsville *Gazette*, January 6, February 24, 1894; Topeka *Evening Call*, June 2, 1894; Cleveland *Gazette*, January 7, 1893; Meier, *Negro Thought in America*, 36; Parson's *Weekly Blade*, April 21, 1894.

65. D. Augustus Straker, "The Organization, Object, and Aim of the National Federation of Colored Men of the United States," A.M.E. Church *Review*, XII (1896), 499–511; R.C.O. Benjamin, *Light After Darkness: Being An Up-to-Date History of the American Negro* (Xenia, Ohio, 1896), 38–39, Murray Collection; Thorpe, *The Mind of the Negro*, 370; Frederick Douglass, *Why Is the Negro Lynched* (Bridgewater, Conn., 1895).

66. *Senate Miscellaneous Documents*, 54th Cong., 1st sess., no. 61, January 9, 1896.

67. Louis Harlan, *Booker T. Washington: The Making of a Black Leader, 1856–1901* (New York: Oxford, 1972), 217–225.

68. Booker T. Washington to S. J. Burrows, October 15, 1895, Booker T. Washington Papers, Harvard University; Harlan, *Booker T. Washington*, 225.

69. Harlan, *Booker T. Washington*, 224–227; Indianapolis *Freeman*, September 28, 1895; Washington *Bee*, October 19, 26, November 2, 1895.

7. The Setting Sun

1. Kousser, *The Shaping of Southern Politics*, 42.
2. Ibid., 31.
3. Tindall, *South Carolina Negroes, 1877–1900*, 76; Cleveland *Gazette*, July 13, 1895; Omaha *Enterprise*, August 24, 1895.
4. "Call For a National Convention," September 10, 1895, John E.

Bruce Papers; New York *Times*, October 17, 1895; April 28, 1896; Indianapolis *Freeman*, February 22, 1896.

5. New York *Times*, October 28, 1895; Cleveland *Gazette*, February 22, May 9, 1896; Indianapolis *Freeman*, February 15, 1895; John M. Langston manuscript, November 14, 1896, Langston Papers, Fisk University; Parsons *Weekly Blade*, April 18, 1896; Baltimore *Afro-American*, May 30, 1896; Washington *Bee*, August 17, 1895.

6. Cleveland *Gazette*, June 6, 1895; Parsons *Weekly Blade*, April 4, May 2, 1896; Indianapolis *Freeman*, March 7, 1896; Leavenworth *Herald*, March 7, 1896.

7. James Clarkson to Whitefield McKinley, February 26, 29, 1896, Richard Greener to McKinley, February 20, 1896, Carter G. Woodson Collection, Library of Congress; Clarkson to Booker T. Washington, February 7, 1896, Booker T. Washington Papers, Library of Congress; Indianapolis *Freeman*, March 14, August 3, 1895; New York *Times*, January 18, July 9, 1895; John M. Langston to wife, June 14, 1896, Langston Papers, Fisk University; Alexander Crummell to John Bruce, February 28, 1896, John E. Bruce Papers.

8. New York *Times*, March 15, June 6, 10, 11, 1896; Washington, *Bee*, March 21, 1896; Cleveland *Gazette*, May 9, June 20, 1896; Omaha *Enterprise*, June 20, 1896; Indianapolis *Freeman*, June 13, 1896.

9. Indianapolis *Freeman*, June 13, 1896; Washington *Bee*, June 27, 1896; Richmond *Planet*, June 27, 1896; Morgan, *From Hayes to McKinley*, 483–485.

10. J.E.W. Thompson to Cleveland, April 2, 1896, Cleveland Papers; Omaha *Enterprise*, May 2, 1896.

11. Omaha *Afro-American Sentinel*, July 18, 1896.

12. Leavenworth *Herald*, March 21, 1896; Gaither, *Blacks and the Populist Revolt*, 92; Willard H. Smith, "William Jennings Bryan and Racism," *Journal of Negro History*, LIV (April 1969), 127–149; Indianapolis *Freeman*, August 1, 1896; Richmond *Planet*, August 1, 1896; Cleveland *Gazette*, September 5, 1896; Jeffrey J. Crow, " 'Fusion, Confusion and Negroism': Schisms Among Negro Republicans in the North Carolina Election of 1896," *North Carolina Historical Review* (Autumn 1976), 365–368; William J. Gaboury, "George Washington Murray and the Fight for Political Democracy in South Carolina," *Journal of Negro History*, LXII (July 1977), 258.

13. Cleveland *Gazette*, April 11, 1896; Omaha *Sentinel*, June 20, 1896; Parsons *Weekly Blade*, July 4, 1896; Richmond *Planet*, August 8, 1896; Topeka *Weekly Call*, August 21, 1896; Indianapolis *Freeman*, October 24, 1896.

14. New York *Times*, September 2, 1896; Omaha *Enterprise*, August

29, October 13, 1896; Washington *Bee*, August 22, 1896; George E. Taylor, "National Appeal to the Negro: Why We Should Favor the Chicago Platform," August 8, 1896, Murray Collection.

15. Indianapolis *Freeman*, August 22, 1896; Washington *Bee*, August 22, 1896; Kansas City *American Citizen*, October 9, 1896.

16. Clarence A. Bacote, "Negro Officeholders in Georgia Under President McKinley," *Journal of Negro History*, XLIV (1959), 232; Cleveland *Gazette*, September 26, 1896; Omaha *Enterprise*, July 25, August 1, 1896; Washington *Bee*, August 8, October 10, 1896.

17. New York *Times*, September 3, 1896.

18. Parsons *Weekly Blade*, September 12, November 7, 1896; Richmond *Planet*, August 15, 1896; Adams, "The Negro and the Agrarian Movement," 215–216; Rice, *The Negro in Texas*, 50–51, 85; Indianapolis *Freeman*, August 1, 1896.

19. Cleveland *Gazette*, July 11, October 17, 31, 1896; Parsons *Weekly Blade*, July 18, 1896; Wilmington *Afro-American Presbyterian* quoted in Indianapolis *Freeman*, July 25, 1896; Omaha *Afro-American*, October 3, 1896.

20. Raleigh *Gazette*, October 31, 1896.

21. Richmond *Planet*, July 25, 1896; Cleveland *Gazette*, August 8, 29, 1896; Paul Dunbar, "The Real Question," *Harper's Weekly*, IV (October 31, 1896), 1078.

22. Lewis L. Gould, *The Presidency of William McKinley* (Lawrence: Regents Press of Kansas, 1980), 11; Washington *Bee*, August 8, 29, October 17, 1896; Cleveland *Gazette*, September 19, 1896; Kansas City *American Citizen*, October 16, 1896; Bruce to Roscoe Bruce, 1896, Blanche K. Bruce Papers; Richard Greener to Whitefield McKinley, September 13, 1896, Woodson Collection. Prominent among the independent campaigners were Harry C. Smith who campaigned in Ohio, John C. Buchner in Illinois, John Walker in Illinois, Iowa, and Kansas, and T. T. Allain and Hale G. Parker in Louisiana. See Cleveland *Gazette* for campaign months.

23. Omaha *Afro-American*, July 18, 1896; Cleveland *Gazette*, July 18, 25, August 22, October 13, 1896; Indianapolis *Freeman*, October 24, 1896.

24. Cleveland *Gazette*, July 25, October 31, 1896; Bruce to Josephine Bruce, October 19, 1896, Blanche K. Bruce Papers.

25. Kousser, *The Shaping of Southern Politics*, 92, 193; Parsons *Weekly Blade*, November 7, 1896; Indianapolis *Freeman*, November 7, 1896.

26. Cleveland *Gazette*, November 7, 1896; Washington *Bee*, November 7, 28, 1896; Kansas City *American Citizen*, November 13, 1896; Iowa *Bystander*, November 20, 1896; Alexander Crummell to John Bruce,

December 5, 1896, John E. Bruce Papers; Gould, *The Presidency of William McKinley*, 28; Indianapolis *Freeman*, May 23, November 14, 1896.

8. The Cancer of Disappointed Hopes

1. James Bryce, "Thoughts on the Negro Problem," *North American Review*, CLM (1891), 649; Kousser, *The Shaping of Southern Politics*, 250; Woodward, *Origins of the New South*, 342; Gaither, *Blacks and the Populist Revolt*, 65.

2. Foner, *Life and Writings*, 477.

3. P. J. Sturges to Douglass, October 8, 1890, Douglass Papers, Library of Congress.

4. Amale Andrell (?) to Douglass, January 18, 1893, Douglass Papers, Library of Congress.

5. Kleppner, *The Third Electoral System*, 180; Dann, *The Black Press*, 169.

6. DeSantis, *Republicans Face the Southern Question*, 184.

7. Indianapolis *Freeman*, November 7, 1896.

Bibliography

A. Primary Materials

1. Manuscript Collections

Chester A. Arthur papers, Library of Congress, Washington, D.C.
Blanche K. Bruce papers, Founders Library, Howard University, Washington, D.C.
John E. Bruce papers, Schomburg Collection, New York Public Library, New York, New York.
Zachariah Chandler papers, Library of Congress, Washington, D.C.
Grover Cleveland papers, Library of Congress, Washington, D.C.
Frederick Douglass papers, Founders Library, Howard University, Washington, D.C.
Frederick Douglass papers, Library of Congress, Washington, D.C.
Frederick Douglass papers, Schomburg Collection, New York Public Library, New York, New York.
Frederick Douglass papers, Widener Library, Harvard University, Cambridge, Massachusetts.
George T. Downing papers, Widener Library, Harvard University, Cambridge, Massachusetts.
T. Thomas Fortune papers, Schomburg Collection, New York Public Library, New York, New York.
James A. Garfield papers, Library of Congress, Washington, D.C.
Ulysses S. Grant papers, Library of Congress, Washington, D.C.
Richart T. Greener papers, Schomburg Collection, New York Public Library, New York, New York.

Archibald Grimke papers, Founders Library, Howard University, Washington, D.C.

Francis Grimke papers, Founders Library, Howard University, Washington, D.C.

Benjamin Harrison papers, Library of Congress, Washington, D.C.

Rutherford B. Hayes papers, Rutherford B. Hayes Library, Fremont, Ohio.

John M. Langston papers, Fisk University Library, Fisk University, Nashville, Tennessee.

John M. Langston papers, Founders Library, Howard University, Washington, D.C.

William McKinley papers, Library of Congress, Washington, D.C.

Montgomery Family papers, Library of Congress, Washington, D.C.

Daniel Murray Collection, Library of Congress, Washington, D.C.

J.C. Napier papers, Fisk University Library, Fisk University, Nashville, Tennessee.

Pinckney Benton Stewart Pinchback papers, Founders Library, Howard University, Washington, D.C.

Hiram Revels papers, Schomburg Collection, New York Public Library, New York, New York.

Ruffin Family papers, Founders Library, Howard University, Washington, D.C.

John Sherman papers, Library of Congress, Washington, D.C.

T. McCants Stewart papers, Founders Library, Howard University, Washington, D.C.

Mary Church Terrell papers, Library of Congress, Washington, D.C.

Robert H. Terrell papers, Library of Congress, Washington, D.C.

Henry M. Turner papers, Founders Library, Howard University, Washington, D.C.

W. H. Wallace papers, Southern Historical Collection, University of North Carolina at Chapel Hill, Chapel Hill, North Carolina.

Henry C. Warmouth papers, Southern Historical Collection, University of North Carolina at Chapel Hill, Chapel Hill, North Carolina.

Booker T. Washington papers, Library of Congress, Washington, D.C.

Booker T. Washington papers, Widener Library, Harvard University, Cambridge, Massachusetts.

Carter G. Woodson Collection, Library of Congress, Washington, D.C.

2. Official Government Records and Documents

Bureau of the Census. *Tenth Census of the United States: 1880.*
——. *Eleventh Census of the United States: 1890.*

Collector of Customs Applications, Treasury Department Records, Record Group 56, National Archives, Washington, D.C.
Collector of Internal Revenue Applications, Treasury Department Records, Record Group 56, National Archives, Washington, D.C.
Congressional Record, 1875–1897.
House Miscellaneous Documents, 52nd Cong., 1st sess., 1891, no. 1.
Senate Miscellaneous Documents, 51st Cong., 1st sess., 1890, no. 82.
————, 54th Cong., 1st sess., January 9, 1896, no. 61.

3. Political Party Records

Proceedings of the Republican National Convention of 1876. Concord, N.H.: Republican Press Association, 1876.
Proceedings of the Republican National Convention of 1830. Chicago: John B. Jeffrey Printing and Publishing House, 1881.
Proceedings of the Republican National Convention of 1884. Chicago: Rand, McNally and Co., 1884.
Proceedings of the Republican National Convention of 1888. Chicago: Rand, McNally and Co., 1888.
Proceedings of the Republican National Convention of 1892. Minneapolis: Charles W. Johnson, 1903.
Proceedings of the Republican National Convention of 1896. N.p.:n.d.

4. Newspapers

Alabama

Huntsville *Gazette,* 1881–1894.

Arkansas

Little Rock *Weekly Mansion,* 1883–1884.

California

San Francisco *Èlevator,* 1876–1892.
San Francisco *Vindicator,* 1887–1889.

District of Columbia

Washington *Bee,* 1882–1897.
Washington *Colored American,* 1894.
Washington *Grit,* 1883–1884.
Washington *Leader,* 1889.

Washington *National Leader*, 1888–1889.
Washington *People's Advocate*, 1879–1884.

Georgia

Savannah *Tribune*, 1876, 1886–1889, 1891–1897.
Savannah *Weekly Echo*, 1883–1884.

Illinois

Chicago *Conservator*, 1882, 1883, 1886.
Chicago *Eagle*, 1892.
Springfield *State Capital*, 1891–1892.

Indiana

Indianapolis *Freeman*, 1886–1897.

Iowa

Des Moines *Iowa State Bystander*, 1896–1897.

Kansas

Atchison *Blade*, 1892–1894.
Baxter Springs *Southern Argus*, 1891.
Coffeyville *Afro-American Advocate*, 1891–1893.
Kansas City *American Citizen*, 1889–1897.
Lawrence *Historic Times*, 1891.
Leavenworth *Advocate*, 1888–1891.
Leavenworth *Herald*, 1894–1897.
Nicodemus *Cyclone*, 1887–1888.
Nicodemus *Enterprise*, 1887.
Nicodemus *Western Cyclone*, 1886–1887.
Parsons *Weekly Blade*, 1892–1897.
Topeka *American Citizen*, 1888–1889.
Topeka *Baptist Headline*, 1893–1894.
Topeka *Colored Citizen*, 1878–1879.
Topeka *Evening Call*, 1893.
Topeka *Kansas Blackman*, 1894.
Topeka *State Ledger*, 1892–1897.
Topeka *Times-Observer*, 1891–1892.
Topeka *Tribune*, 1880.
Topeka *Weekly Call*, 1891.
Wichita *Kansas Headlight*, 1894.
Wichita *National Baptist World*, 1894.
Wichita *People's Friend*, 1894.

Louisiana

New Orleans *Weekly Louisianian* or *Louisianian*, 1876–1882.
New Orleans *Weekly Pelican*, 1886–1889.
Vidalia *Concordia Eagle*, 1877, 1879, 1880, 1883.

Maryland

Baltimore *Afro-American*, 1895–1897.

Michigan

Detroit *Plaindealer*, 1883–1897.

Minnesota

Minneapolis *Observer*, 1890.
St. Paul *Appeal*, 1889–1892, 1894–1897.
St. Paul and Minneapolis *Broad Axe*, 1891–1897.
St. Paul *Negro World*, 1892.

Nebraska

Omaha *Afro-American Sentinel*, 1896–1897.
Omaha *Enterprise*, 1895–1897.

New Jersey

Trenton *Sentinel*, 1880–1882.

New York

New York *Age*, 1887–1892.
New York *Freeman*, 1884–1897.
New York *Globe*, 1880–1884.
New York *Times*, 1876–1897.

North Carolina

Charlotte *Afro-American Presbyterian*, 1889.
New Bern *People's Advocate*, 1886.
Raleigh *Gazette*, 1891, 1893, 1894.
Weldon *Republican and Civil Rights Advocate*, 1884.

Ohio

Cleveland *Gazette*, 1883–1897.
Columbus *Free American*, 1887.

Oklahoma

Langston *City Herald*, 1891–1893.

Pennsylvania

Harrisburg *State Journal*, 1883–1893.

Tennessee

Knoxville *Negro World*, 1887, 1891.
Maryville *Republican*, 1876.

Texas

Galveston *Freeman's Journal*, 1889.

Utah

Salt Lake City *Broad Ax*, 1895.

Virginia

Alexandria *People's Advocate*, 1876.
Boydton *Midland Express*, 1891.
Hampton *Southern Workman*, 1886–1890.
Richmond *Planet*, 1885–1897.
Richmond *Virginia Star*, 1877–1882.

West Virginia

Martinsburg *Pioneer Press*, 1890, 1892.

Wisconsin

Milwaukee *Wisconsin Afro-American*, 1892.

5. Periodicals

A.M.E. Church *Review*, 1884–1897.
A.M.E. Zion *Church Quarterly*, 1892–1894.

6. Articles

Bryce, James. "Thoughts on the Negro Problem." *North American Review*
    CLIII (1891), 641–660.
Douglass, Frederick. "The Cause of Republican Defeat." *Frank Leslie's
    Illustrated Newspaper*, CXXI (1890), 302.

Dunbar, Paul. "The Real Question." *Harper's Weekly*, IV (October 31, 1896), 1078.

Godkin, E. L. "The Republican Party and the Negro." *Forum*, VII (1889), 246–257.

Price, J. C. "The Negro in the Last Decade of the Century." *Independent*, XLI (1891), 5.

"Progress Among the Negro." *Nation*, XLVIII (June 6, 1889), 461–462.

Scarborough, W. S. "The Future of the Negro." *Forum*, VII (1889), 80–89.

Smalls, Robert. "Election Methods in the South." *North American Review*, CLI (1890), 593–600.

Watson, Tom. "The Negro Question in the South." *Arena*, VI (1891), 540–550.

7. Books

Aptheker, Herbert, ed. *A Documentary History of the Negro People of the United States*. 2 vols. New York: Citadel Press, 1951.

Brotz, Howard, ed. *Negro Social and Political Thought, 1850–1920*. New York: Basic Books, Inc., 1966.

Bruce, Henry C. *The New Man: Twenty-Nine Years a Slave; Twenty-Nine Years a Free Man*. York, Pa.: Anstadt and Sons, 1895.

Bruce, John E. *Short Biographical Sketches of Eminent Negro Men and Women*. Yonkers, N.Y.: Gazette Press, 1910.

Dann, Martin E., ed. *The Black Press, 1827–1890: The Quest for National Identity*. New York: G. P. Putnam's Sons, 1971.

Douglass, Frederick. *Address by Hon. Frederick Douglass—Delivered at the Metropolitan A.M.E. Church*. Baltimore: Press of Thomas and Evans, 1894.

———. *The Lessons of the Hour*. Boston, 1895.

———. *The Life and Times of Frederick Douglass*. Boston: DeWolfe, Fiske, and Company, 1895.

———. *Why the Colored American Is Not Represented at the World's Columbian Exposition*. Chicago, 1893.

Foner, Philip, ed. *The Life and Writings of Frederick Douglass*. New York: International Publishers, 1945.

Fortune, T. Thomas. *Black and White: Land, Labor and Politics in the South*. New York: Ford, Howard and Hulbert, 1884.

———. *The Negro in Politics*. New York, 1886.

Gibbs, Mifflin W. *Shadow and Light: An Autobiography*. New York: Arno Press, 1968.

Gilbert, Peter, ed. *The Selected Writings of John Edward Bruce: Militant Black Journalist.* New York: Arno Press, 1971.

Israel, Fred L. *The State of the Union Messages of the Presidents, 1790–1966.* New York: Bowker, 1966.

Johnson, William Henry. *The Autobiography of Dr. William Henry Johnson.* New York: Haskell House, 1970.

Langston, John Mercer. *Freedom and Citizenship: Selected Lectures and Addresses.* Miami: Mnemosyne Publishing Company, Inc., 1969.

————. *From the Virginia Plantation to the National Capital or the First and Only Negro Representative in Congress From the Old Dominion.* Hartford: American Publishing Company, 1894.

Lott, Davis Newton, ed. *The Inaugural Addresses of the American Presidents, from Washington to Kennedy.* New York: Holt, Rinehart, and Winston, 1961.

Lynch, John Roy. *The Facts of Reconstruction.* New York: Neale Publishing Company, 1915.

————. *Reminiscences of an Active Life: The Autobiography of John Roy Lynch.* Chicago: University of Chicago Press, 1970.

Meltzer, Milton, ed. *In Their Own Words: A History of the American Negro, 1865–1916.* New York: Thomas Y. Crowell Company, 1965.

Payne, Daniel. *Recollections of Seventy Years.* Nashville: Publishing House of A.M.E. Sunday School Union, 1885.

Penn, I. Garland. *The Afro-American Press and Its Editors.* Springfield, Mass.: Willey, 1891.

Porter, Kirk and D. Bruce Johnson, eds. *National Party Platforms.* New York: Macmillan, 1956.

Richardson, James D. *A Compilation of the Messages and Papers of the Presidents, 1789–1902.* Vol. VII-IX. New York: Bureau of National Literature and Art, 1903.

Straker, D. Augustus. *The South Investigated.* Detroit: Ferguson Print, 1888.

Taylor, Charles H. J. *Whites and Blacks.* Atlanta: James P. Harrison and Company, 1889.

Williams, Charles R., ed. *Dairy and Letters of Rutherford Birchard Hayes.* Columbus: Ohio State Archaeological and Historical Society, 1922–1926.

Williams, George Washington. *The Negro as a Political Problem.* Boston, 1884.

Yates, Walter L., ed. *He Spoke, Now They Speak: A Collection of Speeches and Writings of and on the Life and Works of J. C. Price.* Salisbury, N.C.: Rowan Publishing Co., 1952.

B. Secondary Materials

1. Periodical Articles

Abramowitz, Jack. "Crossroads of Negro Thought, 1890–1895." *Social Education*, XVIII (1954), 117–120.
———. "John B. Raynor—A Grass-roots Leader." *Journal of Negro History*, XXXVI (1951), 160–193.
———. "The Negro in the Agrarian Revolt." *Agricultural History*, XXIV (1950), 89–95.
———. "The Negro in the Populist Movement." *Journal of Negro History*, XXXVIII (1953), 257–289.
Bacote, Clarence A. "Negro Officeholders in Georgia under President McKinley." *Journal of Negro History*, XLIV (1959), 217–235.
———. "Some Aspects of Negro Life in Georgia, 1880–1908." *Journal of Negro History*, XLIII (1958), 186–213.
Beatty, Bess. "John Willis Menard: A Progressive Black in Post-Civil War Florida." *Florida Historical Quarterly*, LIX (October 1980), 123–143.
Blakely, Allison. "Richard T. Greener and the 'Talented Tenth's' Dilemma." *Journal of Negro History*, LIX (1974), 305–332.
Brewer, W. M. "Henry Highland Garnet." *Journal of Negro History*, XIII (1928), 36–52.
Carl, Robert B. "Race Relations in the Agrarian Revolt: The Georgia Experience, 1889–1896." *Atlanta Historical Bulletin* (Winter 1977), 33–62.
Casdorph, Paul D. "Norris Wright Curney and Texas Republican Politics, 1883–1896." *Southwestern Historical Quarterly*, LXIII (1965), 455–464.
Chafe, William H. "The Negro and Populism: A Kansas Case Study." *Journal of Southern History*, XXXIV (1968), 402–419.
Cheek, William F. "A Negro Runs for Congress: John Mercer Langston and the Virginia Campaign of 1888." *Journal of Negro History*, LII (1967), 14–34.
Collins, Ernest M. "Cincinnati Negroes and Presidential Politics." *Journal of Negro History*, XLI (1956), 131–137.
Crofts, Daniel W. "The Black Response to the Blair Education Bill." *Journal of Southern History*, XXXVII (1971), 41–65.
Crow, Jeffrey J. " 'Fusion, Confusion and Negroism': Schisms Among Republicans in the North Carolina Election of 1896." *North Carolina Historical Review* (Autumn 1976), 364–384.

Crowe, Charles. "Tom Watson, Populists and Blacks Reconsidered."
    Journal of Negro History, LV (1970), 99–116.
DeSantis, Vincent P. "Negro Dissatisfaction with Republican Policy in
    the South." *Journal of Negro History*, XXXVI (1951), 148–159.
————. "The Republican Party and the Southern Negro, 1877–1897."
    Journal of Negro History, XLV (1960), 71–87.
Dilliard, Irving. "James Milton Turner: A Little Known Benefactor of
    His People." *Journal of Negro History*, XIX (1934), 372–411.
Drake, Donald. "Militancy in Fortune's New York *Age*." *Journal of Negro
    History* LV (1970), 307–322.
Fishel, Leslie H. "The Negro in Northern Politics." *Mississippi Valley
    Historical Review*, XLII (1955), 466–489.
————. "Repercussions of Reconstruction: The Northern Negro, 1870–
    1883." *Civil War History*, XIV (1968), 325–345.
Gaboury, William J. "George Washington Murray and the Fight For
    Political Democracy in South Carolina." *Journal of Negro History*,
    LXII (1977), 258–270.
Gatewood, Willard B. "William D. Crum: A Negro in Politics." *Journal
    of Negro History*, LII (1968), 301–320.
Going, Allan J. "The South and the Blair Bill." *Mississippi Valley Historical
    Review*, XLIV (1957), 267–290.
Goldstein, Leslie F. "Violence as an Instrument for Social Change: The
    Views of Frederick Douglass, 1819–1895." *Journal of Negro His-
    tory*, XLI (1976), 61–72.
Goldstein, Michael L. "Preface to the Rise of Booker T. Washington:
    A View From New York City of the Demise of Independent
    Black Politics." *Journal of Negro History*, LXII (1977), 81–100.
Higgins, Billy D. "Negro Thought and the Exodus of 1879." *Phylon*,
    XXII (1971), 39–52.
Houston, G. David. "A Negro Senator." *Journal of Negro History*, XII
    (1922), 243–256.
Huggins, Nathan I. "National Character and Community." *Center Mag-
    azine*, VII (1974), 51–66.
Johnson, Pauline C. "Robert Purvis." *Negro History Bulletin*, V (1941),
    65–66.
Klingman, Peter D. "Josiah T. Walls and the Black Tactics of Race in
    Post Civil War Florida." *Negro History Bulletin*, XXXVII (1974),
    242–247.
Lewis, Elsie M. "The Political Mind of the Negro, 1865–1900." *Journal
    of Southern History*, XXI (1955), 189–202.
McDaniel, Ruth Currie. "Black Power in Georgia: William A. Pledger

and the Takeover of the Republican Party." *Georgia Historical Quarterly*, LXII (1978), 225–239.

Mann, Kenneth Eugene. "John Roy Lynch: U.S. Congressman from Mississippi." *Negro History Bulletin*, XXXV (1972), 64–66.

Meier, August. "The Negro and the Democratic Party, 1875–1915." *Phylon*, XVII (1956), 170–181.

Meier, August, and Elliott Rudwick. "Black Man in the White City: Negroes and the Columbian Exposition, 1893." *Phylon*, XXVI (1965), 64–66.

Miller, Floyd J. "Black Protest and White Leadership: A Note on the Colored Farmers Alliance." *Phylon*, XXXIII (1972), 169–174.

Phillips, Glenn O. "The Response of a West Indian Activist: D. A. Straker, 1842–1908." *Journal of Negro History*, LXVI (Summer 1981), 128–139.

Rogers, William W. "The Negro Alliance in Alabama." *Journal of Negro History*, XLV (1960), 38–44.

Saunders, Robert M. "The Southern Populist and the Negro in 1892." *University of Virginia Essays in History*, XII (Charlottesville: University of Virginia Press, 1966–1967).

———. "The Southern Populists and the Negro, 1893–1895." *Journal of Negro History*, LIV (1969), 241–253.

Simms-Brown, R. Jean. "Populism and Black Americans: Constructive or Destructive?" *Journal of Negro History*, LXV (Fall 1980), 349–359.

Spriggs, William Edward. "The Virginia Colored Farmers' Alliance: A Case Study of Race and Class Identity." *Journal of Negro History*, LXIV (Summer 1979), 191–204.

Taylor, Joseph H. "Populism and Disfranchisement in Alabama." *Journal of Negro History*, XXXIV (1949), 410–427.

Thornbrough, Emma Lou. "American Negro Newspapers, 1880–1914." *Business History Review*, XI (1966), 467–490.

———. "The National Afro-American League, 1887–1908." *Journal of Southern History*, XXVII (1961), 494–512.

Tindall, George B. "The Question of Race in the Convention of 1895." *Journal of Negro History*, XXXVII (1952), 277–303.

Toll, William. "Free Men, Freedmen, and Race: Black Social Theory in the Gilded Age." *Journal of Southern History*, XLIV (1978), 571–597.

Watts, Eugene J. "Black Political Progress in Atlanta: 1868–1895." *Journal of Negro History*, LIX (1974), 268–286.

Woods, Randall B., "C.H.J. Taylor and the Movement For Black Political Independence, 1882–1896." *Journal of Negro History*, LXVII (Summer 1982), 122–133.

2. Books

Athearn, Robert G. *In Search of Canaan: Black Migration to Kansas, 1879–80*. Lawrence: University of Kansas Press, 1978.

Callcott, Margaret Law. *The Negro in Maryland Politics, 1870–1912*. Baltimore: Johns Hopkins Press, 1969.

Cartwright, Joseph H. *The Triumph of Jim Crow: Tennessee Race Relations in the 1880s*. Knoxville: University of Tennessee Press, 1976.

DeSantis, Vincent P. *Republicans Face the Southern Question: The New Departure Years, 1877–1897*. Baltimore: Johns Hopkins Press, 1959.

Factor, Robert L. *The Black Response to America: Men, Ideals, and Organization from Frederick Douglass to the NAACP*. Reading, Mass.: Addison-Wesley, 1970.

Franklin, John Hope. *From Slavery to Freedom: A History of Negro Americans*. New York: Vintage Books, 1969.

———. *George Washington Williams: A Biography*. Chicago: University of Chicago Press, 1985.

Gaither, Gerald. *Blacks and the Populist Revolt: Ballots and Bigotry in the "New South."* University: University of Alabama Press, 1977.

Gerber, David. *Black Ohio and the Color Line, 1860–1915*. Urbana: University of Illinois Press, 1976.

Goodwyn, Lawrence. *Democratic Promise: The Populist Moment in America*. New York: Oxford University Press, 1976.

Grossman, Lawrence. *The Democratic Party and the Negro: Northern and National Politics, 1868–1892*. Urbana: University of Illinois Press, 1976.

Hare, Maud Cuney. *Norris Wright Cuney: A Tribune of the Black People*. Austin: Steck-Vaughn Co., 1968.

Harlan, Louis R. *Booker T. Washington: The Making of a Black Leader, 1856–1902*. New York: Oxford University Press, 1972.

Haskins, James. *Pinckney Benton Stewart Pinchback*. New York: Macmillan, 1973.

Hirshon, Stanley P. *Farewell to the Bloody Shirt: Northern Republicans and the Southern Negro, 1877–1893*. Bloomington: Indiana University Press, 1962.

Holt, Thomas. *Black Over White: Negro Political Leadership in South Carolina During Reconstruction*. Urbana: University of Illinois Press, 1977.

Klingman, Peter. *Josiah Walls: Florida's Black Congressman of Reconstruction*. Gainesville: University Presses of Florida, 1976.

Kousser, J. Morgan. *The Shaping of Southern Politics: Suffrage Restriction and the Establishment of the One-Party South, 1880–1910*. New Haven: Yale University Press, 1974.

Lamson, Peggy. *The Glorious Failure: Black Congressman Robert Brown Elliott and the Reconstruction in South Carolina*. New York: W. W. Norton, 1973.

Litwack, Leon F. *Been in the Storm So Long: The Aftermath of Slavery*. New York: Alfred A. Knopf, 1979.

Logan, Frenice A. *The Negro in North Carolina, 1877–1894*. Chapel Hill: University of North Carolina Press, 1964.

Logan, Rayford W. *The Betrayal of the Negro: From Rutherford B. Hayes to Woodrow Wilson*. New York: Macmillan, 1965.

Meier, August. *Negro Through in America, 1880–1915*. Ann Arbor: University of Michigan Press, 1964.

Meier, August and Elliott Rudwick, eds. *Making of Black America: Essays in Negro Life and History*. 2 vols. New York: Atheneum, 1969.

Nowlin, W. F. *The Negro in American National Politics*. Boston: The Stratford Company, 1931.

Painter, Nell I. *Exodusters: Black Migration to Kansas After Reconstruction*. New York: Alfred A. Knopf, 1976.

Ponton, Mungo M. *The Life and Times of Bishop Henry M. Turner*. Atlanta: A. B. Caldwell, 1917.

Quarles, Benjamin. *Frederick Douglass*. Washington, D.C.: Associated Publishers, 1948.

Rice, Lawrence D. *The Negro in Texas, 1874–1900*. Baton Rouge: Louisiana State University Press, 1971.

Rose, Willie Lee. *Slavery and Freedom*. New York: Oxford University Press, 1982.

Schweninger, Loren. *James T. Rapier and Reconstruction*. Chicago: University of Chicago Press, 1978.

Sinkler, George. *The Racial Attitudes of American Presidents from Abraham Lincoln to Theodore Roosevelt*. New York: Doubleday and Company, 1971.

Smith, Samuel Denny. *The Negro in Congress, 1870–1901*. Chapel Hill: University of North Carolina Press, 1940.

Suggs, Henry Lewis. *The Black Press in the South, 1865–1979*. Westport, Conn.: Greenwood Press, 1983.

Taylor, A. A. *The Negro in Tennessee, 1865–1880*. Washington, D.C.: Associated Publishers, 1941.

Thornbrough, Emma Lou. *T. Thomas Fortune, Militant Journalist*. Chicago: University of Chicago Press, 1972.

Thorpe, Earl E. *The Mind of the Negro: An Intellectual History of Afro-Americans*. Baton Rouge, La.: Ortlieb Press, 1961.

Tindall, George B. *South Carolina Negroes, 1877–1900*. Columbia: University of South Carolina Press, 1952.

Uya, Okon Edet. *From Slavery to Public Service: Robert Smalls, 1839–1915*. New York: Oxford University Press, 1971.

Walls, W. J. *Joseph Charles Price: Educator and Race Leader*. Boston: Christopher Publishing House, 1943.

Wharton, Vernon. *The Negro in Mississippi, 1865–1890*. Chapel Hill: University of North Carolina Press, 1947.

Williamson, Joel. *After Slavery: The Negro in South Carolina During Reconstruction, 1861–1877*. Chapel Hill: University of North Carolina Press, 1965.

Woodward, C. Vann. *Origins of the New South, 1877–1913*. Baton Rouge: Louisiana State University Press, 1951.

―――. *The Strange Career of Jim Crow*. New York: Oxford University Press, 1955.

―――. *Tom Watson: Agrarian Rebel*. New York: Macmillan, 1938.

Wynes, Charles E. *Race Relations in Virginia, 1870–1902*. Charlottesville: University of Virginia Press, 1961.

3. Unpublished Material

Adams, Olin Burton. "The Negro and the Agrarian Movement in Georgia, 1874–1908." Ph.D. diss., Florida State University, 1973.

Fishel, Leslie. "The North and the Negro, 1865–1900: A Story in Race Discrimination." Ph.D. diss., Harvard University, 1953.

St. Clair, Sadie Daniel. "The Public Career of Blanche K. Bruce." Ph.D. diss., New York University, 1947.

White, Edward. "The Republican Party in National Politics, 1888–1891." University of Wisconsin, 1941.

Index

About the Author

BESS BEATTY, Assistant Professor of History at Oregon State University, has published articles on southern and black history in *Labor History*, the *Journal of Southern History*, and *North Carolina Historical Review*.

DATE DUE

OCT 24 '89			
261-2500			Printed in USA